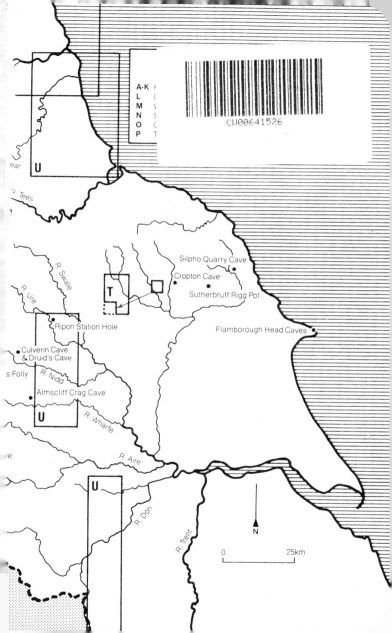

A·K
L
M
N
O
P

R. Tees

R. Swale

R. Ure

Silpho Quarry Cave

Cropton Cave

T

Sutherbruff Rigg Pot

Ripon Station Hole

Flamborough Head Caves

Culverin Cave
& Druid's Cave

s Folly R. Nidd

Almscliff Crag Cave

U

R. Wharfe

R. Aire

U

R. Don

R. Trent

N

0   25km

NORTHERN CAVES

Volume 1
Wharfedale and the
North-East

by

D. Brook, G.M. Davies, M.H. Long, P.F. Ryder

Dalesman Books

1988

The Dalesman Publishing Company Ltd.,
Clapham (via Lancaster), LA2 8EB

First published 1988
© D. Brook, G.M. Davies, M.H. Long, P.F. Ryder 1988
ISBN 0 85206 927 8

NORTHERN CAVES

A comprehensive guide to the caves of northern England.

Vol 1   Wharfedale and the North-East

Vol 2   The Three Peaks (in preparation)

Vol 3   The Three Counties System and the North-West
(in preparation)

Printed in Britain by Knight & Forster Ltd., Leeds

CONTENTS

MAPS & SURVEYS

Each area commences with a map. Other maps and surveys are listed below.

Maps and surveys drawn by G.M. Davies

Cover picture of Out Sleets Beck Pot by M.H. Long

INTRODUCTION

SEVENTEEN years ago, preparation of *Northern Caves* began. The series has been improved as it progressed, but we were conscious that more could be done. Numerous discussions with cavers and the publisher over a period of several years have led to the changes which this volume incorporates, to set the new standard for the work as it approaches the beginning of its third decade, in the 1990s.

The guide is now to be divided into three volumes, rather than the seven previously intended. By that means the cost of covers and introductory pages for four extra volumes is saved. A more expensive cover therefore becomes possible without increasing the overall cost of the work. The durability of the books is thus improved, and the number of volumes needed for a visit to the Dales is reduced. Other changes have also been made, some obvious and others less noticeable.

The first part of the new series covers the former Volume 1 area and that part of the old Volume 5 area roughly east of the Pennine watershed. Volume 2–'The Three Peaks'–will comprise the old Volumes 2 and 3, with the Bruntscar area from Volume 4A. Volume 3 –'The Three Counties System & the North-West'–will include the remainder of Volumes 4A, 4B and 5, together with the caves of Morecambe Bay and Furness.

Exploration continues at a good pace, and it is encouraging to note the progress made, as indicated by the number of entries in the guide. In this volume, Wharfedale and Littondale have seen the most steady progress, from 188 entries in 1972, to 229 in 1975, 265 in 1979, and 293 in the present volume. A great deal of potential remains and those who have the determination to search for new caves will never be without a challenge.

We thank all those whose comments and suggestions have helped us in deciding how to change the series. We are also grateful to the following people for the information and help which they have given: John Cordingley, Roger Davies, Julian Griffiths, John and Peter Hodgkins, John Holmes, Martin Holroyd, Keith McBride, Lank Mills, Alan Speight, John Thorp, Steve Warren, Ian Watson.

February 1988

Caving Club Abbreviations

ACVSU	Ampleforth College Venture Scout Unit
BPC	Bradford Pothole Club
BACC	Bishop Auckland Caving Club
BCC	Burnley Caving Club
BSA	British Speleological Association
BUSS	Birmingham University Speleological Society
CDG	Cave Diving Group
CNCC	Council of Northern Caving Clubs
CUCC	Cambridge University Caving Club
CPC	Craven Pothole Club
DCC	Durham Cave Club
DUSA	Durham University Speleological Association
EMRG	Earby Mine Research Group
EPC	Earby Pothole Club
GC	Gritstone Club
HRCG	Heath Rovers Caving Group
HWCPC	Happy Wanderers Cave and Pothole Club
KCC	Kendal Caving Club
LUCC	London University Caving Club
MSG	Moldywarps Speleological Group
MUSS	Manchester University Speleological Society
NCC	Northern Cave Club
NCFC	Northern Cavern and Fell Club
NPC	Northern Pennine Club
ULSA	University of Leeds Speleological Association
UWFRA	Upper Wharfedale Fell Rescue Association
WRPC	White Rose Pothole Club
YRC	Yorkshire Ramblers Club
YSS	Yorkshire Speleological Society
YURT	Yorkshire Underground Research Team

Access and the CNCC

A REFERENCE to a cave or pothole in this guidebook does not imply any right of access or that permission to visit can be obtained. Ask the appropriate person before going to any of them; most people are reasonable and will allow access if you have the courtesy to ask.

Some caving areas require advance application for permits and it is not always possible to include all necessary details in this guidebook. Where indicated it is essential to refer to the Northern Caving Handbook, published by the Council of Northern Caving Clubs and available from caving shops in the Dales. This Handbook also gives full details about CNCC, its membership requirements and club addresses, as well as the background to specific access agreements negotiated with landowners who imposed restrictions. Under the terms of these agreements the Council has the thankless task of controlling access by prior booking for member clubs. In case of difficulty obtaining the CNCC Handbook contact: Council of Northern Caving Clubs, c/o The Sports Council (NW Region), Byrom House, Quay Street, Manchester M3 5FJ.

The Caving Code

ALWAYS tell a responsible person where you are going and when you expect to return. Use your common sense before calling the cave rescue to an overdue party.

Practise the Country Code – close gates, cover up digs, and don't knock walls or fences down. Take any litter home.

Ensure that all equipment is sound and that the party is properly equipped with safety helmets, adequate clothing, good lamps with reserves, and food if necessary. For ladder pitches everyone must have a whistle and use the standard code – one blast, stop; two blasts, haul in; three blasts, pay out. Keep lifelines taut and only use appropriate knots.

Treat caves with care – their great interest and scientific value depend on them staying as unspoilt as possible. Preserve all underground phenomena, such as calcite formations, and protect cave life, particularly by not polluting water or cave deposits. Spent carbide must always be taken out. In known or potential archaeological sites don't do any digging; any accidental find of archaeological material must not be touched and should be reported immediately to a museum or similar authority.

If you want to go caving, join a club and gain experience with reliable companions and equipment.

ACCIDENT PROCEDURE – SEE OUTSIDE BACK COVER

Geological Information

AT THE beginning of many descriptions is a note of the bed in which the cave lies. The names of Carboniferous limestones are abbreviated in accordance with the conventions used by the British Geological Survey and, if no bed is listed, the cave is in Great Scar Limestone – which is here taken to include the lower beds of the Yoredale Series in those places where they are, for caving purposes, effectively part of the Great Scar; note that no bed is listed in the North York Moors area, where all the caves are in Corallian Limestone of Jurassic age, or for caves in the Magnesian Limestone section. If the bed is simply described as 'Limestone', the cave is in Carboniferous limestone, but the exact bed is unknown.

The names of similar beds vary from place to place, as do the beds themselves. A simplified correlation of the Carboniferous limestones of interest to cavers is given below for the main part of the caving area covered by this volume. The vertical sequence is correctly shown, and beds on the same line are equivalents. Caves are not known in every bed and the intervening sandstones, shales, etc., including some thin limestones, have been ignored. Beds other than limestones are named in full where possible. The Askrigg Block names apply in the areas up to and including Gretadale, and the Alston Block names apply in the Teesdale, Weardale and Alston areas.

ASKRIGG BLOCK		**ALSTON BLOCK**	
ML	Main Limestone	**GL**	Great Limestone
UnL	Underset Limestone	**4FL**	Four Fathom Limestone
3YL	Three Yard Limestone	**3YL**	Three Yard Limestone
5YL	Five Yard Limestone	**5YL**	Five Yard Limestone
MdL	Middle Limestone	**ScL**	Scar Limestone
SiL	Simonstone Limestone	**TBL**	Tynebottom Limestone
HScL	Hardraw Scar Limestone	**JL**	Jew Limestone
HwL	Hawes Limestone	**SmL**	Smiddy Limestone
		PgL	Peghorn Limestone
GScL	Great Scar Limestone	**RnL**	Robinson Limestone
		MSL	Melmerby Scar Limestone

Using this Guide

THIS book is intended as guidance for the wise, not the obedience of fools.

LOCATIONS

The national grid reference (NGR) gives the location of the south-west corner of the 100m square in which the entrance lies, in accordance with convention. Altitudes are given to help in locating entrances on maps and in relation to one another; it should be noted that relatively few entrances have been precisely located by levelling and altitudes are generally approximations, although they should be sufficiently accurate for most purposes.

GRADING

The grades usually apply only to the normal route to the deepest or furthest point of a cave. In complex systems they can only be a rough guide; where convenient some sections of caves may have their own grade, which also includes the easiest route from the surface to that section. Alternatively the cave is given a varying grade and the comparative difficulties of different routes should be apparent from the text. The grades only apply to those caves or parts of caves which are accessible to non-divers.

When planning trips think of the return journey and remember that the grades only apply to fit, competent and properly equipped parties; novices in particular will find the caves harder than indicated and for most systems there must be sufficient experienced and competent cavers in the party.

Grade I   Easy cave; no pitches or difficulties.

Grade II   Moderate caves and small potholes.

Grade III   Caves and potholes without any particularly hazardous, difficult or strenuous sections.

Grade IV   Caves and potholes which present some hazard, difficulty or large underground pitch.

Grade V   Caves and potholes which include very strenuous sections or large and wet underground pitches.

SUMPS

Detailed descriptions of sumps are not given as this guide is intended to be used in conjunction with the CDG's Northern Sump Index and its Newsletters. It is essential that anyone contemplating diving consults these publications for the more comprehensive information they contain.

Free dives are always a hazard – conditions in sumps alter, lines may snag or break, air in airbells may be foul, and route finding can be difficult. Only go with a competent diver who knows the sump well.

FLOODING

Any stream cave or pothole can flood rapidly and unpredictably; so can many which are usually dry. The warnings are for guidance and cannot cover all circumstances – no warning does not mean no hazard. If in doubt – stay out.

OTHER HAZARDS

Minimise objective dangers by using fail-safe techniques in which the party is competent. Safety should be uppermost in the thoughts of all cavers. Lifelines should be used on ladder pitches, and secondary belays should be used as necessary.

Potential hazards for the careless or unwary caver are too numerous to mention and are present in any cave or pothole, whatever its grade. Route finding in complex systems also defies adequate description and there is no substitute for an experienced leader.

ARTIFICIAL AIDS

References in these guidebooks to artificial aids such as bolt belays, iron ladders, fixed lines in sumps, shoring in digs, etc., does not imply that such aids are safe. All artificial aids should be regarded with suspicion; they have usually been provided only for the short-term convenience of the persons who originally placed them. The use of small bolts to facilitate exploration or single rope techniques has increased to such a degree that it would be impossible for a guide of this sort to be up-to-date on their placing. For that reason, and the more important one that small bolts are likely to be relatively impermanent, they have generally not been mentioned. Deterioration of all artificial aids is inevitable and it is up to every individual potholer or group leader to decide whether or not to rely upon any such fixtures.

SINGLE ROPE TECHNIQUES

The descriptions and tackle lists in this guide generally refer to the traditional route down a pitch – usually the most direct – and may not be appropriate for SRT descents. Early SRT routes followed the traditional routes and encountered problems such as volume of water, rope abrasion and sharpness of rock, making rope protection essential. Modern SRT routes are attempts to avoid such hazards: they may vary greatly in route and rope needs from the traditional way. For example, a pitch might involve a traverse with six or seven bolts, a Y hang, two re-belays, a deviation belay, and could need a rope two or three times as long as the vertical drop. SRT routes and rope lengths will alter depending on the whims of the rigger; as bolts rust and are replaced; and as better routes are found. By contrast, the details of a traditional route will usually remain unchanged – save that alternative belays may be used. It is consequently impractical to describe SRT routes and keep the guide to a reasonable length. SRT cavers, while using the general description of a pothole, must be sufficiently competent to establish their own routes and tackle requirements for pitches as the descent progresses.

IMPORTANT

While every reasonable effort has been made to ensure the information in this guidebook is accurate, neither the authors nor the publisher can accept responsibility for any errors, inaccuracies or omissions.

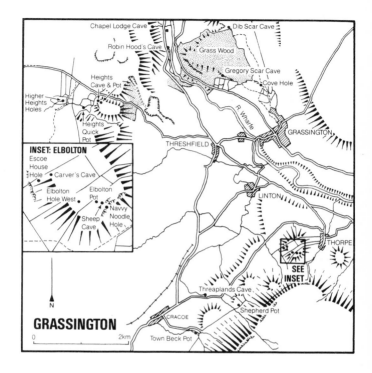

GRASSINGTON

CARVER'S CAVE   NGR SE 005616   Grade I
Alt. 328m   **Length 12m**

    Reef Limestone. Obvious entrance in large shakehole adjoining wall, straight up hill from Escoe House Hole. Low crawl over angular limestone breakdown leads to flat out crawl up mud slope into small chamber where it is possible to stand up. Passage continues uphill to where the way on is completely blocked.

Permission – Holly Tree House, Thorpe.

CHAPEL LODGE CAVE   NGR SD 975662   Grade I
Alt. 235m   **Length 50m**
Explored 1972, CPC; extended 1978/1985, UWFRA.

Entrance at foot of small scar at head of normally dry channel on hill
behind Chapel Lodge. Excavated squeeze down slope enters impressive
passage 3m wide and 1.2m high which quickly becomes a crawl over gours to
where route splits. To left lowers and chokes where massive collapse blocks
way on, while across pool to right leads to climb up into very wide bedding.
Route across this to left becomes too low, but straight ahead leads to further
climb and squeeze up into a beautifully decorated chamber (care!) with no
apparent way on.
Permission – Chapel Lodge Farm.

COVE HOLE   NGR SD 998649   Grade I
[Fairy Hole] [Tom Lee's Cave]
Alt. 210m   **Length 9m**
Prominent cave entrance in Cove Scar can be seen from road. After 9m,
cave passage leads out into field. Further 2.7m cave NNW.
Permission –Town Head Farm, Grassington.

DIB SCAR CAVE   NGR SD 992662   Grade I
Alt. 260m   **Length 4.5m**
Obvious rock shelter in dry valley above the Scar.

ELBOLTON HOLE WEST   NGR SE 006615   Grade III
Alt. 340m   **Length 45m**   **Depth 30m**
Reef Limestone. Fenced shaft by wall W of cairn on Elbolton Hill. Mined
shaft enters natural cave at bottom. First chamber at foot of entrance shaft is
large, with steep slope of mud and boulders down to large pool. A careful
climb up mud slope at far side of chamber leads through to the second
chamber, and beyond is a short passage to the final chamber.
Tackle – 30m ladder; 10m belay; 40m lifeline.
Permission – Holly Tree House.

ELBOLTON POT   NGR SE 007615   Grade III
Alt. 340m   **Length 150m**   **Depth 41m**
Re-discovered 1950, UWFRA; connected to Navvy Noodle Hole 1980,
UWFRA.
Reef Limestone. Entrance in mined passage 15m W of cairn on Elbolton
Hill. Obvious pitch leads straight into chamber from which four passages
radiate. W can be followed for 45m before it becomes choked. S passes
through a small chamber to a short canal and sump, dived for 3m past
awkward squeeze to airbell in narrow rift. After duck through to further

the other two ways quickly unite in an alternative route to the Grand Canyon which can also be reached via the last passage out of the first chamber, and down the 2nd pitch. At the end of the Grand Canyon is the 3rd pitch, and below, a pool and a boulder choke. Other passages lead off, but all quickly become choked or are too tight.

A dig from Navvy Noodle Hole which linked the two caves has now collapsed.

Tackle

Pitch	Ladder	Belay	Lifeline
1st	17m	9m	30m
2nd	6m	4.5m	12m
3rd	8m	2.5m	12m

Permission – Holly Tree House, Thorpe.

ESCOE HOUSE HOLE   NGR SE 004616   Grade II
Alt. 290m   Length 40m   Depth 18m

Reef Limestone. Straight above, but over the wall from, obvious mine level on Elbolton Hill. Large open shaft. Two rift passages at bottom quickly close down. Third passage is crawl on E side leading to short chimney and second cavern. Three small crawls lead off: two become too small. To W leads to 2nd pitch, and climb down to loose boulder floor which was excavated by UWFRA in 1980 to establish connection to Escoe House Level – since collapsed again.

Tackle

Pitch	Ladder	Belay	Lifeline
Entrance	8m	Stake	10m
2nd	4.5m	3m	8m

Permission – Holly Tree House, Thorpe.

GREGORY SCAR CAVE   NGR SD 991651   Grade I
Alt. 250m   Length 9m

Conspicuous entrance at base of scar in Grass Wood. Low crawl through small arched chambers to choke.

HEIGHTS CAVE   NGR SD 964646   Grade I
[Calf Hole] [Elland Cave] [Skythorns Cave]
Alt. 340m   Length 11m

Chamber with prominent, W facing twin entrances split by central pillar. Mesolithic finds in Craven Museum, Skipton.

HEIGHTS POT   NGR SD 964646   Grade I
[Skythorns Pot]
Alt. 350m   Depth 8m

Small shaft entrance above cave. Climb down does not need tackle and ends in small chamber.

HEIGHTS QUICK POT   NGR SD 961644   Grade I
Alt. 328m   **Depth 9m**

Small sink in shakehole under collapsed wall, midway between Height House and Height Laithe. Now blocked with boulders but formerly, small chamber led into tight, slanting rift.

HIGHER HEIGHTS HOLES   NGR SD 957645
[Skythorns Pots]
Alt. 355m

All entrances in rocky stream sink near old limekiln W of track above Height Laithe.

1. Depth 3m   Grade I
Stream sinks into small, boulder-choked chamber.

2. Depth 6m   Grade I
E of stream sink and just round corner of rock face is small shaft with water entering and fissure descending to low bedding.

3. Length 18m   Depth 15m   Grade III
Extended 1969, BCC.

Just to right of 2 is drop into boulder chamber with further drop down rift to one side. Feet-first crawl to drop onto boulder floor and wriggle to another drop. Two short passages end almost immediately but downwards leads to rift with sump which is liable to back up.
Permission – Bell Bank, Skythorns.

NAVVY NOODLE HOLE   NGR SE 007615   Grade IV
[Elbolton Cave]
Alt. 330m   **Length 73m**   **Depth 32m**
Connected to Elbolton Pot 1980, UWFRA.

Reef Limestone. Follow track up from Thorpe to near cairn at top; entrance is small cave opening at foot of small scar. Pitch leads straight into large chamber where archaeological finds have been made. Passage out on far side leads to 2nd pitch and large passage with two short climbs, to Bat Chamber. At far side a steep slope leads down to a sump pool, the sump being 6m long with a maximum depth of 2m. Free diving is not advisable. Just before sump is hole in passage roof entering crawl down to a narrow sump. Immediately beyond main sump is 3rd pitch into final chamber, with no exit. Choked floor conceals collapsed link to Elbolton Pot.

An awkward climb in the first chamber leads into a muddy passage with a 3m climb down to a further passage which chokes after another 3m climb.

Tackle

Pitch	Ladder	Belay	Lifeline
Entrance	8m	6m	12m
2nd	–	9m handline only	
3rd	12m	4.5m	18m

Permission – Holly Tree House, Thorpe.

ROBIN HOOD'S CAVE   NGR SD 978657   Grade IV
Alt. 180m   **Length 400m**
Extended 1971, CPC and 1972/74, CDG.

WARNING – Parts of this cave are liable to complete flooding.

On river Wharfe side of road just up-dale of old quarry on the left.
Entrance is 1m diameter concrete pipe which passes under the road. 60m of
rough crawling lead to a long pool and chamber. A duck under a flake is
followed by a 3m sump, Connection Duck, with small airspace. A squeeze up
through boulders leads into a 4.5m high aven, and from the gallery above a
low crawl at roof level opens into a deep chimney. Scramble up and along the
rift to a fine gour passage with a squeeze into Arch Chamber. Sandy crawl
leads to a fissure and squeeze down between great flakes of rock to the
Terminal Syphon, which has been dived for 110m to an underwater boulder
choke.

A short traverse on chert ledges from Arch Chamber leads to a crawl up an
inclined passage to a calcited choke. A more serious route at stream level
(from the Connection Duck) goes through boulders just above water level
and then through a nasty duck, The Neck Pincher. This leads to a further
squeeze and a canal passage with a climb up between unstable boulders to
the high level series.

SHEEP CAVE   NGR SE 007615   Grade I
Alt. 335m   **Length 8m**

Reef Limestone. Small cave entrance in shakehole 30m NW of Navvy
Noodle Hole. Short length of small passage opens into a chamber, and
passage out on far side quickly narrows and becomes choked. This is within
6m of inlet passage into Main Chamber of Navvy Noodle Hole.
Permission – Holly Tree House, Thorpe.

SHEPHERD POT   NGR SD 995603   Grade I
Alt. 297m   **Depth 9m**

Reef Limestone. Entrance in shakehole in field 50m from fell wall is 9m
descent between large boulders to choke. No tackle required. In an adjoining
shakehole is another descent, for 6m into a small chamber.
Permission – Threaplands Farm, Cracoe.

THREAPLANDS CAVE   NGR SD 987605   Grade I
Alt. 225m   **Length 550m**
Extended 1956, 1960 and 1961, CDG.

At head of small valley some 200m E of Threaplands Farm, below the
Cracoe – Thorpe Road. Prominent entrance at the rising leads to a low, wet
crawl, which after 52m reaches a sump. This has been dived and is 17m long,
the far end emerging into a stream passage of small dimensions which after
145m, mostly crawling, reaches a junction. The obvious way forward reaches
a 3m sump after 37m. Beyond is a further 9m of passage to a choke. At the
junction, the other way leads off from behind a big boulder, and can be

followed for another 280m to the terminal sump, passing through three nasty ducks.

Note: Stream is water supply for dairy herd at Threaplands Farm and permission to enter cave is not given.

TOWN BECK POT   **NGR SD 985598**   **Grade I**
Alt. 250m   **Length 4.5m**   Depth 4.5m

Hole covered by stones on S side of beck a short way downstream from cross wall. Drop into small chamber with roof which dips steeply to end in shingle-choked crawl.

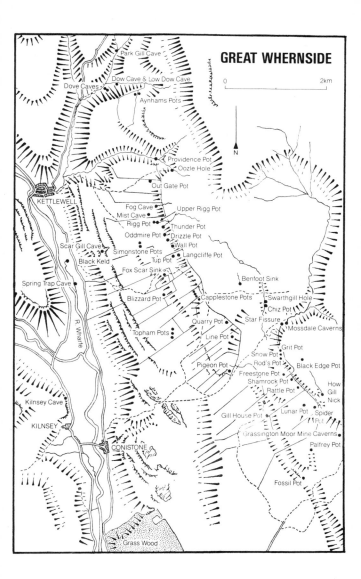

GREAT WHERNSIDE

0   2km

N

Park Gill Cave
Dow Cave & Low Dow Cave
Dove Caves
Aynhams Pots
Providence Pot
Oozle Hole
Out Gate Pot
KETTLEWELL
Fog Cave
Mist Cave
Upper Rigg Pot
Rigg Pot
Thunder Pot
Oddmire Pot
Drizzle Pot
Scar Gill Cave
Wall Pot
Simonstone Pots
Langcliffe Pot
Black Keld
Tup Pot
Fox Scar Sink
Benfoot Sink
Spring Trap Cave
Blizzard Pot
Capplestone Pots
Swarthgill Hole
Chiz Pot
Quarry Pot
Star Fissure
Mossdale Caverns
Topham Pots
Line Pot
Snow Pot
Grit Pot
Pigeon Pot
Rod's Pot
Black Edge Pot
Freestone Pot
Shamrock Pot
How
Gill
Nick
Rattle Pot
Kilnsey Cave
Lunar Pot
KILNSEY
Gill House Pot
Spider
Pot
Grassington Moor Mine Caverns
CONISTONE
Palfrey Pot
Fossil Pot
R. Wharfe
Grass Wood

GREAT WHERNSIDE

AYNHAMS POTS NGR SD 988741 Grade II
Alt. 450m Depth 6m

MdL. SW of large shakehole on S side of Caseker Gill are two small pots on either side of wall, near a wall junction.

1. E of wall is shakehole with gritstone boulders over entrance to shaft. Rift pitch with boulder roof and ends (care!) to choked floor which has been unsuccessfully dug.

2. Over wall to W is line of shakeholes; in the first is a straight choked shaft.

Tackle (both pots) – 8m ladder; stake and sling belay; 9m lifeline.

BENFOOT SINK NGR SE 007705 Grade II
Alt. 480m Depth 24m
Explored 1980 onwards Derbyshire Caving Club.

MdL. Hole near stream sink in massive shakehole drops through series of boulder chambers to a choke.

On Silver Rake 350m to the SE is a vertical walled collapse 7m in diameter and 11m deep which appeared in early 1987.

BLACK EDGE POT NGR SE 019690 Grade 1
Alt. 488m Length 12m Depth 4.5m

Gritstone. Huge sinkhole in the peat plateau. Hole under gritstone cliff drops into a complex among gritstone boulders. No obvious way forward.

BLACK KELD NGR SD 974709 Grade IV
Alt. 198m Length 396m Depth 9m
Explored 1949, CDG; extended 1975-77 CUCC.

This important rising for Langcliffe Pot and Mossdale Caverns is reached via track running past Cruts Barn, on opposite side of road to Scar Gill House. Resurgence pool lies below a small scar and there is no enterable passage for the non-diver. Access is not allowed at present.

The cave is basically a bedding complex on two levels, the lower level being submerged.

Submerged Passages – 152m long

Full details are in CDG Newsletter No. 45, October 1977, but may be summarised as follows. From entrance two routes lead off at 2.5m depth, To right is 33m of sump into Lake 1. To left a separate line leads off for 116m to

Lake 2; the last 60m pass through a boulder area which should be treated with extreme caution as it may be prone to collapse.

Dry Series – 244m long

These passages are best entered via Lake 1 where a scramble out of deep water gains access to start of hands and knees crawl in a passage about 3m wide and 1m high. Easy going for 30m to a waist deep pool at a strong cross joint where two ways lead off. Left is a low bedding plane, but more obvious way is a flat-out crawl to the right. This continues for 30m through a series of revolting muddy pools to a sharp left turn, followed by several squeezes, to enter a small chamber.

Two upper passages from chamber both close down quickly. At floor level the flat-out crawl continues over gours to an area of pools with minimal airspace (nose in roof!). After 15m of wallowing a roof tube can be entered and a short crawl leads forward to a sudden enlargement at Stretch Cavern.

Right from Stretch Cavern is stooped walk to drop on left into small static sump. To left is walking passage to descent of boulders back to pool level. Above descent is bedding connecting to Lake 2 via extremely tight squeeze; below descent is large and confusing bedding plane. Several routes lead back towards low bedding at strong cross joint 30m from Lake 1, but only one can be forced through. Main route is right to pool at another cross joint, where way to right leads up into higher bedding plane and series of small chambers connected by sandy crawls. Small tube to right links back to Stretch Cavern but main way is left, to enlarge and emerge near roof level in large chamber at Lake 2.

BLIZZARD POT NGR SD 992703 Grade II
Alt. 415m   **Length 10m**
Explored 1985, CPC.

Entrance in field to N of prominent walled off mine workings. In area marked as area of shakeholes on OS map. Squeeze down into small chamber with narrow fissure in floor. Continues over fissure as tight choked crawl.

CAPPLESTONE POTS NGR SD 998702 Grade II
Alt. 485m   **Depths to 15m**
Explored 1983, CPC.

MdL. Several narrow rifts up to 15m deep in fields to NW of Capplestone Gate. All close down to choked fissures.

Tackle (all pots) – 20m ladder; stake and sling belay; 25m lifeline.

CHIZ POT NGR SE 012700 Grade II
Alt. 442m   **Depth 14m**
Explored 1981, Derbyshire Caving Club.

MdL. Entrance covered by blocks, in left bank of gill some 6m downstream of normal entrance to Swarthgill Hole. Tight squeeze onto a 12m pitch provides an alternative entry to the upstream aven and rift series of Swarthgill Hole.

Tackle – 15m ladder; bar and short spreader belay; 18m lifeline.

DOVE CAVES   NGR SD 981741

Explored by miners; re-discovered 1942, BSA.

Two lead mine levels on E side of Park Gill midway between bottom of Park Rash and Dow Cave, well above stream. Levels intersect natural caverns and lengths stated are mostly mine workings.

Upper Level   **Alt. 345m**   **Length 195m**   **Grade II**

At top of large spoil heap. Wading, initially in waist deep water, for 170m gets shallower as the mined section trends upwards to pass under bridge of calcited boulders after 120m. Next 45m along level is largely mined out of silted up natural passage and ends at miners' working face. Climb up onto calcite boulder bridge (take care to avoid formations) for 12m to chamber 8m long, 6m wide and 3m high. A further boulder slope at N end leads up narrow 5m rift to choke.

Lower Level   **Alt. 330m**   **Length 58m**   **Grade II**

Down spoil heap from Upper Level. Low entrance to flat-out crawl in water followed by sporting low duck under wedged block to a rise up out of water into larger passage. A nicely calcited 8m aven is gained here. Take care not to damage calcited miners stemples. From the base of the aven a three way junction is reached. To right is short tight tube to sump, choked after 2m. Straight on is short miners' trial level in water. To left a duck in cold deep water through keyhole leads to larger passage ending in small aven.

Permission – Grange Farm, Litton.

DOW CAVE   NGR SD 983743   Grade III
Alt. 320m   **Length 3.7km including Providence Pot**

Extended 1953, 1956, 1986, CPC.

WARNING – Hobson's Choice is a climb up through delicately poised boulders and is best left alone. It is also impassable in wet conditions. The whole of the Second Choke area cannot be considered safe under any circumstances due to its unstable nature: the crawls and stream sections are prone to sudden and very high levels of flooding after rain.

A fascinating cave of great character and variety, including the unique Dowbergill Passage. Follow path from bottom of Park Rash upstream and over new footbridge, then round to right and cross beck at prominent boulder slope with entrance at top under scar.

Descend into large stream passage, followed by walking and scrambling for 140m to sandbanks. A further 140m of large walking stream passage leads to mined area. Leave the stream briefly by entering workings (on right), then turn quickly left and up through a dripping chamber and through an eye hole down to main stream passage. Soon after there is a hands and knees crawl. Immediately after straightening up, low in the right hand wall is the tube-like entrance to Dowbergill Passage, a long and complex rift giving a superb through trip to Providence Pot.

Continuing upstream the main cave leads to a large cavern, the First Miners' Chamber. Skirt the large boulder choke to the right, follow stream and then climb up through boulder squeezes – Hobson's Choice – into Depot

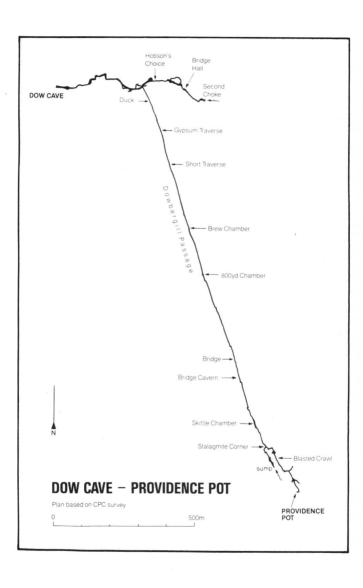

DOW CAVE

Hobson's Choice

Bridge Hall

Second Choke

Duck

Gypsum Traverse

Short Traverse

Dowbergill Passage

Brew Chamber

800yd Chamber

Bridge

Bridge Cavern

Skittle Chamber

Stalagmite Corner

Blasted Crawl

sump

N

DOW CAVE – PROVIDENCE POT

Plan based on CPC survey

0 _____ 500m

PROVIDENCE POT

Chamber. On left is an ascending rift which leads to the Second Miners' Chamber, 8m high with small mine workings but no exit. Straight on from Depot Chamber leads to a series of large caves including the Third Miners' Chamber, Bridge Hall and the main stream passage, until a high rift is encountered, at the end of which is a waterfall. Chimney up the rift out of the range of spray. Above, and behind, is Goliath, a huge stalactite. Traverse off the rift and re-join the stream passage. Round the corner is a further waterfall, easily climbed, giving access to the Roof Gardens, now much despoiled. Straight forward leads to the third waterfall and second choke. From downstream end of Roof Gardens an exposed climb with a difficult move (climbing grade 4c) leads to Clog's Passage – a bouldery tube choked after 17m.

Second Choke is a complex, hazardous breakdown zone. Following main stream, low streamway leads to ascending rift with water cascading down from loose boulders. Climbing up out of main streamway at end of canyon passage several routes interconnect with streamway or close down but a 30m low crawl may be gained which ends at excavated and scaffolded ascent in boulders (Dig A). Very tight squeeze out of scaffolding enters further section of streamway. Crawl in stream for 20m through unstable blocks with unsporting squeezes including the notorious Legbreaker and ascent out of water takes one into Albert Hall – a chamber some 10m long, 5m wide and 3m high. N area closes down between blocks. Three ways forward S – SE join up at various points via Curtain Chamber, Spring Chicken Aven or a low crawl in the stream. Furthest extremity is crawl through pool to choke of very loose blocks.

See under Providence Pot for description of Dowbergill Passage.

Permission – North Cote, Kilnsey.

DRIZZLE POT   NGR SD 994713   Grade II
Alt. 479m   **Depth 11m**

MdL. In shallow shakehole 250m N of boundary wall, and 50m beyond Wall Pot. Entrance covered by large boulders which must be replaced. Large shaft enters reasonable sized chamber with small stream entering part way down one wall, to sink in pool on floor. No passable way on, although an undercut area to one side may repay digging.

Tackle – 12m ladder; stake and sling belay; 20m lifeline.

Permission – West Gate, Kettlewell.

FOG CAVE   NGR SD 992720   Grade III
[Far Rigg Cave]
Alt. 480m   **Length 90m**
Explored 1964, Severn Valley Caving Club.

MdL. Entrance is a prominent stream sink beneath a 2m waterfall. Fissures under waterfall unite in a monotonous low crawl which finally splits into several choked outlets. Water has been tested to Rain Pot.

FOSSIL POT

NGR SE 019667

Grade II

Alt. 325m

Length 12m

Depth 14m

Explored 1955, CPC.

In dry valley leading to Gill House. Entrance (blocked at present) in valley floor near old lead mine workings. Narrow rift pitch into larger passage with sandy floor. A short, tight crawl leads to a parallel rift. Replace boulders over entrance.

Tackle – 14m ladder; stake and sling belay; 15m lifeline.

FOX SCAR SINK

NGR SD 993707

Grade I

Alt. 445m

Depth 3m

Excavated 1986, CPC.

SiL. Wet weather sink below N end of Fox Scar, Conistone Moor. Entrance rift closes down to narrow fissure.

FREESTONE POT

NGR SE 016688

Grade I

Alt. 449m

Length 15m

Depth 15m

MdL. In depression 100m long above Bycliffe Sink. Entrance chute beneath small cliff enters a series of boulder chambers situated beneath each other. No tackle required.

GILL HOUSE POT

NGR SE 012681

Grade II

Alt. 370m

Length 140m

Depth 15m

MdL. Entrance fenced round in field 90m S of Gill House, in dry stream bed. Pitch leads to large cave filled with debris. W passage ends in a small chamber with water entering through roof. E passage ends in boulder fall. Small passage, to the N, meanders on as a 36m low wet crawl becoming too low. Pool near bottom of pitch leads to standing height rift passage which ends in an aven, the floor of which is choked by huge boulders. Pot is now blocked at foot of entrance pitch.

Tackle – 8m ladder; 3m belay; 11m lifeline.

GRASSINGTON MOOR MINE CAVERNS

NGR SE 026676

Explored by lead miners.

MdL. A series of phreatic caverns about 600m long and at a depth of about 60m from the surface, found by workings from Old Turf Pits Shaft. The caverns are now inaccessible due to massive collapse of the shaft and workings.

GRIT POT

NGR SE 014691

Grade II

Alt. 462m

Depth 8m

MdL. Very narrow strenuous pitch choked at the bottom.

Tackle – 8m ladder; stake and sling belay; 12m lifeline.

HOW GILL NICK   NGR SE 023683   Grade I
Alt. 455m   Length 12m

MdL. Large shakehole with small stream sink. Extensively excavated by CPC from 1954/1958. In S side a series of open joints form a small dry bedding complex.

KILNSEY CAVE   NGR SD 973684   Grade II
Alt. 190m   Length 52m

Small entrance near right end of Kilnsey Crag where stream emerges in wet weather. Just inside entrance is junction; the route to the right being too tight almost immediately, while the left passage can be followed through a low canal with pools to where way on is blocked by a calcite barrier.

LANGCLIFFE POT   NGR SD 995710   Grade V
Alt. 488m   Length 9.6km   Depth 116m

Explored 1936 and 1954, CPC; main explorations 1968, YURT and 1968/70/72, ULSA.

WARNING – Parties may be cut off by floods beyond Hammerdale Dub and Nemesis. A trip into the far reaches is one of the most serious undertakings in British caving. The choke beyond Nemesis is liable to move and block the way in – or out.

MdL– HScL. Entrance shakehole is NE of Fox Scar and 50m S of the wall. Hole among limestone slabs is top of entrance pitch. First section of 15m is usually wet but the last section of 12m is dry and broken to the floor of a large multiple aven. Downstream it is soon easiest to traverse 2m above the water to a drop at the start of a canal. Craven Crawl – 200m of wet crawling – was the termination of the cave until 1968. At Number One Junction stooping height inlet enters which can be explored for 300m to a boulder choke. Downstream, Stagger Passage is 600m of stooping and walking, passing the inlet of Strid Passage to Hammerdale Dub and a junction with a much larger passage.

Inlet Series

Upstream, Skirfare Inlet is roomy for 800m until it splits into two. Straight ahead the Thunder Inlet comprises 275m of crawls and narrow rifts to a partial blockage. To the left, The Roads, is a more pleasant passage on two levels which unite as a 3m high tunnel. The water rises from thin fissures but a series of crawls over calcite and boulders emerge in the streamway of Strid Passage. The water can be followed down a wet crawl for 500m to its junction with Stagger Passage, or a more attractive passage upstream passes under a series of avens. The largest of these, Slaughter Aven, is gained by climbing a rift out of the streamway. Beyond the avens a boulder choke is passed into a very wet passage which has not been forced to any conclusion. Oddmire Pot entrance drops in to Slaughter Aven.

The Main Drain

Below Hammerdale Dub, 215m of large stream passage with occasional boulder falls ends where the water sinks into two low crawls. Ahead a dry passage threads its way between boulders for 150m until it rejoins the water

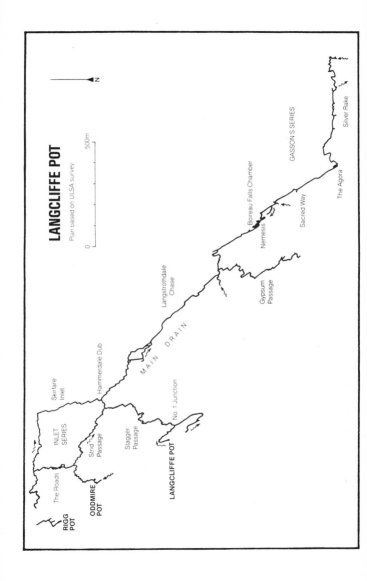

LANGCLIFFE POT

Plan based on ULSA survey

0   500m

N

RIGG POT

ODDMIRE POT

LANGCLIFFE POT

The Roads

INLET SERIES

Skirfare Inlet

Strid Passage

Stager Passage

Hammerdale Dub

No 1 Junction

M A I N   D R A I N

Langstrothdale Chase

Gypsum Passage

Nemesis

Sacred Way

Boireau Falls Chamber

GASSON'S SERIES

The Agora

Silver Rake

emerging from the Wet Way, which provides a damp alternative to the boulder crawl. The united passages now form Langstrothdale Chase – 1.2km of uninterrupted streamway well supplied with boulder obstacles. At Mile House two passages enter. The first is a small inlet explored for 60m and the second is Gypsum Passage, a large dry gallery with a loose boulder choke 30m forward. Pass this with care at high level into a fine continuation and a second choke where a small stream sinks. The inlet gradually diminishes in size to a muddy crawl and climb up into a splendid traverse. The stream emerges from a low, wet crawl, a high level route soon silts up, and the main passage terminates after a struggle through boulders.

At the end of Langstrothdale Chase, 370m downstream of Mile House, the water sinks into a lower bedding plane and the deserted continuation degenerates into a crawl forward into Boireau Falls Chamber, 18m in diameter and 6m high. Here the stream re-appears and cascades into the boulders flooring the chamber.

Gasson's Series

Beneath Boireau Falls Chamber a complex boulder choke is passed to an open passage and 21m pitch, laddered from a false boulder floor. This drops into Nemesis, a chamber 18m high and long and 6m wide. The outlet with the water leads to a group of chambers and a massive complex boulder choke which can be passed to a high streamway. Only 60m forward the water turns right into a pool, creating a short duck. The stream then quickly descends through chaos to Poseidon Sump, which is choked. Ahead the deserted continuation is floored by sand and is a procession of fine rifts and chambers for 400m until a final traverse and boulder slope enters the Agora, 11m wide and high and 24m long. At the far end a route down under fine formations becomes a steep, greasy stalactite slope into Aphrodite Avenue – a splendid high canyon. For some distance the passage is floored with gour pools but gradually boulder falls become more common and the passage larger. Eventually the way forward is sealed by a wall of sand and boulders but a smaller descending passage reaches Dementor Sump which has been dived to a boulder choke after 15m, with tight passage continuing. The sump is fed by a large inlet passage which can be explored by climbing a 3m waterfall but after 300m it ends in a choke of large boulders.

Tackle

Pitch	Ladder	Belay	Lifeline
Entrance	26m	4.5m	30m
Nemesis	22m	6m	36m

Permission – Mile House, Coniston.

LINE POT   NGR SE 006695   Grade II
Alt. 470m   **Depth 15m**
Explored 1958, CPC.

MdL. Entrance on top of scar to the W of Mossdale track. Small hole in line of shakeholes is covered by a limestone slab. Pitch bells out to impressive dimensions before closing in to a choked fissure after corkscrew descent.

Tackle – 15m ladder; 4m belay; 20m lifeline.

LOW DOW CAVE   NGR SD 983743   Grade I
Alt. 310m   Length 12m

At edge of boulder pile below Dow Cave. Crawl through clean boulders into short but sweet streamway ending in massive blocks.
Permission – North Cote, Kilnsey.

LUNAR POT   NGR SE 021682   Grade III
Alt. 435m   Depth 27m
Explored 1955, CPC.

MdL. Near SE corner of former Porphyry Dam. First 3m in small shaft with numerous ledges on to sloping boulder in roof of big 18m shaft. Floor is boulders with 6m of descending rift passage which becomes too tight and choked.

Tackle – 25m ladder; 3m belay; 30m lifeline.

MIST CAVE   NGR SD 990718   Grade II
Alt. 477m   Length 21m
Explored 1986, YURT.

MdL. Shakehole with small rising, 250m NW of Rigg Pot, contains entrance under limestone outcrop. Crawl over collapsed roof slab into small streamway. Downstream is too tight; upstream continues to a left bend and partly silted passage on right, but eventually becomes low and narrow.

MOSSDALE CAVERNS   NGR SE 016697   Grade V
Alt. 430m   Length 10km   Depth 60m
Explored 1941, BSA; extended by BPC, ULSA and others.

WARNING – Liable to total flooding. Only stable entrance is blocked – all others are unstable and dangerous. All expeditions into this system under present conditions are inadvisable and permission to descend is not given.

MdL. New entrance to left of scar is blocked. Other entrances are located around stream sink under overhang. Several routes via crawls and boulder chambers unite in Assembly Hall. Down S boulder slope is flat roofed streamway down to Blackpool Sands.

Western Passages
To right in Assembly Hall, passages radiate to the Trenches and Table Chamber where the Broad Street stream is encountered. Upstream beyond squeezes a deep canal appears to sump and numerous side passages form a dry oxbow series to the S. Down Broad Street, Far Western Passages are 2m above stream on the right. They run SE for 300m until the high rift passage dwindles into low crawls which sub-divide.

Broad Street to Cigarette Junction
Continuing down Broad Street the stream enters a waist deep canal leading to Blackpool Sands where the water deepens. The Swims consist of 150m of wide, wet passages to a scramble over blocks into Boulder Hall, 15m wide, 9m high and 50m long – the largest chamber in the system. Across Boulder

Hall the stream enters Confusion Passages, a region of wide bedding planes and diverging joint passages. On the far left is Confusion Cavern, a rift chamber 37m long, 20m high and 6m wide, but the way forward is to keep right and rejoin the stream. Above a dry oxbow to the right is flat roofed Gypsum Aven, and beyond the water flows into Broadway and hence to Cigarette Junction.

Cigarette Junction to Rough Chamber

At Cigarette Junction the dry passage ahead soon splits into Middle and Right Passages while the stream runs left into a series of crawls to the Syphon Passage. This has been forced in dry conditions to a tight waterlogged fissure and high level boulder choke crawls. Syphon Passage is now totally silted up and water flows beyond it to Rough Passage.

Before Syphon Passage the roomy dry corridor of Straightway runs SE joining up with the Middle and Right Passages. The latter is the easiest route from Cigarette Junction to Rough Chamber, proceeding via Wiggle Junction and the Serpent. Just before the Serpent, Ourobourous Passage is a rift in the right wall. Narrow at first, it soon becomes walking size but ends after 140m in a boulder choke. At the end of Straightway, the continuation enters Great Aven, which is 25m high, while left leads to a roomy rectangular cavern – Rough Chamber.

Rough Passage

Under the floor of Rough Chamber a low crawl enters the False Marathon Network but the obvious exit from the chamber is a rift. Suddenly this drops to a crawl of Rough Passage and turns right, but ahead a climb over a chockstone reveals Shingle Passage, which originally ended in a pool. A simple duck gains a continuation and high on the left a bored tube connects with the beginning of Syphon Passage. Shingle Passage becomes an awkward rift ending in Fungus Chamber. Rough Passage is a hands and knees crawl relieved by occasional stooping sections and a slide under a boulder. A side passage on the right intersects the False Marathon Network which finally becomes very low downstream. The large side passage on the left is Oomagoolie Passage – a 300m offshoot running NW. It begins as a crawl but eventually enlarges to a roomy passage ending in the Piccadilly Circus boulder choke. This has been linked to Fungus Chamber in Shingle Passage. Rough Passage continues past Waterfall Junction with its attendant oxbow until finally, 215m from Rough Chamber, Kneewrecker Junction is gained.

Kneewrecker Series

The left branch at the junction is Kneewrecker – a 250m long, wet awkward crawl which suddenly ends at a T-junction with the impressive Relief Passage. To the N this highway passes under a high aven and becomes very narrow while a W branch is choked by fill. To the S, Relief Passage intersects large caverns at False Fourways, but a crawl in the stream leads on to the true Fourways Junction.

Fourways

Straight ahead the water flows into the continuing crawl of Far Syphon Passage which eventually sumps. S a dry crawl and climb intersect the

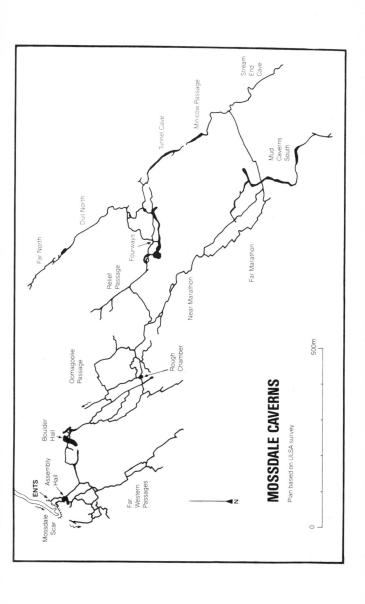

ENTS

Mossdale Scar

Assembly Hall

Boulder Hall

Far Western Passages

Oomagoolie Passage

Rough Chamber

Relief Passage

Far North

Dull North

Fourways

Tunnel Cave

Near Marathon

Minicow Passage

Far Marathon

Mud Caverns South

Stream End Cave

MOSSDALE CAVERNS

Plan based on ULSA survey

N

0   500m

Fourways South sand caverns at a T-junction. To the right these open up into a massive bedding chamber which connects with False Fourways, while left diminishes to the crawl of Imperial Way. N branch from Fourways is easy going for 90m to where two tunnels enter at floor level on the right. These unite and soon open out into Tunnel Caves, where a trickle of water flows in a handsome but muddy streamway. Finally the trickle sinks into boulders and the continuing dry cavern ends in a wall of mud and boulders. A narrow fissure at roof level is the oral connection with Minicow Passage in Marathon Series. The water in Tunnel Caves emerges from a boulder choke above which is an extensive series of crawls and chambers. The most westerly crawl connects with Imperial Way in Fourways South. Continuing along Fourways North the passage becomes very variable in size due to large mudbanks. This Dull North Passage leads 300m to Far North Chamber where a small stream can be found flowing in boulders beneath the floor.

Far North

Wriggle down into low crawl at far end of North Chamber. Passage becomes too low after 37m but route under right wall pops out above awkward climb down to stream. Water runs into jagged tortuous passage and reappears in North Chamber. Upstream over mud barrier is large passage to a boulder choke at low level bypassed at high level into a wide cavern sloping back to the stream once more. Odd scrambles in a fine passage lead to a final cavern beyond a short crawl. Inlet is a squeeze to a sump and a wide dry passage is terminated by a boulder choke.

Marathon Series

The right branch at Kneewrecker Junction is Near Marathon Passage which consists of 300m of crawling and sideways walking. For 60m the passage is dry until an inlet passage 75m long brings in the water from the False Marathon Network. Downstream is a wet oxbow containing a nasty duck but this can be avoided by a dry, rough bypass. Near Marathon ends when the streamway lowers to a squeeze and a shingle slope on the right marks the Parting of the Ways. Up the slope is Leakey's Marathon, 300m of sideways crawling in a monotonous passage which turns into a rift after the entry of a muddy inlet. The rift then rejoins the main Marathon stream. The squeeze in the waterway is the start of Far Marathon East which is shorter and less energetic than Leakey's Marathon. After the initial squeezes it becomes an easy crawl as far as a cross rift, where it lowers to a flat out crawl for 75m until the junction with Leakey's Marathon. A short wet passage now leads to an aven which is a 6m chimney up into High Level Mud Caverns. A sump has now appeared just before the aven, perhaps because of silting in Stream End Cave; that part of the cave described from here on is presently inaccessible.

High Level Mud Caverns

S branch is 245m of walking and crawling in a wide passage to a boulder choke. Keeping up to the left passes two blockages but ends in an unstable chamber. N branch of High Level Mud Caverns soon sub-divides. A crawl on the right enters the Sanctuary – a 9m high aven, while right drops into a clean washed passage ending in a slot in the floor and a mud choke. The slot communicates with Far Marathon East but is impassable.

Far Stream Cave to Stream End Cave
Below the 6m chimney a short crawl drops into a pleasant streamway – Far Stream Cave – which gives easy walking to Minicow Junction where an inlet enters. This is Minicow Passage which may be followed up through a 'mini-swim' to a boulder choke. Passing this, alternative climbs of 6m enter a large high level cavern preceded by a high aven. The stream is rejoined eventually but emerges from a series of sumped passages and a further difficult climb regains the high level cavern. The passage ends in a blank wall with an oral floor connection with Tunnel Caves. Downstream at Minicow Junction the Stream End Cave achieves impressive proportions before it ends in a large, muddy boulder choke with two roof chambers.
Permission – This cave is within the Conistone Common. The owner of the shooting rights and gaitholders' spokesman is A.F.D. Roberts, 'Mossdale', Conistone.

ODDMIRE POT   NGR SD 994713   Grade V
Alt. 480m   **Length – see Langcliffe Pot**
Explored 1977, WRPC.

MdL. An alternative entrance to Langcliffe Pot via the Inlet Series, and thus cutting out the flood-prone Craven Crawl. Excavated entrance cunningly hidden behind large boulder at S side of horseshoe shaped shakehole with stream falling down rock face to E, 32m N of Drizzle Pot. Care needed at top as slippery shelf gives straight onto broken 21m pitch into Slaughter Aven of Langcliffe Pot. Grade assumes trip is to far reaches of Langcliffe Pot.

Tackle – 23m ladder; spreader belay; 30m lifeline.

Permission – West Gate, Kettlewell.

OOZLE HOLE   NGR SD 994727   Grade II
Alt. 480m   **Length 55m**
Explored 1974, KCC.

MdL. Obvious entrance just above stream in true left bank of Dowbergill Wham. Initially walking size, the excavated passage degenerates into a low crawl, which is now very silted up, until a T-junction is reached, at a small stream passage. Downstream with the water can only be followed for 12m to where it is too small, while an abandoned downstream route continues for 9m to a complete choke. Upstream quickly splits, one way choking at once, whilst the other leads to the bottom of a 4.5m shaft which most likely connects with an old bellpit on the surface above.
Permission – North Cote, Kilnsey.

OUT GATE POT   NGR SD 990724   Grade II
Alt. 470m   **Depth 20m**
Explored 1956, CPC.

MdL. Tight entrance under limestone slabs is difficult to find. Pitch is constricted halfway down by a bottleneck and at present is blocked by jammed boulders at this point. At bottom low bedding caves and further short pitch in floor are choked. One ladder for both pitches.

Tackle – 20m ladder; stake and sling belay; 25m lifeline.

PALFREY POT   NGR SE 021674   Grade II
Alt. 380m   **Depth 12m**

MdL. On E side of shallow valley, entrance partly covered by large slabs. Straight descent in rift to a boulder floor. Climb up at E end leads to short crawl and a parallel shaft with easy climb down to floor and choke.

To the W in the main Folds valley is Nelson's Level, which intersects a natural rift and bedding plane after 180m and a stream inlet passage after 250m.

Tackle – 12m ladder; stake and sling belay; 15m lifeline.

PARK GILL CAVE   NGR SD 985749   Grade II
Alt. 380m   **Length 22m**
Explored 1968, YURT.

SiL. Resurgence below small dry gorge near head of Park Gill. Easy crawl round to right, through wallow to junction. Ahead is 5cm airspace, becoming lower while dry passage to right soon becomes silted up. Water sinks a short distance higher up the gill.

PIGEON POT   NGR SE 005688   Grade I
Alt. 430m   **Depth 6m**
Explored 1975, CUCC.

MdL. Entrance over wall on W side of Mossdale track. Short crawl down drops into tight rift which is choked at the bottom.

PROVIDENCE POT   NGR SD 992728   Grade III
Alt. 400m   **Length 344m: 3.7km including Dowbergill**   **Depth 30m**
                 Passage and Dow Cave
Explored 1954, CPC.

Prominent lidded entrance in stream bed in Dowbergill just before gill forks. Climb down dug shaft to small 3m crawl. Drop of 1.5m into small chamber is followed by a short rift into the main passage. Continue through 54 Cavern and scramble through boulders, keep to the right then up slope in large aven; 6m up this is 25m passage, becoming too small (scaling pole needed). From aven down to an easy squeeze, through to slanting mud and boulder passage, then into July Grotto and forward to T-junction. Right is small inlet passage for 20m, which becomes too tight. Left is Terminal Chamber and then narrow tube up calcited slope into Blasted Crawl. This is now a muddy wallow with crawling size canal passages, eventually debouching into The Palace. This large chamber is descended to an eyehole and a steep slope (climb down staircase to the right) into The Dungeon. Drop down calcite boss into Depot Chamber, turn right under formations into a small crawl which enters the Dowbergill Passage at Stalagmite Corner. Upstream for 90m in large stream passage is sump, dived for 44m past two airbells before being blocked by gravel.

N.B. Take careful note of crawl entrance at Stalagmite Corner for the return journey.

Dowbergill Passage   **Grade IV**
WARNING – In wet weather much of the stream route is impassable and long, exhausting traverses become necessary; the Duck also sumps.

The traverse of Dowbergill Passage from Dow Cave to Providence Pot, or in the reverse direction, remains one of the classic caving expeditions in the district. It has also been the scene of many cave rescues. The survey plan of a simple straight line joining the two caves belies the intricate and at times exasperating problem of route-finding within a 20m vertical range in the high rift passages. It is strongly recommended that parties contemplating the through trip should acquaint themselves with both ends of the passage before attempting a complete traverse. It is suggested that Providence Pot and the S part of Dowbergill Passage at least to the rock window in Bridge Cavern, and Dow Cave and the N part of Dowbergill Passage at least as far as Brew Chamber, be each explored beforehand. Parties exploring from Dow Cave should always make sure that the Providence Pot entrance is open. The following description is the easiest route, from Providence Pot to Dow Cave.

From Stalagmite Corner proceed downstream over blockfalls into easy walking passage with stream to left in low bedding. A squeeze between boulders leads to Skittle Chamber. From here follow 245m of boulder strewn passages, including a crawl in the stream after 15m, until a short traverse is reached. After this a boulder fall appears to block the way. This can be forced through a squeeze but a slit to the left gives access to a parallel rift and then a window on the right drops into Bridge Cavern – a large 3m wide and 4.5m high passage with a loose block floor which continues for some distance. The Bridge, at the Dow Cave end of the Chamber, is a 2m arch of several suspended boulders. Under this, and a little way forwards, on the right, is a descent down a boulder slope into a chest deep canal, followed by a shallower stream cave. A narrow rift stream passage section is followed for 230m via several small boulder obstacles to an obvious oxbow. Another 90m of stream passage follows and then a low crawl on the left gives access to a parallel passage; 25m along this is the 8.5m wide 800 Yards Chamber. From here there are two ways on.

The stream level is tortuous at one point but soon eases until a boulder pile forces an ascent. A wide direct traverse (or easier higher level) from 800 Yards Chamber also reaches the same place and continues across a holdless section (Greg's Horror) to a false floor and descent to stream. Easy going ends at another boulder choke below Brew Chamber.

The boulder pile is 15m high and by an exposed climb it can be surmounted. A simpler way is to crawl through choke 4.5m above stream sink and follow fissure passage to a chimney and straddle down onto blocks. Further descent leads to traverse line 6m above stream and a way over blocks before dropping to water level.

Continue in stream along narrow passage to a rock window and chest deep water below the Terrible Traverse. The beginning of Gypsum Traverse is marked by an obvious slanting climb up to a shale bed and a route forward over a false floor. Not recommended is the waterway, which degenerates into a tortuous crawl cum traverse. From Gypsum Traverse scramble down into chamber and slide past huge slab to Hardy's Horror – a short hand traverse and drop onto a boulder in a pool. A bypass is possible by diving a 1m sump to the same pool and a fine passage continues to a duck under a mass of flowstone. Above the flowstone (scaling pole required) is the Buddhist's Temple – a well decorated aven. Beyond the Duck a gothic canal gradually lowers until a chute rises into Dow Cave.

For those traversing in the opposite direction, points to note include a squeeze at stream level before a slanting traverse up to Brew Chamber (easier route); the exit from Bridge Cavern at the far end, on the right; and the location of Stalagmite Corner, low down on the left hand side.

QUARRY POT   NGR SE 005697   Grade II
Alt. 495m   **Depth 17m**
Explored 1958, CPC.

MdL. SE of Capplestone Gate and 100m from shakehole marked "Quarry" on map. Takes bog drainage. Entry through boulders into chamber with one solid wall. The whole pot comprises three superimposed boulder chambers which are entered via the intervening boulder chokes. No tackle required.

RATTLE POT   NGR SE 018685   Grade II
Alt. 455m   **Depth 8m**

MdL. Oval shakehole with covered shaft at N end. Very narrow rift with small bedding cave at the bottom. No tackle required.

RIGG POT   NGR SD 992716   Grade IV
Alt. 478m   **Length 150m**   **Depth 34m**
Explored 1938, CPC; extended 1968 and 1970, ULSA.

MdL. About 800m SE of Rain Slack Well. A prominent stream sink. Entrance a hole in boulders over a rift. A climb down and then short boulder slope to head of pitch (usually dry). Passage straight ahead is choked by boulders. At N end of chamber below pitch is excavated crawl to two more large avens and entry to series of crawls. Hands and knees crawl to T-junction. Upstream a stalactite over a pool bars progress but downstream a canal has been forced for 60m until the air space becomes very low.

Tackle – 20m ladder; 6m belay; 25m lifeline.

Permission – West Gate, Kettlewell.

ROD'S POT   NGR SE 015690   **Grade II**
Alt. 462m   Depth 6m

MdL. Shaft in a very small shakehole. Narrow 6m ladder climb in a choked rift.

Tackle – 8m ladder; 3m belay; 12m lifeline.

SCAR GILL CAVE   NGR SD 981711   **Grade I**
Alt. 340m   Length 6m

In scree filled gill above the Scar. Shattered rock shelter.

SHAMROCK POT   NGR SE 017687   **Grade I**
Alt. 455m   Depth 7m

MdL. Twin entrances unite at 3m into a climb down into boulder floored chamber 3.5m long.

SIMONSTONE POTS   NGR SD 988712   **Grade II**
Alt. 440m   Depth 6m
Explored 1968, YURT.

SiL. Two small but awkward shafts on Langcliffe Pasture. One requires a ladder or handline.

Tackle – 8m ladder; stake and sling belay; 12m lifeline.

SNOW POT   NGR SE 014691   **Grade I**
Alt. 462m   Depth 9m

MdL. Entrance on small plateau, where gritstone and limestone meet. Very narrow rift beginning to widen out at bottom which has a boulder floor. Rope descent.

SPIDER POT   NGR SE 022682   **Grade I**
Alt. 430m   Length 15m   Depth 8m

MdL. Entrance is shakehole in SE corner of Lunar Pot field. A spiralling chute enters a chamber with two choked outlets.

SPRING TRAP CAVE   NGR SD 975705   **Grade I**
Alt. 195m   Length 370m
Explored 1949, NPC; extended 1965 and 1972, CDG.
WARNING – In flood Sump 1 may become 150m long, extending to second junction.

On E bank of Black Keld, just over wall from pumphouse. Low entrance leads to cross rift and step into hands and knees crawl for 27m to sump. This has been passed and is 45m long, to an open canal passage at the far side

1.2m high. After 45m the way splits, to the left continuing as a canal until it becomes too tight after 30m where the water emerges from an impenetrable bedding plane. Right at the junction is dry, and can be followed for 30m to a further junction. The right fork leads to Pot Sump which has been dived for 15m before it becomes too tight, while a passage over the pot passes through a low, heavily silted squeeze to a mud choke and a well decorated aven series.

The main passage from the second junction continues for a further 120m, rising gradually all the way until Sump 2 is reached. This has been dived for 15m to a small airbell and chamber above. No underwater continuation is apparent.

Permission – Mile House, Kettlewell.

STAR FISSURE   NGR SE 016697   Grade I
Alt. 430m   **Length 12m**   **Depth 8m**

MdL. Immediately S of the pool sink at W end of Mossdale Scar. Drop into small boulder ruckle with blind crawls. Further descent to stream in fissure passage, which chokes under the sink. Water runs into boulder ruckle.

SWARTHGILL HOLE   NGR SE 012701   Grade III
Alt. 442m   **Length 470m**   **Depth 24m**
Explored 1959, CPC; 1979, GC.

WARNING – Lower sections flood in wet weather.

MdL. A confused system of high joints linked by small streamways. Entrance is rift in E bank of Swarth Gill – covered by boulders. Rope is useful on first part of pitch and ladder on last section into chamber. Passages at two levels lead off to a series of inlets and avens, but downstream is a spiral crawl to a wet junction. The inlet is a meandering crawl with a branch chamber to the right before the stream rises from a choke, passed by a crawl on the right and a fissure passage ending at a second choke. A passage 8m downstream of the first choke links back to the foot of the entrance shaft.

Downstream from the inlet junction, a frothy canal leads to a further junction and complex oxbows into Aven Series on the left. Crawl into canal may be avoided by high level route to the left, which reunites in Flake Cavern. Stream flows into low bedding plane in first boulder chamber beyond Flake Cavern, and is last seen amongst the chaos of the terminal choke in the second boulder chamber. Top of entrance pitch blocked at present.

Tackle – 9m ladder; 9m belay; 15m lifeline.

THUNDER POT   NGR SD 993716   Grade I
Alt. 480m   **Depth 6m**
Explored 1964, ULSA.

Complex sink area. Narrow rift beneath boulder at N sink is climbable when stream is diverted but is choked by shingle. Another small shaft at the S sink and a boulder choked chasm at the W sink.

TOPHAM POTS   NGR SD 994695   Grade II
Alt. 383m   **Depth 5m**
Explored 1986, CPC

Several small rifts in New Close Allotments on W side of Tophams Road, Conistone Moor. All close down at around 5m depth.

Tackle (all pots) – 8m ladder; stake and sling belay; 10m lifeline.

TUP POT   NGR SD 995711   Grade I
Alt. 480m   **Depth 8m**

MdL. About 60m W of Langcliffe Pot. A 3m wide shaft in shallow shakehole. Climb down at N end to floor of rubble which chokes the pot. At present much scrap iron clutters the hole.
Permission – Mile House, Kettlewell.

UPPER RIGG POT   NGR SD 992716   Grade II
Alt. 480m   **Depth 9m**

MdL. Narrow wet rift, 9m deep, about 9m upstream of Rigg Pot. Choked by pebbles.

Tackle – 9m ladder; stake and sling belay; 12m lifeline.

WALL POT   NGR SD 994713   Grade III
Alt. 479m   **Depth 27m**
Explored 1948 and 1954, CPC.

MdL. S of Rain Pot between Rigg and Langcliffe Pots, 200m N of wall. First 8m pitch into rift chamber; at N end narrow slit is top of 18m pitch. Stream sinks in gravel floor.

Tackle

Pitch	Ladder	Belay	Lifeline
Entrance	8m	3m	10m
2nd	20m	6m	25m

Permission – West Gate, Kettlewell.

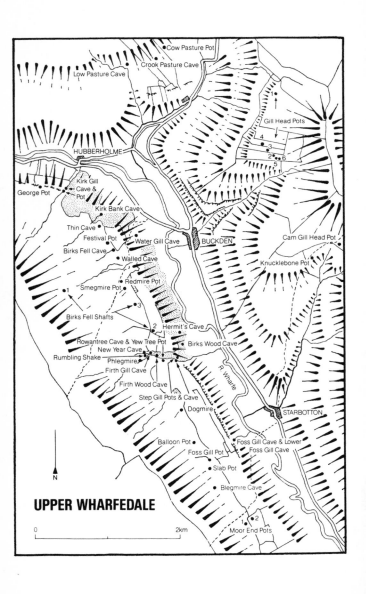

Cow Pasture Pot
Crook Pasture Cave
Low Pasture Cave

Gill Head Pots
4
3
2 • 6
5

HUBBERHOLME

Kirk Gill
Cave &
Pot
George Pot
Kirk Bank Cave

Thin Cave
Festival Pot • Water Gill Cave
Birks Fell Cave
• Walled Cave
• Redmire Pot
•1 Smegmire Pot
•3
Birks Fell Shafts
2 • Hermit's Cave
Rowantree Cave & Yew Tree Pot
New Year Cave
Rumbling Shake • Phlegmire
Firth Gill Cave
Firth Wood Cave
Step Gill Pots & Cave
• Dogmire

Balloon Pot
• Foss Gill Pot
• Slab Pot
• Blegmire Cave

•1 •2
Moor End Pots

BUCKDEN

Cam Gill Head Pot

Knucklebone Pot

Birks Wood Cave

R. Wharfe

STARBOTTON

Foss Gill Cave & Lower
Foss Gill Cave

N

UPPER WHARFEDALE

0   2km

UPPER WHARFEDALE

BALLOON POT   **NGR SD 942744**   **Grade II**
Alt. 420m   **Depth 6m**
Obscure entrance in line of shakeholes N from Foss Gill Pot, with no sign of bed rock. Awkward climb down into long rift containing remains of Met. Office weather balloon, and ending in a choke at foot of debris slope. Permission – Bushey Lodge, Starbotton.

BIRKS FELL CAVE   **NGR SD 931769**   **Grade IV**
Alt. 362m   **Length 3.6km**   **Depth 142m**
Explored 1932, YRC; extended 1947, BPC; 1968/69 and 1973, CPC.

WARNING – Flooding in the Canal and in The Wet Bedding Caves will seal off sections of the cave. There are loose boulders in many places.

Entrance in a shallow valley, just before a small waterfall, about 100m W of wall corner. One of the finest sporting potholes in the north; includes sections of large rift passage streamway, crawling, traversing and climbing. It is at present the deepest pothole in the area covered by this volume of the guidebook and the lower passages to the final sump are strenuous.

Easy going in a rift passage from eyehole entrance for 230m to a small chamber out of which a flat out crawl, The Bradford Crawl, gives way to easier passage to Tree Chamber. Rift passage for a short distance is followed by a deepening canal. Keyhole on right at the end of The Canal gives access to the flat out Connection Crawl, 15m long and having 9m long inlet on right. Crawl emerges into large passage and on right of exit are squeeze and 2m climb into chamber 12m by 4.5m; above a fine flow are two roof passages.

Just downstream in main passage is inlet on right to Basin Aven, where a short climb reaches a low crawl which becomes too small. First pitch in main streamway can be by-passed by traversing over the top and climbing down narrow parallel rift to the right. Stream passage leads into Slipped Floor Chamber, 67m long, 6m wide, 4.5m high. Way on is down The Dig, just before the end of the chamber, a 3m drop into the stream passage. Sporting cascades follow until Shooting Box Aven is reached. Downstream from Shooting Box Aven a fine canal passage goes to Aven Two. Scaling gear is needed to reach the passages above each of these avens.

Downstream out of Aven Two, climb up rubble slope and then through keyhole, down to streamway. This area is dangerously unstable. Stream passage to 40 Years' Corner, decorated with many fine formations. On to First Wet Bedding Cave, 9m long, then climb up on left via rift, into Dry

Fault Chamber. Climb down to enter Second Wet Bedding Cave, 100m long. Climb up on the right, just before the end, to Moon Milk Cave, dry with stream passage below, and then carefully negotiate a series of unsafe boulder chambers. Crawl under The Block—a massive boulder, down to the small hole below it, and into the stream passage. Follow stream down to Cascade Pitch (bolt belay results in ladder hanging directly in flood water, but no natural belay nearby) followed by two short drops. Follow high narrow rift passage at stream level, through a duck under a chockstone, and then climb up into Bridge Aven. Climb down to the stream again and enter The Grand Gallery, 170m long and up to 20m high rift passage with 60m long high level oxbow and knee deep water. This culminates in Whitehall with its many fine formations. Out of this chamber, straight on leads to Perfection Oxbow, which contains gour pools and eventually rejoins the main stream passage after 45m. (The Oxbow continues over the top of the short climb down into the main stream passage for a further 40m, ending in a calcite choke.)

Main passage leads out of Whitehall on the left and a well decorated stream rift continues to Elbow Bend. Straight forward here leads to a choked bedding cave, only 20m from the end of Hermit's Cave. Left, round Elbow Bend, via a descending rift passage, leads to The Thrutch, a narrow rift, shortly followed by Shale Crawl, a 90m long wallow in 50cm deep water, to Shale Cavern. Out of this chamber is Shale Pitch leading to a tight rift passage. A hole on the right after 90m leads to a waterlogged passage and The Styx sump. Straight on are The Traverses, which provide strenuous progress as far as a small, climbable pitch. Climb up again into a bedding crawl which after 6m drops down The Slimy Slit to The Sewer Series. Canal passage leads to the final sump after 110m, only 120m from and at the same level as the rising in the valley floor.

Shooting Box Aven Series

Scale aven for 16m. Rift passage upstream to chamber with 3.5m waterfall. Hard climb up the waterfall gives more rift passage to junction. Right too small to follow. Left to large bedding chamber with obscure 2.5m climb on the left. Canal passage to junction. Right too narrow; left passage goes for 110m, ending in choke. Just before the end a passage on the right gives access to two avens.

Aven Two Series

Scale aven, 15m. Rift passage to chaotic boulder area, then well decorated stream passage to crawl leading to even bigger stream passage, 6m high. A very tight tube gives access to the 18m high Aven Three, above which is a further 300m of passage, mostly a low canal ending 30m beyond a duck at a sump.

Tackle

Pitch	Ladder	Belay	Lifeline
1st	9m	3m	12m
Cascade	6m	9m	12m
Shale Pitch	15m	6m	20m
Slimy Slit	6m	3m	9m

Permission—CNCC.

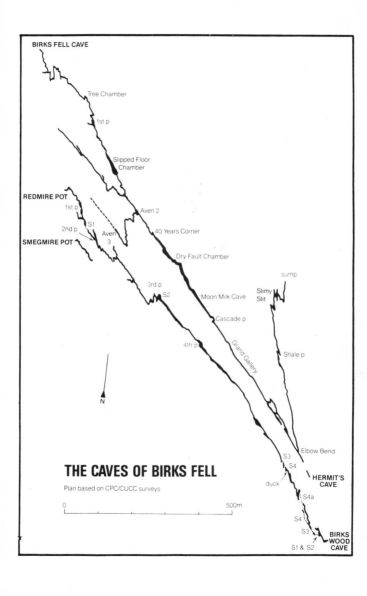

BIRKS FELL CAVE

Tree Chamber

1st p

Slipped Floor
Chamber

REDMIRE POT

1st p

S1

2nd p

Aven 3

SMEGMIRE POT

Aven 2

40 Years Corner

Dry Fault Chamber

3rd p

S2

Moon Milk Cave

Cascade p

4th p

Grand Gallery

sump

Slimy
Slit

Shale p

Elbow Bend

S3

S4

duck

S4a

S4

S3

S1 & S2

**HERMIT'S
CAVE**

**BIRKS
WOOD
CAVE**

N

THE CAVES OF BIRKS FELL

Plan based on CPC/CUCC surveys

0   500m

BIRKS FELL SHAFTS   Grade II
Explored 1970, CPC.

1. NGR SD 924764   **Alt. 470m**   **Depth 11m**
   MdL. Large stream sink in conspicuous shakehole. Pitch enters large chamber with rift descent into narrow passage which becomes too tight.

2. NGR SD 936759   **Alt. 360m**   **Depth 4.5m**
   Narrow fissure under wall by flood sink. Squeeze down into boulder floored passage. Becomes too tight in both directions.

3. NGR SD 934763   **Alt. 380m**   **Depth 4.5m**
   Squeeze down between timbers into small chamber under adjacent shakehole. No exit apparent.

Tackle – 8m ladder; stake and sling belay; 9m lifeline.

Permission – Redmire Farm, Buckden.

BIRKS WOOD CAVE   NGR SD 940757   Grade IV
Alt. 250m   **Length 255m – 1.6km including Redmire Pot.**
Explored 1960 & 1971, CPC; extended and linked to Redmire Pot 1976-77, CUCC.

   At top of waterfall by side of track. Inside the entrance is a 1.5m free dive into a small chamber and canal passage leading upstream. After 27m a bedding chamber on the left is followed by a duck and ascending fissure which becomes too narrow. The main way on is halfway along the canal where a small roof level bedding on the left leads to a drop into a pool and a duck into a narrow canal, which is followed by Sumps 1 and 2, 11m and 4.5m long. These sumps lead to a large airbell and on no account should they be free-dived as they are tight and awkward.

   From the airbell Sump 3, 12m long, leads to a low stream passage with Sump 4 only 18m upstream. This sump is 25m long and leads to a tight airbell, The Wretched Wriggle, ending at the as yet undived Sump 5. Happily, these nasty sumps are bypassed by a small passage leading off on the right 9m upstream of Sump 3. A squeeze upwards and an awkward crawling traverse lead to 67m of strenuous progress along a narrow rift ending at the static Sump 4A. This is 25m long and emerges at the bottom of the final climb in Redmire Pot.

Permission – Redmire Farm, Buckden.

BLEGMIRE CAVE   NGR SD 945738   Grade I
Alt. 440m   **Length 6m**
Explored 1976, CUCC.

   Entrance in smaller part of a double shakehole on bench above Foss Gill Pot. Descending rift passes squeeze to crawl ending in choke. Small stream normally sinks here.

CAM GILL HEAD POT   NGR SD 962770   Grade III
Alt. 550m   **Depth 17m**
. Explored 1969, GC.

ML. In shallow shakehole just above wall which runs round head of Cam Gill. Small entrance is top of pitch into roomy chamber. At foot are three ways on. A 2.5m climb down to one side leads to choked rifts in the floor; a narrow slot leads to further choked rift behind the SW wall; the last way is a window on to a further pitch into a rift passage. The foot of the rift is choked, but a short traverse is possible at roof level.

Tackle

Pitch	Ladder	Belay	Lifeline
Entrance	12m	6m	20m
2nd	4.5m	Foot of first ladder	8m

COW PASTURE POT   NGR SD 938799   Grade I
Alt. 420m   **Depth 6m**

SiL. Entrance 100m NE of small scar on Cow Pasture Narrow rift choked at the bottom.

CROOK PASTURE CAVE   NGR SD 935797   Grade II
Alt. 400m   **Length 17m**
Explored 1968, YURT.

SiL. Rising from small scar on Cow Pasture N of Cray. Entrance is narrow crawl on right, and sideways crawling past two awkward corners ends where passage side has collapsed.

DOGMIRE   NGR SD 940748   Grade I
Alt. 415m   **Depth 6m**
Explored 1977, CUCC.

Rift shakehole below stream sink at foot of next valley N of Foss Gill Pot. Short crawl leads to climb down into small chamber. Right is an inlet which is too low. Rift ahead is obstructed by silt, although it is possible to see further.

FESTIVAL POT   NGR SD 930771   Grade II
Alt. 366m   **Length 25m**   **Depth 6m**
Explored 1951, EPC.

Entrance 120m NW of Birks Fell Cave is 3m pitch into small chamber and through squeeze into very low passage which chokes.

Tackle – 4.5m ladder; 3m belay; 6m lifeline.

Permission – Redmire Farm, Buckden.

FIRTH GILL CAVE   NGR SD 936755   Grade II
Alt. 340m   Length 30m
Explored 1957, HRCG.

In Firth Gill above wood. Low entrance and flat crawl for 18m to rift. Tight crawl to upstream chamber with 6m waterfall.

FIRTH WOOD CAVE   NGR SD 937755   Grade II
Alt. 335m   Length 30m
Explored 1967, WRPC.

About 100m from top of wood in Firth Gill is small rising on the N bank, 15m above the main stream. A low wet crawl with very little airspace leads round several bends to where one can stand. Beyond, more crawling in a water-filled rift passage for 9m, becoming too narrow.

FOSS GILL CAVE   NGR SD 948744   Grade III
Alt. 260m   Length 245m
Explored 1957, CDG; extended 1969, CPC.

WARNING – Entrance quickly sumps in wet weather.

Prominent rising at opposite side of valley to Starbotton. Low bedding plane drops into 1st canal, deep and with very cold water. Canal quickly ends where main passage turns right; short passage on left here leads to 2m drop and choke, which is the same as that met at end of Lower Foss Gill Cave. On upstream quickly meets 2nd canal, shorter and shallower, ending where streamway turns right to intersect large, bouldery passage. To right here is low canal ending in choke but main way is left, past boulders to 3rd canal, the longest but not out of depth. This canal ends at wide, block-strewn passage with short branch to left at end of canal, leading to choke.

Wide passage leads to T-junction with stream welling up out of very deep, narrow rift in floor. To right is high fissure leading to 3m climb up into continuation which is too narrow 18m from climb. Left at T-junction is crawl into wide bedding plane, with way to 2.5m deep well on right, and continuing crawl in canal past a squeeze and over mudbanks to where flake of rock blocks passage.

Permission – Bushey Lodge Farm, Starbotton.

FOSS GILL POT   NGR SD 944742   Grade IV
Alt. 415m   Length 137m   Depth 47m
Explored 1914, YRC; extended 1968, NCC.

On plateau edge above Starbotton, where large stream sinks. Entrance is a large rift with an easy boulder slope descent of 14m to head of 1st pitch. At foot, high rift leads to tight crawl and larger passage to top of 2nd pitch. Chamber below has narrow fissure on one side where water sinks, while a 3m climb down leads to an open passage running back under the upper series. After 20m a canal is met and 12m on is a T-junction. To the left is an inlet with stream falling out of a tight rift, and a passage beyond through a further canal to a flat out crawl which gets too low. Right at the junction leads through more canal and a 1m long duck, to a final boulder chamber with three muddy tubes leading out, all of which quickly end.

Tackle

Pitch	Ladder	Belay	Lifeline
1st	12m	6m	20m
2nd	11m	6m	20m

Permission – Bushey Lodge Farm, Starbotton.

GEORGE POT   NGR SD 921779   Grade II
Alt. 350m   **Depth 8m**
Explored 1957, CPC.

In large shakehole 320m W of Kirk Gill; entrance covered by slabs and wire netting. Straight descent into large chamber with no way on.

Tackle – 8m ladder; stake and sling belay; 9m lifeline.

GILL HEAD POTS
[Out Moor Pots]
Explored, YRC.

ML. Main group of shafts is on Out Moor to the N of Buckden Gavel Mine.

1. NGR SD 953792   Alt. 535m   Depth 9m   Grade II
Isolated shaft at stream sink above Cow Close Gill. Climb down shattered rock past two large chockstones to a rubble floor where water seeps away.

2. NGR SD 953783   Alt. 555m   Depth 6m   Grade I
Long shakehole with remarkable linear cliff. Hole at S end is chute down unstable slope into a square chamber with three impenetrable rifts leading off.

3. NGR SD 953784   Alt. 555m   Depth 9m   Grade II
Small shakehole by junction of walls. Top section of pot is loose and earthy to a bottleneck 3m down. Rope useful for remainder of the shaft.

4. NGR SD 952785   Alt. 550m   Depth 6m   Grade II
Tight shaft by ruined wall. Difficult to ascend.

5. NGR SD 954783   Alt. 555m   Depth 14m   Grade III
Small shakehole 30m NW of No. 6. Zig-zag climb down chimney for 6m to a rubble floor. Narrow rift to second shaft which is best tackled with a rope. Ends in choke.

6. NGR SD 954783   Alt. 555m   Length 34m   Depth 14m   Grade III
Impressive sink by wall. Climb into open pot and down massive wall into waterfall chamber with short inlet. Opposite is dry passage under skylight to a choke. At NW corner a pitch leads to a blockage and narrow slot at high level into a deep long rift. Very awkward to reverse.

Tackle

Pitch	Ladder	Belay	Lifeline
1st	6m	3m	9m
2nd	9m	1m	18m

HERMIT'S CAVE NGR SD 940759 Grade I
Alt. 250m Length 15m
Explored 1958, CPC.

Rift cave entrance in scar just below the track. Rift gets smaller and ends, after two squeezes, in a choke. End is approximately 20m from Elbow Bend in Birks Fell Cave.

There are several other small bone caves in this scar, one of which is the home of a fox.

Permission – CNCC.

KIRK BANK CAVE NGR SD 929775 Grade II
[Birk Bank Cave] [TW3]
Alt. 335m Length 190m Depth 20m
Explored 1965, UWFRA.

On NW bank of gorge in Kirk Bank Wood. Entrance is a 3m deep slot under a cliff. Below the slot a fine passage rapidly lowers after the water sinks into the floor. A low crawl with bends opens out above a gully 5m deep, which can be climbed. The water is now rejoined in a block-strewn chamber and the exit passage is well endowed with large formations until a high level route bypasses a grovel in the stream. The water sinks into shingle on the left and a 15m long bedding plane crawl rejoins it just before a very low, wide canal which is the limit of exploration.

Permission – Mr Travers, 44 Stoney Ridge, Bingley, Yorkshire.

KIRK GILL CAVE NGR SD 924778 Grade I
Alt. 340m

In Kirk Gill. Entrance is where small stream emerges. A through circuit to Kirk Gill Pot. (See description below.)

KIRK GILL POT NGR SD 924778 Grade II
Alt. 350m Length 213m Depth 9m
Explored 1957, CPC.

Entrance shaft is in a cross rift, 10m above a small scar. A 3.5m drop into a streamway is followed by a rift passage which gains in height to walking size. This meanders on as a narrow rift for 80m to a 3.5m waterfall. Traverse over this and descend round the back of a huge flake of rock. At the bottom, to the right, step through a rock window to re-join stream passage. Traverse past cross rifts for 15m then drop into Kirk Gill Cave and entrance is reached after sharp bend and 30m stream passage.

From foot of entrance shaft, squeeze over boulders enters upstream crawl which passes tight, 20m long inlet and reaches a chamber. Rift leads to 3m waterfall and higher passage to final chamber, where water enters from boulder-choked passage 4.5m up.

Permission – The Grange, Hubberholme.

KNUCKLEBONE POT   NGR SD 958768   Grade II
Alt. 520m   **Length 27m**   **Depth 12m**
Explored, 1951 CPC; extended 1975, BPC.

MdL. Near head of Cam Gill, in a shakehole part way up the steep left bank. Pitch with small stream entering lands in narrow rift, and ensuing crawl passes several tight bends to where passage becomes impassable.

Tackle – 12m ladder; stake and 3m belay; 15m lifeline.

LOWER FOSS GILL CAVE   NGR SD 948744   Grade II
Alt. 257m   **Length 21m**

Conspicuous entrance on left side of waterfall below Foss Gill Cave. Crawl through pool and then over rocks into aven with a squeeze into a further small chamber and choke.

LOW PASTURE CAVE   NGR SD 933797   Grade I
Alt. 400m   **Length 4.5m**

SiL. Entrance 50m N of prominent resurgence in Crook Gill. Small stream in base of shakehole can be followed upstream in crawl to low sump.

MOOR END POTS
1. NGR SD 949733   **Alt. 420m**   **Depth 11m**   Grade II
Explored 1971, UWFRA.

Beyond small plantation NW of Moor End Farm, where small stream sinks. Excavated entrance rift with pitch at far end under bank leads to small chamber with inlet part way up one wall. Passage on from chamber is low, wet crawl, which soon sumps.

Tackle – 11m ladder; stake and sling belay; 15m lifeline.

2. NGR SD 950733   **Alt. 410m**   **Depth 27m**   Grade III
Explored 1972, UWFRA.

Small covered slot in side of same gully as 1, but below wall. Very awkward section at top of pitch, involving tight sideways squeeze, opens out into larger shaft broken by several ledges. Landing is in a choked rift where digging failed to locate a way on. Entrance and top section liable to be blocked by recently tipped rubbish.

Tackle – 27m ladder; stake and sling belay; 40m lifeline.

Permission – Bushey Lodge Farm, Starbotton.

NEW YEAR CAVE   NGR SD 936756   Grade II
Alt. 350m   **Length 9m**
Explored 1967, WRPC.

At head of Firth Gill above wood where broken down wall meets track. Low wet crawl ends at restricted sump after only 9m. This has been dived but was too tight some 1.5m in, the way being blocked by boulders.

Permission – Redmire Farm, Buckden.

PHLEGMIRE   NGR SD 935755   Grade I
Alt. 380m   **Length 6m**
Explored 1976, CUCC.

Collapse above Firth Gill Caves exposed short crawl in stream which becomes choked by cobbles. Stream sink is 30m further S.

REDMIRE POT   NGR SD 933766   Grade V
Alt. 367m   Length 1.3km; 1.6km including Birks Wood Cave   Depth 117m
Explored 1970, CPC; major extensions 1977-78, CUCC.

WARNING – The trip to the bottom is very strenuous and should only be attempted by cavers experienced both in free diving and in the use of breathing apparatus.

Entrance 80m from wall in a small shakehole. Please replace cover.

Entrance Series
Short crawl to 2.5m climb down into rift streamway; 30m of narrow passage to cascades and 1st pitch. At bottom of pitch is 3m climb down and duck into 45m of easier passage to a duck followed by Sump 1. Just before the duck a small inlet on the right becomes too narrow after 20m. Sump 1 is 12m long and cannot be passed without breathing apparatus. Dive down to 2.5m where a squeeze beneath two ribs of rock on the right leads to a wriggle up over a shingle bank to emerge in a constricted sump pool. After 37m of narrow rift is 2nd pitch into an impressive stream passage.

Main Streamway
Upstream from foot of 2nd pitch can be followed for 15m to a large aven, down which pours the stream from Smegmire Pot, supplying the bulk of the water. Beyond this aven is a tiny crawl and wriggle up into a tiny inlet.

Downstream from the pitch lies Grantchester Meadows, 90m of imposing passage leading to The Z's, a series of acute bends in the rift. Small inlet at roof level on left here has been explored for 30m. On downstream is 75m of walking rift passage leading to a junction with a small inlet on the right which has been explored for 15m. The walking continues beyond the junction for a further 75m, the last 30m being superbly decorated with helictites up to a foot long (care!). This section ends where the stream makes a sharp left hand bend and drops into a crawl which lasts for 15m and enlarges at a series of cascades and a 3m climb leading to the 3rd pitch into a large chamber, The Lorelei, originally discovered from Birks Wood Cave.

Lower Series
At the foot of the pitch a climb down through boulders leads to Sump 2. This is a free dive of 6m, emerging at a low airspace chamber and duck into a low canal, The Vizier's Vent, followed by 90m of crawling to easier, stooping passage 30m long to 4th pitch. This is best rigged dry by traversing out and to the right. At the bottom of the pitch climb over boulder slope in shattered rift and rejoin stream. Walking for 15m to climb down into chamber followed by squeeze over boulder and traverse down in a narrow fissure emerging in a further long, shattered rift well decorated with helictites. Easy walking for

60m leads to a climb up over boulders and squeeze down, regaining the stream where 45m of walking and crawling emerge at the head of a pitch. No need to descend pitch (which is not included in tackle list) as stream route below is choked, and way on is traverse over pitch to a roof bedding and 15m crawl to short climb down into the top of a narrow rift. Traverse forward to wider section and slide down the rift to a false boulder floor. From here a strenuous 6m long crawling traverse in a narrow fissure emerges at a second false floor, followed by an awkward squeeze over a boulder and down a 3m climb (difficult on return). After another 15m of narrow rift a cascade drops into a large chamber which provides welcome relief.

Beyond the chamber is a 3m climb down into yet more narrow rift passage. Roof tube above is well decorated but ends at two silt-choked chambers after 60m. At floor level 90m of tortuous passage leads to Sump 3, an easy free dive of 1.5m. Sump 4, a free dive of 0.6m follows immediately and is succeeded by a 6m long low airspace section which may sump in wet weather. The next 45m is mostly crawling and leads to the final climb of 4.5m down to the end of the 25m long Sump 4A of Birks Wood Cave. Beyond the climb the roof tube continues as a muddy crawl which has been pushed to a narrow rift above the airbell between Sumps 4 and 5 of Birks Wood Cave.

Tackle

Pitch	Ladder	Belay	Lifeline
1st	9m	1.5m	15m
2nd	8m	Spreader	12m
3rd	12m	6m	20m
4th	9m	3m	15m

Adequate breathing apparatus is needed for Sump 1, and hood and mask for Sumps 2, 3 and 4; weights are useful in Sump 2.

Permission – Redmire Farm, Buckden.

ROWANTREE CAVE   NGR SD 938755   Grade III
Alt. 343m   **Length 855m**
Explored 1976, CPC.

Entrance above rising near Yew Tree Pot drops into passage leading upstream to cascade, followed by wide bends and canal. Ahead is an oxbow and then passage of varied height leads to wide, watery bedding plane. At far end are massive dropped blocks but route over these gains straight high fissure which becomes smaller and emerges in Thunder Aven, with inlet stream. Handy Aven is adjacent and beyond is narrow rift to 4m climb, succeeded by small winding passage to flat crawl, becoming too low. In roof above climb is chamber and narrow passage linking with streamway through a slit.

Bolting up Handy Aven gained reasonable-sized streamway with formations. Inlet on left quickly narrows and streamway passes this and Little Surprise Inlet – small passage on left to tight, wet fissure – to enter Crab's Claw Cavern, a high inlet aven. Passage beyond is low, wet and choked – almost directly below sinks.

RUMBLING SHAKE   NGR SD 936755   Grade I
Alt. 350m   **Depth 6m**
Explored 1967, WRPC.
   About 15m S of New Year Cave. A 6m descent through boulders to a small choked chamber. Now fallen in.

SLAB POT   NGR SD 944740   Grade II
Alt. 427m   **Depth 8m**
Explored 1968, BSA.
   In small shakehole at foot of gully, some 200m S of Foss Gill Pot. Top of shaft is covered by tremendous stone slab. An easy ladder climb into a small chamber with passage out on either side. Downstream becomes too tight immediately; upstream soon ends at a constricted sump.
   In the same area are three further small holes, all easily climbable, and choked at the bottom. Another shaft requires a ladder to a choked chamber.

Tackle – 8m ladder; stake and sling belay; 12m lifeline.

Permission – Bushey Lodge, Starbotton.

SMEGMIRE POT   NGR SD 933764   Grade III
Alt. 365m   **Length 95m**   **Depth 6.4m**
Explored 1975, CUCC.
   Entrance below sink of second stream SE of Redmire Pot, covered by stone slab which must be replaced.
   Drop into small chamber where water enters from impassable slot. Downstream a tight, waterlogged squeeze on an awkward right-hand corner is passed to a flat-out canal with minimal airspace. After 30m the passage enlarges to hands and knees until the stream sinks in boulders. An oxbow on the left, where water enters from the roof, contains loose boulders (care!) and rejoins the stream in a trench which becomes too tight at all levels. Water has been tested to Smeg Aven in the Redmire Pot – Birks Wood Cave system.
Permission – CNCC.

STEP GILL CAVE   NGR SD 940755   Grade I
Alt. 260m   **Length 12m**
Explored, HRCG.
   Large cave entrance with stream emerging, just below waterfall. Passage size quickly decreases to hands and knees crawl above cascade, and way forward is completely choked.
Permission – Redmire Farm, Buckden.

STEP GILL POTS   NGR SD 940755   Grade I
Alt. 280m
1. Explored 1956, HRCG.   **Depth 15m**
   Between second waterfall and footbridge, entrance partly hidden by large

boulder. Climbable descent over blocks into narrow rift leads to further climb down into a rift chamber with bedding plane out under one wall. Soon becomes too low to follows.

2. Depth 6m

Just down-valley from entrance to 1, at end of small gully. Easy climb down leads into a sloping boulder floored rift which chokes completely after 9m.

Permission – Redmire Farm, Buckden.

THIN CAVE   NGR SD 929773   Grade I
Alt. 347m   **Length 6m**
Explored 1976, UWFRA.

Entrance in small steep-sided shakehole below track, with small stream emerging from over-tight upstream passage to sink in entrance. Short crawl leads to inverted T-section passage which is passable to where large dropped block bars the way. Beyond appears too tight for further progress.

Permission – Redmire Farm, Buckden.

WALLED CAVE   NGR SD 931768   Grade I
Alt. 357m   **Length 25m**
Explored 1932, YRC.

Obvious entrance in small valley over the hill from Birks Fell Cave entrance is 2m climb down into bedding cave which becomes too tight to follow after 25m.

Permission – Redmire Farm, Buckden.

WATER GILL CAVE   NGR SD 934772   Grade II
Alt. 271m   **Length 100m**
Explored 1959 and 1968, CPC.

At the top of Water Gill behind Redmire Farm. Low wet crawl for 17m. Through boulder choke to another crawl, then into a small chamber. A climb above the stream passage, which eventually gets too small, gives access to small grottoes with fine formations. Cave now permanently closed as it is a farm dairy water supply.

YEW TREE POT   NGR SD 938755   Grade II
Alt. 335m   **Depth 15m**
Explored 1957, HRCG.

Above track in Firth Gill on S slope. Large stream rises from boulders and sinks by a pothole. A 6m climb down cascade leads to waterfall chamber. Wet squeeze under wall to a further 6m climbable rift. Stream sinks into boulder floor.

Permission – Redmire Farm, Buckden.

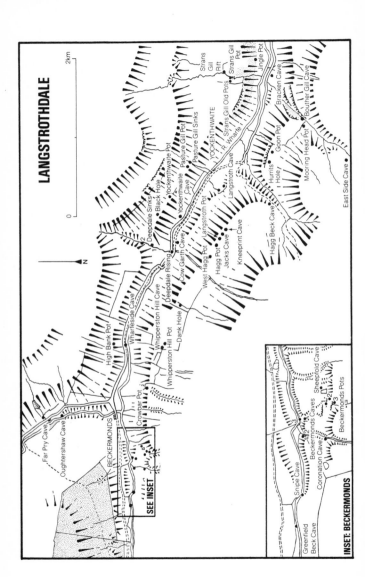

LANGSTROTHDALE

0   2km

N

Strans Gill Pot
Strans Gill Rift
Jingle Pot
Strans Gill Old Pots
Bracken Cave
Boulther Gill Cave
Deepdale Sinks
Yockenthwaite Pot
Pasture Gill Pot
Black Hole
Pasture Gill Sinks
YOCKENTHWAITE
Yockenthwaite Cave
Goon Pot
Hurnts Hole
R. Strans Gill
R. Wharfe
Mooring Head Pot
Cow Garth Cave
Langstroth Cave
Deepdale Rising
West Hagg Pot
Langstroth Pot
Hagg Pot
East Side Cave
Dank Hole
Jacks Cave
Kneeprint Cave
Hagg Beck Cave
Whipperston Hill Cave
Whipperston Hill Pot
Wharfeside Cave
High Bank Pot
Far Pry Cave
Oughtershaw Cave
Crowbar Pot
BECKERMONDS
SEE INSET

INSET: BECKERMONDS

Snipe Cave
Sheepfold Cave
Beckermonds Caves
Beckermonds Pots
Coronation Cave
Greenfield Beck Cave

LANGSTROTHDALE

BECKERMONDS CAVES

1. NGR SD 868800   **Alt. 325m**   **Length 60m**   **Grade II**

S of Greenfield Beck, at first bend 1.2km W of farm. Enter through oxbow, then right along narrow passage containing pools to low boulder strewn chamber where the stream sinks.

2. NGR SD 867800   **Alt. 322m**   **Length 40m**   **Grade II**

In small dry valley S of main beck. Difficult squeeze down through cascade into chamber with inlet on left. Winding crawl downstream to sump with draughting roof passage.

Just up the gill from this there is a letter-box into a low bedding plane which emerges into the stream bed after 12m.

3. NGR SD 868800   **Alt. 317m**   **Length 4.5m**   **Grade I**

Undercut in shale bed in S bank of beck below 1. Cave is dead end most notable for remarkable amplification of noise of nearby waterfall.

Permission – Economic Forestry Group, Kendal.

BECKERMONDS POTS

1. NGR SD 868799   **Grade II**
Alt. 345m   **Length 45m**   **Depth 18m**

Explored 1949, NPC.

In shallow dry valley 200m S of Greenfield Beck. A 4.5m rope pitch enters a narrow descending passage to wet 6m pitch (ladder, belay and lifeline required). Large passage into 12m high chamber where No. 2 Pot enters.

Tackle – 8m ladder; stake and sling belay; 9m lifeline.

2. NGR SD 868799   **Grade II**
Alt. 352m   **Length 67m**   **Depth 24m**

Explored 1949, NPC; extended, KCC.

Scramble down shakehole into boulder chamber. Inlet ends after 45m of varied going but downstream is large passage to 18m pitch with long belay in roof. Thread ladder through window on left for dry descent into chamber in No. 1 Pot, where the water sinks.

Tackle – 20m ladder; 9m belay; 25m lifeline.

3. NGR SD 868798   **Alt. 360m**   **Length 25m**   **Grade II**

Explored 1971, CPC.

Tight entrance pitch of 3m into bank E of stream sink. Water enters via aven on right. Downstream narrow winding passage and cascade to chamber

with run-in on left which blocks further progress.
Permission – Economic Forestry Group, Kendal.

BLACK HOLE   NGR SD 899797   Grade II
Alt. 360m   **Depth 6m**
Explored 1968, BSA.

In shallow gully 300m NW from Yockenthwaite Pot. Entrance covered by corrugated iron sheet and rocks, which must be replaced. Easy climb down 2.5m leads to large ledge with stream emerging from impassable bedding passage in N wall. A further descent of 3.5m opens into rift with floor of rocks and gravel. Water disappears into very low bedding under wall. The hole is in very dark limestone with abundant fossils.

Tackle – 8m ladder; stake and sling belay; 12m lifeline.

Permission – Yockenthwaite Farm.

BOUTHER GILL CAVE   NGR SD 911778   Grade II
Alt. 350m   **Length 67m**

Resurgence entrance in N bank just at the top of a waterfall in Bouther Gill. Walking stream passage to short climb, then canal and small duck into large chamber with lake. Climb up far side of chamber (scaling pole) gives access to two avens. Tight underwater slot in lake would require digging.

BRACKEN CAVE   NGR SD 916782   Grade III
Alt. 255m   **Length 460m**
Explored and extended 1959, 1970-71, CPC.

Timbered entrance in the middle of field into 140m of low wet crawling in a rift stream passage to a lofty chamber. Above the cascades sandy crawl regains the stream in a canal and then over rocks to a wide bedding cave with a duck into small chamber. The Ripple Tube then leads to 60m low passage which develops into a very low crawl with small air space.

CORONATION CAVE   NGR SD 867799   Grade II
Alt. 350m   **Length 150m**
Explored 1953, EPC.

In a small valley 170m W of Beckermonds Pots. Entrance in left bank is 1.2m drop into streamway, followed by 75m of narrow, meandering passage to 4.5m high chamber. Beyond chamber, passage reduces in size to a flat out crawl over shingle in stream, to final sump.
Permission – Economic Forestry Group, Kendal.

COW GARTH CAVE   NGR SD 896795   Grade III
Alt. 290m   **Length 169m**
Explored 1984, BPC.

WARNING – Entrance beddings sump quickly, and water displaced further upstream can cause levels to rise.

Covered entrance lies at foot of bank, 20m from road, opposite Cow

Garth Barn, and drops into low bedding. Water encountered here will prevent access unless it is pumped out. Flat out crawling leads to a dog-leg and awkward duck. Beyond, the passage enlarges to meet a small inlet on right, and then a further tight section and duck reach junction with larger passage, which is blocked to left. Main way continues to further junction – again blocked to left, while to right gradually lowers to a choke. Permission – Raisgill Farm

CROWBAR POT   NGR SD 877798   Grade II
Alt. 365m   **Length 36m**   **Depth 8m**
Explored 1968, MUSS.

In dry valley below small stream sink. A 6m climbable pitch drops into a stream passage which can be followed for 15m in a straight line down-valley to a chamber 8m high, with short upper passage running up towards surface. From the chamber a wet crawl leads to a small sump after a further 15m.

DANK HOLE   NGR SD 887794   Grade II
Alt. 380m   **Depth 6m**
Explored 1974, MUSS.

Shaft top covered with boulders against W bank of stream, adjacent to point where dry weather flow normally sinks. A squeeze down past a large wedged rock leads to straight descent to the floor of a small rift. An impassably low bedding passage takes the water, but lack of space prevents excavation of the silt and rocks blocking it.

Tackle – 8m ladder; stake and sling belay; 10m lifeline.

DEEPDALE RISING   NGR SD 894795   Grade I
Alt. 275m   **Length 35m**   **Depth 12m**
Explored 1957 and 1973, CDG.

Below road on bank of Wharfe almost opposite confluence of Deepdale Beck. Wet crawl beneath road leads to sump after 11m. Sump is 9m long, easiest on the right, leading to a large cross rift airbell with no dry land and a tight roof level crawl to the left, quickly becoming too low. Beneath the airbell a flooded rift drops to 9m depth with two ways on. In the W wall a bedding plane inlet is obstructed by cobbles, while a shingle floored passage under the E wall descends to 12m depth and is choked with gravel.

DEEPDALE SINKS   Grade II
1. NGR SD 895798   **Alt. 300m**   **Depth 9m**
Explored 1987, UWFRA.

In corner of scar on left bank of gill, covered by rocks, which must be replaced. Extremely awkward, tight descent in narrow shaft enlarges at foot where small climb down enters series of blocked rifts.

2. NGR SD 895800   **Alt. 323m**   **Depth 8m**
Explored 1982, UWFRA.

Small walled up hole in face of scar on right bank at foot of waterfall. Two small steps lead to drop into rift with stream entering and exiting via impassable slots.

Tackle (either hole) – 8m ladder; bar and spreader belay; 12m lifeline.

Permission – East Deepdale Farm.

EAST SIDE CAVE   NGR SD 906773   Grade I
Alt. 468m   **Length 18m**
Explored 1987, YURT.

MdL. From upper reaches of Bouther Gill, follow small gully on NW side up to a rising. Hole just behind resurgence enters small passage which enlarges quickly at T-junction. Left chokes after 3m; right is roomy passage to abrupt choke of large boulders.

FAR PRY CAVE   NGR SD 873812   Grade II
Alt. 370m   **Length 40m**   **Vertical range 4.5m**
Explored 1973, YURT.

In N side of small gill opposite Oughtershaw Hall is narrow 1m drop into small stream passage. Downstream easy crawling for 9m to where floor drops and it is possible to stand. Roof lowers and 4.5m sideways crawl leads to small aven and acute corner where passage continues narrow. Upstream short flat out crawl and easier going past inlet on left and tree roots to step up in floor and choked bedding. Inlet can be followed for 10m before splitting up and becoming too tight.

GOON POT   NGR SD 907782   Grade II
Alt. 378m   **Depth 12m**
Explored 1975, UWFRA.

Entrance covered over with slabs and turf in small shakehole in centre of row between two small stream sinks above Raisgill Wood. Tight start soon opens out into comfortable pitch with two small inlet streams spraying the ladder. Outlet from small chamber at foot is far too tight.

In the same row of shakeholes are four other holes up to 4.5m deep which do not require any tackle.

Tackle – 12m ladder; stake and sling belay; 20m lifeline.

Permission – Raisgill, Hubberholme.

GREENFIELD BECK CAVE   NGR SD 862800   Grade III
Alt. 330m   **Length 45m**   **Depth 6m**
Explored 1971, University of Bradford Union Potholing Club.

Bedding plane entrance is 60m downstream of main sink. Wet crawl into low passage containing the stream, which can be followed down to a pitch. A further bedding plane on the right becomes too low. Belay ladder to flake on the left. Landing in chamber 8m long, 4.5m wide and 8m high with water sinking into floor.

Tackle—4.5m ladder; 1m belay; 9m lifeline.

Permission—Economic Forestry Group, Kendal.

HAGG BECK CAVE   NGR SD 900782   Grade IV
Alt. 395m   **Length 150m**   **Depth 8m**
Explored 1968, BSA.

In shallow gully on N side of track leading from Raisgill over Horse Head to Halton Gill. Close to track is entrance fissure which leads down boulder slope to head of 2m climb down into larger cross passage. To left quickly closes. To right leads round sharp corner to crawl to further corner. Excavated section down rocks follows to more crawling and small aven chamber where there is standing room. Beyond, crawling for another 30m in a sinuous passage leads to a mud bank and flat out crawl in sludge. At a corner to the left, mud gives way to deep water and a bad duck which is only negotiable on one's back. At far end short canal leads to a walking size passage with good stalagmite banks, and then the cave suddenly ends at a choke. It is possible to climb up in rift to one side to where daylight is visible, although an exit cannot be made.

The rising for the cave is situated part way down the side of Hagg Beck, and two short sections of passage can be entered, both quickly becoming choked. Just above the gully entrance is an active sink which can be entered for 9m to where it becomes an impassable tight slot.

Permission—Raisgill, Hubberholme.

HAGG POT   NGR SD 895789   Grade I
Alt. 390m   **Depth 11m**
Explored 1967, YURT.

Stream sinks in rocky shakehole 70m W of Langstroth Pot. Descent of 2.5m into rift with floor formed by steep boulder slopes, down to silt choke where stream flows into joints.

Permission—Raisgill, Hubberholme.

HIGH BANK POT   NGR SD 882803   Grade II
Alt. 350m   **Length 9m**   **Depth 8m**

Small hole, covered by old bed end, near large boulder at top of steep hillside above Wharfeside Cave. Pitch onto boulders with obvious passage into aven chamber and climb down to boulder choked crawl back under entrance. At floor level behind foot of ladder is squeeze into small chamber with 10cm descending fissure. Two very small pots in gullies further E.

Tackle—6m ladder; 4.5m belay; 10m lifeline.

HURRITS HOLE   NGR SD 905783   Grade II
Alt. 378m   **Depth 8m**
Explored 1970, UWFRA.

Large rift covered with assorted timber and corrugated iron sheets which must be replaced. Straight descent lands on choked floor, with very narrow slot dropping to further depths at W end.

Tackle – 8m ladder, stake and sling belay; 12m lifeline.

JACKS CAVE   NGR SD 896788   Grade I
Alt. 390m   **Length 6m**

Small cave entrance approximately 100m SE of Langstroth Pot. Restricted passage to where acute bend prevents further exploration.
Permission – Raisgill, Hubberholme.

JINGLE POT   NGR SD 918785   Grade II
Alt. 280m   **Depth 15m**

On N bank of River Wharfe, 0.8km upstream of Hubberholme in wood behind Sanders Barn. Entrance hard to locate, and is rift opening covered with timbers and rocks. Straight ladder descent to sloping floor ending in choke. A small stream enters part way down one wall, to sink in floor.

Tackle – 15m ladder; 6m belay; 25m lifeline.

Permission – Scar House, Hubberholme.

KNEEPRINT CAVE   NGR SD 897787   Grade II
Alt. 390m   **Length 30m**   **Depth 6m**
Explored 1967, HWCPC.

Entrance lies in a grassy shakehole with no signs of bed rock, 200m SE of the entrance to Langstroth Pot. A short easy climb down 3.6m leads to a meandering rift passage which can be followed by a sideways walk to two short cascades. Below, it is necessary to crawl in places, and the end is reached in a small silted up chamber after a particularly low squeeze.
Permission – Raisgill, Hubberholme.

LANGSTROTH CAVE   NGR SD 902789   Grade II
Alt. 285m   **Length 320m**
Explored 1963, EPC.

Close to rising at head of small stream just up-valley from Yockenthwaite bridge. Timbered entrance drops 1.2m into bedding passage which can be followed upstream as a crawl over sharp, clean-washed rock for 110m to a junction with a passage on the left. This leads to an alternative entrance, and concealed behind rocks at the junction is a small inlet passage. This is tight and awkward, and 55m from the start it splits, the left branch ending shortly in a choke; the right branch continues for a further 70m of well decorated small streamway to end at a very tight duck. The main passage can be followed upstream from the second entrance in a stooping height passage which gradually enlarges, containing several deep pools on the floor, and some fine formations.

After 90m a small chamber is reached and the passage beyond becomes a crawl in a deepening canal until a final cross rift is entered at a sump. Sumps

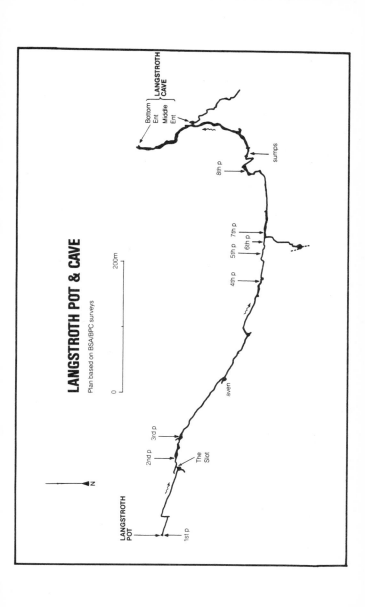

LANGSTROTH POT & CAVE

Plan based on BSA/BPC surveys

0 _____ 200m

N

LANGSTROTH
POT

1st p

The
Slot

2nd p

3rd p

aven

4th p

5th p   7th p
        6th p

8th p

sumps

Bottom
Ent
Middle
Ent

LANGSTROTH
CAVE

of 4.5m, 3m and 2m emerge at bottom of Langstroth Pot. Free-diving is inadvisable, as air in intervening airbells is liable to become foul.
Permission – Raisgill, Hubberholme.

LANGSTROTH POT   NGR SD 896788   Grade IV
Alt. 390m   **Length 1.1km**   **Depth 90m**
Explored 1967, BSA (largely explored by CDG through sumps in Langstroth Cave); extended 1980, Scunthorpe Caving Club.

In shallow gully just below small stream sink by stunted tree. Almost straight opposite Yockenthwaite Pot on far side of valley. A short tight crawl, best entered feet first, leads to top of short pitch into small chamber. Way on leads down series of short climbs past aven inlet to a low duck. Beyond this the passage is a narrow rift, followed by traverse on ledges to climb down to stream. A squeeze down step leads to duck and canal, giving way to walking size passage. A well decorated section leads to involved crawl over and through collapsed boulders, until, after a step to the right, a small chamber with an inlet is reached. A 2.5m climb down leads to the floor, and The Slot, an awkward fissure only 23cm wide. A traverse at roof level for 12m leads to climb down to stream and head of 2nd pitch with belay up on left. The top of the pitch is very narrow, and is awkward on the return. The shaft opens out at a ledge halfway down, and the landing is in a high rift chamber.

A climb up leads over fallen blocks and a short traverse reaches the 3rd pitch, with good belay on left. Again the landing is in a high rift chamber, and from here a high but narrow passage meanders onwards for the next 120m to an aven chamber in a recess on the right. The first part of the passage has a very fine array of helictites. Beyond the aven, more meandering passage follows to a sudden corner to the left and a lowering of the roof. Alternating sections of stooping and crawling lead to the 4th pitch, with belay on shelf on left. At foot is chamber with small inlet passage, and the way continues downstream in a large passage 1.5m wide and 6m high. The 5th and 6th pitches follow fairly quickly, and below the 6th pitch a large inlet enters on the right.

The inlet is a fine swirling canyon passage some 15m high at the junction, and it can be followed up two short climbs to an awkward crawl, which after 90m emerges in a large chamber with two inlets entering, and a remarkable straw stalactite some 4.5m long. Both passages beyond can be followed for a considerable distance, one finally getting too tight, while the other is choked after a climb up a mud wall into a well decorated section.

Back in the Main Passage the head of the 7th pitch is quickly reached with a bolt belay on the right wall. The passage below reaches large proportions until a spill-in of debris leaves either a low crawl to the right or a climb over the debris as the way on. Goat Inlet enters low down against the right wall here and starts as a 6m sump (not free diveable) leading to a 3m high meandering passage which ends after 50m at another sump. This has been penetrated through a constriction to an airbell after 8m

Beyond Goat Inlet the main passage gets smaller and a canal with fine formations is soon reached. At the far end is a small chamber with a short silted passage on the left, and after two short steps, the top of the 8th and final pitch is reached. The chamber at the bottom is large, with an aven inlet, and a high rift passage leads to an acute bend and the final sump. Sumps of 2m, 3m and 4.5m emerge in Langstroth Cave. Free diving is inadvisable as air in intervening airbells is liable to become foul.

Tackle

Pitch	Ladder	Belay	Lifeline
1st	4.5m	Stake and sling	8m
2nd	17m	Sling	20m
3rd	12m	Sling	20m
4th	8m	Sling	12m
5th	6m	Sling	12m
6th	4.5m	3m	–
7th	6m	Short spreader	12m
8th	17m	Short spreader	21m

Permission – Raisgill, Hubberholme.

MOORING HEAD POT   NGR SD 910778   Grade II
Alt. 370m   **Depth 9.5m**

W of Bouther Gill Cave near wall leading to barn. Walk-down pot with pitch between boulders in floor. Short blocked crawl in boulders just above choked floor of pot.

Tackle – 6m ladder; 9m belay; 9m lifeline.

OUGHTERSHAW CAVE   NGR SD 873809   Grade I
Alt. 330m   Length 6m
Explored 1968, YURT.

Entrance in scar in grounds of Oughtershaw Hall. Roomy crawl and squeeze into small chamber with 7cm high inlet sump.

PASTURE GILL POT   NGR SD 905793   Grade IV
Alt. 356m   Length 760m   Depth 104m
Explored 1967, BSA.

WARNING – The entrance pitch and Near Rift have dangerous loose rocks. A small rise in water level would make Tadpole Passage and the duck beyond The Far Rifts impassable.

Up gill running down beside Yockenthwaite to area of obvious sinks, then over wall to NW for 50m to fenced shaft. Top of entrance pitch is down through unstable boulders and demands great care, to a landing in a boulder floored rift. Stemples hold back excavated material and these should not be used as belay for 2nd pitch which follows immediately. Below this, small step leads down into large stream passage which can be followed upstream in two separate passages towards the gill until they both become too tight. Downstream is easy walk of 8m to head of 3rd pitch, best laddered dry via a 3m pot and window, reached by a short crawl to the left. At foot is circular chamber with rift passage leading out, and 12m on is 4th pitch, with bolt belay on shelf at roof level on left.

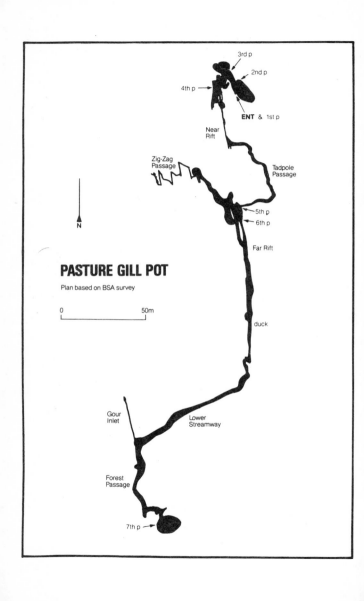

3rd p

2nd p

4th p →

ENT & 1st p

Near
Rift

Tadpole
Passage

Zig-Zag
Passage

→ 5th p

→ 6th p

Far Rift

N

PASTURE GILL POT

Plan based on BSA survey

0   50m

duck

Gour
Inlet

Lower
Streamway

Forest
Passage

7th p →

A dry alternative route to the 4th pitch can be followed by a dangerous traverse in an excavated shale bed, passing two holes in the floor, to an aven chamber. To one side of this is head of By-pass Pitch of 32m to a boulder floor, with a further pitch of 9m reached through a very tight squeeze down between big boulders. This lands in the Near Rift, 15m downstream from the foot of the 4th pitch. The Near Rift continues for 40m and involves awkward traversing over and through loose rocks, which must be treated with caution. At far end a short climb down leads to start of Tadpole Passage, a low, wet crawl 75m long with a duck half way along. Passage gradually enlarges and several cascades allow walking to 5th pitch, with belay point on right wall. The small circular chamber below has two ways out, the water flowing in a bedding passage to the 6th pitch, while an easy climb up leads into the Far Rifts, and a by-pass to the 6th pitch.

At the upstream end of the Far Rift, 2m wide and 23m high, a small aven can be climbed to a bedding crawl and an awkward climb up into Zig-zag Passage. This can be followed by crawling and traversing through 75m of uncomfortable passage to a further climbable aven of 11m with a short length of passage above, which quickly becomes too tight.

Downstream in the Far Rift is a climb down a tremendous sloping slab and traverse through fissure to further large rift and lowering of the roof to a crawl in water and a duck. Beyond, passage quickly enlarges at an aven, followed by walking in a clean washed, well decorated streamway. The roof gradually lowers giving a hands and knees crawl for the next 60m to a series of cascades, below which more walking leads to an inlet on the right, Gour Passage, which ends after 30m of tight sideways crawling, at a small aven. The main passage continues with a large number of tree roots entering through cracks in the walls and roof, and a final length of crawling leads to the top of the 7th and final pitch. Landing is in a chamber 12m across with a large boulder slope on one side, and containing the final sump – 10m in diameter. This has been dived, and the water appears to flow off down through boulders in the 3m deep pool.

Tackle

Pitch	Ladder	Belay	Lifeline
Entrance	11m	Stake and sling	15m
2nd	9m	Small bar and short spreader	15m
3rd	15m	3m	25m
4th	41m	Short spreader	50m
5th	6m	Sling	10m
6th	8m	4.5m	12m
	(can be by-passed without tackle)		
7th	12m	9m	20m

By-pass Pitch Route

1st	32m	Small bar and short spreader	36m
2nd	11m	4.5m	15m

Zig-zag Passage Avens

1st	8m	Sling	12m
2nd	11m	Sling	15m

Permission – Top Farm, Yockenthwaite.

PASTURE GILL SINKS   NGR SD 905793   Grade II

1. Alt. 340m   **Depth 4.5m**

At foot of the largest waterfall in the gill, entrance covered by large boulders. An awkward climb down into a tight rift with no way on.

2. Alt. 355m   **Depth 3.6m**

Immediately at top of largest waterfall. Easy climb down into small rift, with bedding outlet which is too tight to enter.

3. Wheel Sink Alt. 355m   Length 15m   Depth 14m

Entrance in W bank covered by large iron wheel. A 12m pitch lands in a small chamber with floor of gritstone boulders. A wet crawl leads out of this with water entering through the roof until after 15m the passage narrows and the way on is blocked by shingle. This is within 8m of the upstream passage below the 2nd pitch in Pasture Gill Pot.

Tackle (Wheel Sink) – 14m ladder; 3m belay; 20m lifeline.

Permission – Top Farm, Yockenthwaite.

SHEEPFOLD CAVE   NGR SD 869799   Grade II

Alt. 345m   Length 9m

In small rocky shakehole within a few metres of NE corner of an old sheepfold. Easy descent down slope of mud and rocks leads directly to low stream passage. Upstream is far too tight, while downstream under the right wall can be followed into a low unstable boulder chamber. At far side is window through to annexe, and the stream can be seen flowing off down impenetrable rifts.

Permission – Economic Forestry Group, Kendal.

SNIPE CAVE   NGR SD 864800   Grade II

Alt. 325m   Length 15m

Explored 1975, YURT.

Entrance below dry waterfall in bed of Greenfield Beck, 400m upstream of rising near Beckermonds Caves. Meandering, flat out crawl becoming very low.

STRANS GILL OLD POTS   NGR SD 916788   Grade II

Alt. 355m

1. Depth 14m

Entrance 50m W of Strans Gill is open hole with wall round. Easy scramble down slope on W side leads to low entrance under rock face. Dangerous climb down, over and through loose boulders, leads to small chamber with one solid wall.

2. Depth 8m

On W bank of Strans Gill in corner of wire fence. Now completely covered and turfed over, showing no sign of its existence. Easy climb leads to boulder floor. Further short climb to sloping mud bank, which completely blocks the way on. This point is very close to passage at head of aven in upper passage of Strans Gill Pot.

Permission – Yockenthwaite Farm.

STRANS GILL POT   NGR SD 916788   Grade V
Alt. 353m   **Length 500m**   **Depth 105m**

Explored 1967, BSA; extended 1973, GC; 1984, CDG.

WARNING – Even a small amount of water flowing down the entrance pitch would make it impassable. Dam should be checked before entering hole. Passage between bottom of Charity and Sluice impassable if much water enters system.

Entrance covered by slabs in small dammed-off enclosure by right bank of Strans Gill, above wood. Top part of 1st pitch is extremely tight – 19cm – to a ledge, then opens out into small chamber. Passage out is tight crawl for 6m to Hope Pitch, again very tight at top, with belay on left. Chamber at bottom is in washed out shale bed, and crawl leads out, passing three avens, to a narrow rift passage. Part way along is start of crawl traverse on ledges, leading past a very tight section to a corner and The Opera Box at top of Charity Pitch, with bolt belays for ladder and double line. Pitch is large rift with big ledge 15m down. Fissure in floor of ledge, 9m deep, leads to main inlet and alternative wet route to foot of 3rd pitch.

From foot a crawl down over boulders leads into a low streamway which enlarges after 45m at a collapse chamber. Beyond, more crawling leads to a double cascade and further crawling to an awkward squeeze and 3m climb down to Sluice Pitch with belay on left. This pitch is always extremely wet, and lands in a large, high chamber, The Assembly Hall. By chimneying up rift above Sluice Pitch a crawl leads forward to a balcony from which an alternative dry descent – Balcony Pitch – lands in Assembly Hall. Left of the balcony a very exposed traverse on a shale ledge – Traverse of the Gods – gains pitch into Genesis, an abandoned phreatic passage descending steeply to a choke after 25m.

A number of passages radiate from Assembly Hall. Hidden behind boulders on the left is Sump Passage, a hands and knees crawl upstream for 20m to an inlet sump 45m long and followed by a roomy passage, lowering to a crawl to the second sump, dived to an airbell after 5m. After another 10m the sump dips down and has not been followed further.

Up the boulder slope in Assembly Hall leads into Overtime Series, a high level route to The Passage of Time. Following the stream down under large boulders leads to a junction with two passages on the right. The active inlet, Blackleg Passage continues for 60m of crawling through a nasty duck to a low airspace canal which quickly becomes impassable, while the other passage, Union Street, is normal route to The Passage of Time.

Just past the junction the stream falls away to left down 5th pitch into a rift, and from far end a short, wet crawl leads to the 6th pitch for which there

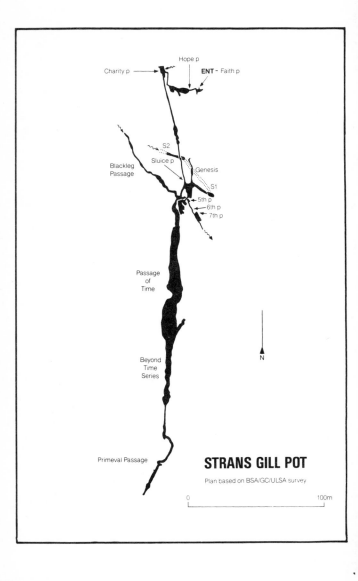

Charity p ← Hope p

ENT - Faith p

S2

Sluice p

Blackleg
Passage

Genesis

S1

5th p
6th p
7th p

Passage
of
Time

N

Beyond
Time
Series

Primeval Passage

STRANS GILL POT

Plan based on BSA/GC/ULSA survey

0   100m

is no natural belay, followed immediately by the 7th and final pitch which is very wet. At foot is rift chamber with small passage forward to final constricted sump, which can be passed in drought to a narrow rift and a choke.

Union Street is hands and knees crawl for 9m to rift passage at start of The Passage of Time, and junction with Overtime Series. Traversing for 11m leads to sudden enlargement and passage becomes 6m wide and 3m high, with a deep fissure in the floor which can be descended in steps for 23m to a sump, at the same level as the final sump in the streamway. The way on continues as a large well decorated passage to a double bend, and here the formations become finer and more abundant until they reach staggering proportions and density, one of the finest arrays yet discovered in the north of England. Just beyond a superb column the passage closes down to a crawl among formations at roof level to a collapsed chamber and further crawl to mud slope down to start of Primeval Passage, 26m of low, wet crawl in deep water to slope up at foot of aven. Difficult 6m climb leads up into a short choked passage. Beyond aven further nasty crawling for 15m leads to a rift and mud slope which completely chokes passage.

Tackle

Pitch	Ladder	Belay	Lifeline
Faith	12m	Crowbar and short spreader	20m
Hope	6m	2.5m	–
Charity	50m	Short spreader	55m
Sluice	11m	Sling	20m
5th	4.5m	3m	8m
6th	6m	Piton	12m
7th	12m	Sling	25m
Balcony	15m	4.5m	25m
(Sluice pitch alternative)			
Traverse of the Gods	3m	Piton and sling	25m

Permission – Yockenthwaite Farm.

STRANS GILL RIFT   NGR SD 917788   Grade II
Alt. 356m   **Depth 11m**

In E bank of gill 40m upstream of Strans Gill Pot. Entrance through oil drum in collapsed bank below broken down wall leads direct to head of pitch in large rift. Water enters from narrow slot half-way down, making bottom 4.5m very wet. Passages out of chamber at foot are impassable narrow rifts.

Tackle – 12m ladder; stake and sling belay; 15m lifeline.

Permission – Yockenthwaite Farm.

WEST HAGG POT   NGR SD 893790   Grade II
Alt. 390m   **Length 9m**   **Depth 4.5m**

Insignificant entrance covered by boulders in shallow stream gully 320m WNW of Langstroth Pot. Drop onto boulders in narrow fissure which

descends into small chamber. Flat crawl leads off and after squeeze turns right and narrows excessively.
Permission – Raisgill, Hubberholme.

WHARFESIDE CAVE   NGR SD 883801   Grade III
Alt. 292m   Length 40m
Explored 1968, ULSA.

The entrance to this extremely tortuous cave is a slot in a cliff adjacent to the Wharfe. It discharges a small stream and a powerful draught. The passage varies in height, from 1m to 1.5m and is a rift throughout. Main characteristics of the cave are sharp wall flakes and vicious bends, one of which marks the present termination of the cave.

WHIPPERSTON HILL CAVE   NGR SD 882796   Grade I
Alt. 360m   Length 6m

Narrow slot entrance covered by boulders (which must be replaced) on shelf on E bank of small stream above sink by wall corner. Easy double climb down leads to small chamber and very low choked bedding outlet through which the noise of water can be heard.

WHIPPERSTON HILL POT   NGR SD 882796   Grade II
Alt. 380m   Length 9m   Depth 8m

Entrance concealed behind large boulder in dry valley running up from obvious rising at wall corner straight up fell from Whipperston Hill Barn. Easy descent of 4.5m leads to rift chamber with a narrow inlet passage entering which can only be followed for a short way before becoming too tight. At the opposite end of chamber is further drop of 1.5m over boulders to a crawl round to the left to a parallel aven. In front the way on is choked with mud and rocks.

Tackle – 8m ladder; 3m belay; 9m lifeline.

YOCKENTHWAITE CAVE   NGR SD 898794   Grade IV
Alt. 270m   Length 150m
Extended 1969/71, BSA and KCC.

WARNING – This cave should only be explored in times of drought.

On N bank of Wharfe just upstream of stone circle, where small stream resurges. Low crawl leads quickly to deep canal and duck, emerging in small chamber with 2m high waterfall on far side. An easy climb up leads to 0.6m high bedding passage with several centimetres of water over floor. After 30m of severe crawling, sometimes with very little air-space, over razor sharp rock, a rib of rock is encountered, and a lowering of the roof. Beyond this, slim cavers can follow a wide meandering canal to where it changes to a low, but fast flowing streamway, before reverting to a deep canal. Deep water leads past several cross rifts to a silt bank and beyond, the passage narrows, with the airspace becoming very small, to where further progress is impossible.
Permission – Yockenthwaite Farm.

YOCKENTHWAITE POT   NGR SD 901796   Grade IV
Alt. 360m   **Length 180m**   **Depth 46m**
Explored 1950, UWFRA; extended 1972, BSA.

On N bank of Wharfe in small thicket, straight up hill from stone circle.
Entrance pitch best laddered from S side, avoiding loose rocks, to landing in
large rift. Excavated hole on left at foot of steep slope leads to low chamber
formed in washed out shale bed. Gully in floor cuts down quickly to head of
2nd pitch, while traverse over top enters small inlet passage which rapidly
becomes too tight. At foot of pitch is small chamber, and water all collects
and flows to restricted opening at top of 3rd pitch, which is awkward to climb
at first. Further stream enters through roof of chamber at bottom, and the
combined waters flow into a narrow rift passage.

Blasting widened the rift sufficiently to pass an acute bend and reach the
4th pitch which is very awkward at top. From foot of shaft stream flows into
impassably tight passage, However, 3m down it is possible to leave the ladder
and crawl across a bedding to a further dry shaft of 8m. The landing is in a
very large rift with a steep boulder floor, and this is the continuation of the
surface rift. Down the slope leads to a climb down on loose boulders to
rejoin the stream, which can only be followed upstream for a short way.
Downstream the water filters away through a severe choke on a fault.

Part way down the slope below the dry pitch an inlet passage can be
reached via a dangerous climb up the right wall. From the top a narrow rift
passage continues, and can only be passed by a sideways traverse spread-
eagled over the slot below. From far end of traverse walking with occasional
traversing to avoid some magnificent formations leads to a squeeze and short
climb down to a pool. Further crawling, walking and traversing, in what has
now become a downstream passage reaches an area of parallel faults, and
just beyond, the floor drops down a series of small steps, and becomes too
tight after a couple of bad corners.

Tackle

Pitch	Ladder	Belay	Lifeline
Entrance	12m	Stake and sling	20m
2nd	6m	3m	12m
3rd	4.5m	Belay to 2nd	8m
4th	12m	Short bar and spreader	20m
Dry pitch	8m	3m	12m

(this pitch can be rigged by tailing the ladder through from the 4th pitch).

Permission–Yockenthwaite Farm.

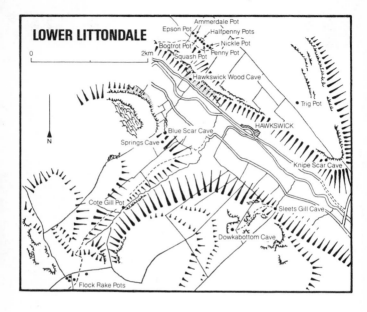

LOWER LITTONDALE

AMMERDALE POT
Alt. 440m

NGR SD 945722
Length 20m

Grade III
Depth 30m

Explored 1976, NCC.

Entrance in second shakehole along row from small stream sink by wall. Easy climb to floor of shakehole is followed by more awkward climb down shored boulder slope (care) to head of first pitch. This can be free-climbed but ladder is advisable. At foot small stream enters from impenetrable rift, and further boulder slope leads to head of 12m second pitch with bolt belay, and a tight take-off. Wet descent for 4.5m to ledge, then dry for remainder in fine shaft. At bottom a tight rift drops into a small chamber, followed by crawl to second chamber and final crawl of 6m to a lowering of the roof.

Strong draught and booming noise warrant further attention.

Tackle

Pitch	Ladder	Belay	Lifeline
1st	6m	1.5m	12m
2nd	12m	Short spreader	20m

Permission – Old Cotes, Arncliffe.

BLUE SCAR CAVE   NGR SD 939705   Grade I
Alt. 290m   Length 20m

Explored 1976, NCC; extended 1984, G.N. Long.

Situated in face of clints above the main rising to S of Blue Scar. Entrance is usually well concealed by a profusion of nettles, and leads into a chamber 6m wide and 8m long. At far end floor drops down slot, and a slope to excavated crawl leading to small aven and continuing muddy passage to where route splits into three impassable fissures.

Permission – Low Ryelands, Arncliffe.

BOGTROT POT   NGR SD 945722   Grade II
Alt. 440m   Depth 14m

In shakehole just to SE of Ammerdale Pot where bog drains into a 3m deep open shaft. Small hole in floor at N end is a 6m pitch, choked at the bottom.

Tackle – 8m ladder; stake and sling belay; 12m lifeline.

Permission – Old Cotes, Arncliffe.

COTE GILL POT   NGR SD 933692   Grade II
Alt. 370m   Length 90m   Depth 13m

Explored 1960, EPC; extended 1977, WRPC.

WARNING – Liable to serious flooding.

The entrance is on NW bank of Cote Gill, just upstream of two waterfalls (usually dry). A narrow 3.5m climb drops into a square streamway which rapidly degenerates into a crawl upstream. About 45m from the entrance the crawl is choked by a mud bank. Downstream the passage is joined by a flat out inlet on an upper level. The combined streams drop down a 3.5m pitch into the 12m long terminal chamber. To the SW this is choked by mud, while the water drops down an excavated slope into a short canal with no passable outlet, even by diving.

Tackle

Pitch	Ladder	Belay	Lifeline
Entrance	4.5m	4.5m	8m
2nd	4.5m	3m	8m

Permission – Arncliffe Cote Farm.

DOWKABOTTOM CAVE NGR SD 951689 Grade III
Alt. 387m   **Length 670m**   **Depth 23m**
Extended 1970, NCC.

Best approached via Sleets Gill and footpath up scars. Entrance is 60m W of wall corner by the big depression of Dowkabottom. A climb down onto collapse debris shows two passages.

The S passage is reached by an easy scramble down slope into chamber from which tall rift passage leads on to second chamber. Beyond this, passage gets smaller to a third chamber, and ultimately chokes 45m from entrance.

A more awkward climb down leads into chamber at start of N passage. At the far side of this chamber a stalagmite slope up leads into long passage with fine flows on walls. Passage narrows, and 150m from the entrance it meets the former sump, now blasted to create a duck. Beyond the duck a climb gains a roof bedding plane and large sloping chamber, from which rift passage continues to crawl and further chamber. Walking size passage gives way to more crawling and traverse over deep pool, until large passage is reached. Easy going to junction with huge passage, choked to right, with inlet in opposite wall. Inlet can be followed to further junction in 20m, the passage to the left quickly becoming choked, while that to the right can be followed in a narrow streamway for considerable distance. The main passage slopes down steeply to the left, and becomes a rift 20m high narrowing into a neck only 1m wide. A dangerous climb into the roof here leads to a further short length of passage and unstable chamber. Beyond neck, passage widens and steep slope on silt and boulders leads round corner to where stream flows off into small passage in left wall. Straight ahead, large passage continues up a boulder slope and through a choke to more large passage and final choke. The stream can be followed down a sloping passage, down a 3m waterfall, and through a low canal to a choke.

Permission – Lainger House, Bordley.

EPSON POT   NGR SD 945722   Grade III
Alt. 448m   **Length 30m**   **Depth 9m**
Explored 1979, BCC; extended 1982, NCC.

Excavated entrance to top of 8m pitch dropping into small chamber. Way on is low crawl and tight rift to where further progress is impossible. The stream is thought to connect with nearby Ammerdale Pot.

Tackle – 8m ladder; stake and long sling belay; 12m lifeline.

Permission – Old Cotes, Arncliffe.

FLOCK RAKE POTS   NGR SD 924681   Grade II
Alt. 505m   **Depths around 6m**

Four small shafts grouped on either side of the wall. All straight descents to choked floors. About 150m E is an open craggy hole 4.5m deep, 3m square, choked at bottom.

Tackle (all pots) – 8m ladder, stake and sling belay; 9m lifeline.

HALFPENNY POTS   NGR SD 946721   Grade I
Alt. 440m

1. Depth 6m
Next shakehole NW of Squash Pot. Climb down at S end of shakehole−which contains a milk churn−is choked at foot. Next shakehole N has a 3m long through cave.

2. Depth 6m
Third shakehole NW of Squash Pot. Climb down boulders is choked at bottom.

HAWKSWICK WOOD CAVE NGR SD 944715 Grade III
Alt. 250m   Length 37m
Explored 1974, Ex BSA.

Excavated entrance at top of small stream channel near northern boundary to Hawkswick Wood. Awkward descent beside large loose boulder leads to bedding passage that can only be entered feet first. A small enlargement a short way in allows one to turn round, and the way continues as a tight crawl over a series of dried up gours. After two tight spots an oxbow to the left is reached, and just beyond the far end is a tight duck in a sludgy pool, followed almost at once by a sump of impossibly small dimensions.

KNIPE SCAR CAVE   NGR SD 968701   Grade I
Alt. 340m   Length 9m

Obvious entrances in left side of scar at S end of ridge between rivers Skirfare and Wharfe. Two entrances unite immediately, then easy crawl to wriggle into low chamber, followed by further wriggle to sharp right bend and uncompromising lowering of roof.

NICKLE POT ·   NGR SD 947720   Grade II
Alt. 440m   Depth 20m
Explored 1950, Baildon Climbing Club

In deep shakehole next to 3.5m deep hole covered with fencing. Just inside is a 3.5m drop landing in a boulder-floored chamber, with some loose blocks. Climbs down of 4.5m and 3m lead to where the rift becomes impenetrable.

Tackle−9m ladder; 6m belay; 20m lifeline.

Permission−Old Cotes, Arncliffe.

PENNY POT   NGR SD 947720   Grade II
Alt. 440m   Depth 12m
Explored 1922, YRC.

In next shakehole SE of Nickle Pot is climbable rift (ladder useful) with stream sinking at N end. Crawl under right wall is too tight after 2m.

Tackle−9m ladder; stake and sling belay; 15m lifeline.

Permission−Old Cotes, Arncliffe.

SLEETS GILL CAVE NGR SD 959692 Grade IV

Alt. 290m   Length 2.4km   Depth 27m   Vertical range 76m
Explored 1906; extended 1968, ULSA and BSA; 1971, NCC; 1972 ULSA.

WARNING – Entrance slope can sump rapidly in wet weather, often after long delay. The whole known cave except The Ramp floods to the roof.

One of the most spectacular caves in the district. Entrance at the head of Sleets Gill, near Hawkswick, is an arch 1.5m high and 3.5m wide. A steep slope of 52m descends 25m and has a low section at the bottom. From the base of the scree slope an uneven passage continues for 30m to a junction with a rift excavated down to water on left. Ahead the main route continues for 80m to a further junction at the start of the main gallery.

To right at junction is passage which is sumped in sections, except during drought, leading to junction with streamway. Impassable sumps are quickly met in both directions.

Main Gallery

This magnificent bored tunnel averages 3.5m high and 4.5m wide for 370m. At first it is lined by mud banks but these are replaced by gour pools and calcite floors for much of its length. Behind a boulder on the right is Boireau's Passage – a 75m long strenuous crawl ending in a boulder choke. About 200m further along a large side passage on the right ends in a static sump. This has been dived to a steep underwater passage. The Main Gallery ends in a boulder choke but 25m back, under the south wall, a slot to a 2.5m drop leads down boulders into a series of low crawls and then a canal. At the end of the canal a large inlet enters on the left and a crawl to the right enters an area of boulder chokes adjacent to the terminal choke of the Main Gallery.

'68 Series

The canal inlet is 60m of very wet crawling which is only safe in dry weather as it carries a considerable stream, hence the name – Hydrophobia Passage. This ends at a junction with a large tunnel. To the right the deserted passage ends in two boulder choked branches. Upstream the water comes from a small passage which eventually sumps. The way on is a large tunnel to the right and up a mud slope to a maze area of dry passages and routes down to the stream. A final boulder strewn crawl suddenly breaks out into a passage 8m square. Here the stream is rejoined and can be followed up to a deep canal and a 4.5m long sump.

Pleasant free dive often has poor visibility on the return, and emerges in a fine canal passage. As the water shallows a steep phreatic ramp on the right can be ascended over slippery mud to a choke over 12m above water level. Beyond, the next passage on the left is sumped. This has been forced past two airbells into a rock strewn bedding 33m from base. The main passage beyond suddenly ends at a boulder choke, with the water issuing from a wet arch to the right. This is an awkward duck into a system of crawls; by keeping left here a manhole up into a large tube is found. To the left, this chokes with boulders (probably the other side of the boulder choke mentioned above), while to the right a streamway lowers over cobbles. Opposite the manhole up

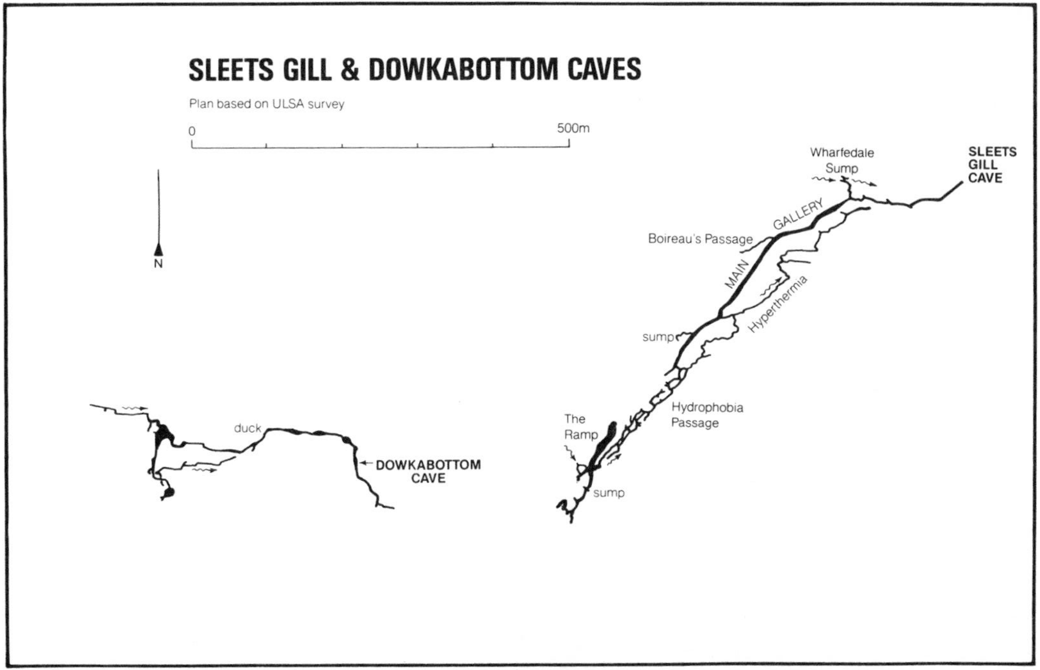

SLEETS GILL & DOWKABOTTOM CAVES

Plan based on ULSA survey

0 _____ 500m

N

SLEETS GILL CAVE

Wharfedale Sump

MAIN GALLERY

Boireau's Passage

Hyperthermia

sump

Hydrophobia Passage

The Ramp

sump

sump

DOWKABOTTOM CAVE

duck

into these passages is a system of large rocky bedding planes, all eventually choked.

At the junction with the large passage before the sump, a steep slope up to the right leads to a T-junction. Left, a wide low passage has a complex inlet in the north wall and ends in a choke of mud covered boulders. Right is The Ramp, where the impressive tunnel rears up at 35° and rises 60m over 90m of passage, to end in a choke of stalagmited boulders.

Hyperthermia

Low outlet from canal at the end of Main gallery unites with a crawl from the base of the 2.5m drop, in a waterlogged struggle for 150m which should only be attempted under dry settled conditions. A muddy side passage on the left connects with the Main Gallery and Hyperthermia then enlarges to a hands and knees crawl with odd pools and flat out sections. A passage to the right has very low airspace after 45m, but beyond a boulder cluttered rift the main route assumes more acceptable proportions before sumping.

Permission –'Mossdale', Conistone.

SPRINGS CAVE   NGR SD 938703   Grade I
Alt. 335m   **Length 8m**

Entrance visible from road in bank S of Blue Scar. Short low crawl leads to circular chamber 3m high. No obvious way on.

Permission – Low Ryelands, Arncliffe.

SQUASH POT   NGR SD 946721   Grade III
Alt. 440m   **Depth 18m**

Explored 1950, Baildon Climbing Club.

Second shakehole N of Nickle Pot. Boulder belay for ladder. Pitch is narrow at top and water falling down shaft sinks in choked floor.

Tackle – 20m ladder; 3.5m belay; 25m lifeline.

TRIG POT   NGR SD 962711   Grade I
Alt. 435m   **Depth 6m**

Explored 1976, CUCC.

Well-concealed entrance in shakehole 60m from trig point on bearing of 320°. Broken climb down into choked chamber with no way out.

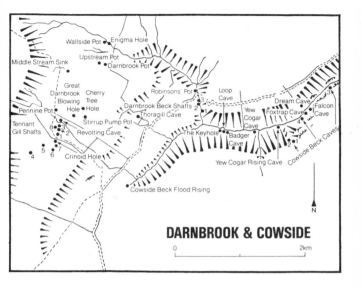

Cowside Beck Caves

Wallside Pot • Enigma Hole
Middle Stream Sink
Upstream Pot
• Darnbrook Pot
Great
Darnbrook Cherry
Blowing Tree
Hole • Hole
Pennine Pot
Tennant
Gill Shafts
Stirrup Pump Pot
Revolting Cave
8 3 2
5 7
4 6 Crinoid Hole
Robinsons' Pot
Loop
Cave
Darnbrook Beck Shafts
Thoragill Cave
Yew
Cogar
Cave
Dream Cave
Foxtrap Cave
Falcon
Cave
The Keyhole
Badger
Cave
Yew Cogar Rising Cave Cowside Beck Caves
Cowside Beck Flood Rising
N

DARNBROOK & COWSIDE

0   2km

DARNBROOK & COWSIDE

BADGER CAVE   **NGR SD 903700**   **Grade II**
Alt. 300m   **Length 15m**
Explored 1977, UWFRA.

Small entrance behind boulders (which must be replaced) at head of slope
up to scar a few metres down-valley from Loop Cave. Tight excavated crawl
can be followed through two squeezes to where way on gets too low.
Permission – Darnbrook House.

CHERRY TREE HOLE   **NGR SD 881704**   **Grade IV**
Alt. 467m   **Length 1.2km**   **Depth 41m**
Explored 1960, CPC; extended 1971, CPC.

A complex system of great variety and considerable potential. Entrance is
in large, square-sided shakehole in which grows a wild cherry tree. Free-
climbable entrance shaft (handline useful). The way leads down through a

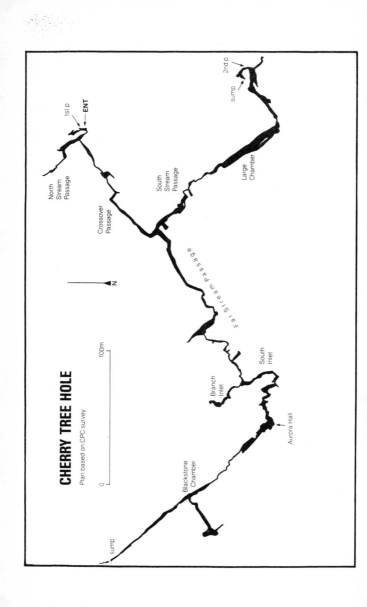

CHERRY TREE HOLE

Plan based on CPC survey

N

0   100m

sump

Blackstone
Chamber

Aurora Hall

Branch
Inlet

South Inlet

Fairstream passage

Crossover
Passage

North
Stream
Passage

1st p

ENT

South Stream
Passage

Large
Chamber

sump

2nd p

dig in boulders to the first ladder pitch. N is a squeeze at head height which leads to a 9m shaft, The Pit. A bedding cave outlet is choked by sand. From the first pitch, a squeeze leads to a 3m blind pitch – Hammer Pot. A figure of 8 passage, the stream in the bottom circle and a crawl along the top circle, follows until a flat block is reached. Straight on is the North Stream Passage (upstream) which ends in a boulder-choked aven after 45m. Left is the dry fault Crossover Passage which leads through a pool to Quicksand Aven. Squeeze down boulders leads to a large rift passage with moonmilk floor. Climb up through boulders then down boulder slope to Main Junction.

Far Stream Passage

Leads upstream from Main Junction through large rifts, avens and cascades for 170m until junction is reached. Right leads to Branch Inlet, small stream passage which sumps after 37m. Sump is 10m long with tight exit, followed by 20m long passage to choke. Left leads to South Inlet canal and stream passage for nearly 60m to aven with formations. Low bedding cave almost filled with water leads to climb through boulders into Aurora Hall, 8m high, 12m long, 6m wide, and the start of The Far North. Climb muddy slope to top, then climb down between flowstone cascades and through extensive shattered section of passage. Hands and knees crawl, then through pools, gives access to Blackstone Chamber with fine formations. Left out of Blackstone Chamber leads to the Terminus and a final decorated aven. Straight on is the Morass Inlet – a low crawl in glutinous mud for 85m to sump.

South Stream Passage

Downstream from Main Junction a fair-sized stream passage descends over boulders and through cascades to a very large fault chamber with many unstable rocks. Climb up at far end in chimney to hands and knees crawl on hard mud to Spiral Chamber with a fine formation. Down muddy hole into fault passage which leads to a pitch and final sump. Before pitch is a low crawl up to the left ending in a choke.

Final sump has been dived for 90m to a low, wide airbell, and a short second sump of 6m which leads to a dry crawl and the third sump. Boulder obstructions were frequent in this, and exploration ends after about 75m at a very narrow section. The rising is 1km away and 60m lower.

Tackle

Pitch	Ladder	Belay	Lifeline
1st	4.5m	1m	6m
South Stream Passage	9m	3m	15m

Permission – Darnbrook House.

COWSIDE BECK CAVES   Grade I

1. NGR SD 914698   **Alt. 410m**   **Length 6m**
Impressive rock shelter entrance in cove E of waterfall.

2. NGR SD 913698   **Alt. 410m**   **Length 9m**
Small entrance in W side of scar leads to chamber with daylight penetrating.

3. NGR SD 918705   Alt. 300m   Length 6m
   Steep climb up gully into lofty fissure passage.

4. NGR SD 915702   Alt. 290m   Length 25m
   Entrance in steep grass slope. Short canal passage and crawl under loose
boulders into a bedding cave which divides and becomes too tight.

COWSIDE BECK FLOOD RISING NGR SD 888691
Alt. 358m   **Length 25m**
Explored 1959, CPC; extended 1976, CDG.

   Large boulder filled rift below wall, 60m up-valley from normal rising at
head of Cowside Beck. Easy climb down enters low bedding chamber with
pool covering floor. Diving has revealed a downstream passage which has
been followed for 6m to a boulder obstruction, while in opposite direction
low submerged bedding has been followed to a large boulder after 3m. Main
route on upstream seems to lie through over-tight slot to the left where
current could be observed.
Permission – Tennant Gill Farm.

CRINOID HOLE   NGR SD 876699   Grade I
Alt. 490m   **Length 15m**   **Depth 6m**
Explored 1974, MUSS.

   The entrance lies in a small shakehole just to the S of the Pennine Way
near a broken down wall. A slide down a mud bank leads into a steeply
sloping phreatic passage large enough to permit walking at the start.
Gradually the way becomes lower until the roof meets the mud floor. Of
interest for the large number of crinoids projecting from the walls.
Permission – Tennant Gill Farm.

DARNBROOK BECK SHAFTS   Grade II
Nos. 1 & 2 Explored 1965, CPC; No. 3 explored 1977, UWFRA.

1. NGR SD 899703   Alt. 315m   Depth 9m
   About 250m downstream from road bridge on E bank. At foot of small
outcrop, covered by boulders. Tight descent to sump pool, with water
entering through boulders from alternative entrance in stream bed. Sump has
been dived for 4.5m to where it was too constricted.

2. George's Shaft   NGR SD 899704   Alt. 315m   Length 30m   Depth 9m
   Obscure entrance covered by debris at foot of wall, 90m upstream from 1.
Fine fluted shaft descends past ledge, to big shelf and further short drop. At
foot are two ways on. To left becomes too tight amost immediately, while
other way emerges beyond squeeze in large mud filled passage. Upstream
quickly ends after crawl, while downstream splits, with muddy crawl up
slope on left to choke, and low gravel floored passage straight ahead which
quickly becomes too low.

3. NGR SD 899704   Alt. 315m   Depth 9m
   On W bank 30m upstream of 2. Shored section enters clean washed shaft
ending on debris slope into chamber formed largely in fill, with no passable

outlet. Entrance has now been blocked at request of farmer.

Tackle (any shaft) – 9m ladder; stake and sling belay; 12m lifeline.

Permission – Darnbrook House.

DARNBROOK POT   NGR SD 885710   Grade III
Alt. 455m   **Length 335m**   **Depth 71m**
Explored 1957, CPC; extended 1964, BSA.

WARNING – the boulder choke at foot of Main Chamber is unstable and should be treated with great caution.

Entrance in shakehole about 90m NNW from wall corner above shooting hut. Easy climb down excavated shaft is followed by tight 9m pitch to streamway. Downstream rift passage leads to crawl, then down through cascades to large Main Chamber, 18m by 12m and up to 15m high. Crawl out at foot of boulder slope leads to continuation of streamway and some fine formations. Passage ends where water sinks in floor and way forward is blocked by choke. Upstream from entrance is Loopway Passage, rift stream passage with several oxbows. Climb up on left after 90m leads to Sentinel Chamber. Back in stream passage turns right and ends in a low crawl which eventually sumps. Sump has been dived for 30m to silt banks which prevent further progress towards the sink, which is 400m away. All the upstream cave is finely decorated.

Tackle – 11m ladder; 6m and stake belay; 15m lifeline.

Permission – Darnbrook House.

DREAM CAVE   NGR SD 914704   Grade I
Alt. 295m   **Length 21m**
Explored 1978, Ilkley Caving Club.

Obscure entrance concealed behind boulders (please replace) at foot of small scar, some 90m up-valley from obvious rising. Horrible muddy crawl along what appears to be the roof of a large, mud-filled phreatic tube.
Permission – The Green Farm, Arncliffe.

ENIGMA HOLE   NGR SD 885713   Grade I
Alt. 435m   **Depth 8m**
Explored 1958, CPC.

Small hole, covered by rocks, part way up true right bank of gill, just before stream bed starts to climb up to a little gorge. Awkward climb (ladder best) descends to where stream enters from impassable inlet, and further wet drop leads to over-tight rift.

Tackle – 8m ladder; 3m belay; 10m lifeline.

Permission – Darnbrook House.

FALCON CAVE   NGR SD 916703   Grade II
Alt. 300m   **Length 30m**
Obvious entrance on ledge at SW end of Yew Cogar Scar above Cowside

Beck. Can be reached by traverse from grass slope at end of scar. Large passage rapidly diminishes in size until the way on is by flat out crawl over stalagmited boulders. After a particularly low section the roof lifts, permitting comfortable crawling in a wide bedding passage to the final choke.

Permission – The Green Farm, Arncliffe.

FOXTRAP CAVE   NGR SD 916703   Grade II
Alt. 295m   Length 230m
Explored 1980, WRPC and CDG.

Small entrance in obvious gully just up-valley from Falcon Cave. Low, muddy crawl for 9m passes a duck to emerge through boulders in a large chamber. A slot down through blocks in the floor leads to sandy slope down to a sump. This has been dived to a large bell after 140m and the continuing duck and second sump have been explored for 50m to where main way on appears to have been lost.

Permission – The Green Farm, Arncliffe.

GREAT DARNBROOK BLOWING HOLE
NGR SD 880703   Grade II
Alt. 485m   **Depth 6m**
Explored 1960, CPC.

Entrance W of Cherry Tree Hole. Small shaft in dug out boulders, with small crawl which has noticeable warm draught, but becomes too small.

Permission – Darnbrook House.

THE KEYHOLE   NGR SD 903700   Grade II
Alt. 305m   Length 6m

Small sloping entrance at foot of scar about 50m up-valley from the more obvious entrances to Loop Cave. Very awkward squeeze at foot of slope is best dealt with feet first, and the ensuing passage is a tight sideways crawl which becomes too tight.

Permission – Darnbrook House.

LOOP CAVE   NGR SD 903700   Grade II
Alt. 300m   Length 45m

Two entrances in small scar on S bank of Cowside Beck 400m downstream of the confluence with Darnbrook Beck. A small stream issues from the larger (E) entrance and it is possible to emerge from the W entrance some 9m away. Part way round the loop in the left wall is a small crawling size passage. For the first 9m to a sharp corner to the left the floor is covered by a layer of stalagmite, and at one time contained some good cave pearls. Beyond the corner the stream is met. To the left, downstream, can be followed through a small tube to end in a little chamber after 12m, while upstream continues round several tight bends to a pool. Forward is a short sump leading to 6m of

passage and a further sump which has a bad bend and constriction 3m in, preventing progress.
Permission – Darnbrook House.

MIDDLE STREAM SINK   NGR SD 878708   Grade II
Alt. 520m   **Depth 8m**
Explored 1958, CPC.

The entrance lies high on Darnbrook Fell in the middle of an area of exposed limestone just below a prominent stream sink. An easy ladder climb lands in a small chamber with a narrow rift descending further on one side and becoming too tight.

Tackle – 8m ladder; sling belay; 12m lifeline.

Permission – Darnbrook House.

PENNINE POT   NGR SD 878703   Grade II
Alt. 500m   **Length 20m**   **Depth 5m**
Explored 1959, CPC.

Entrance in shakehole right beside Pennine Way drops into 9m crawl to top of 4m climb (rope useful). At foot is large chamber (9m x 9m x 4m tall) with a boulder floor blocking all signs of a way on. Start of crawl is likely to be blocked.
Permission – Darnbrook House.

REVOLTING CAVE   NGR SD 878701   Grade III
Alt. 495m   **Length 9m**
Explored 1976, UWFRA.

Entrance in small shakehole within few metres of Tennant Gill. Step down drops into start of low crawl, floored with horrible orange-coloured sludge. A mud duck after 6m leads to tight corner, and impassable bend.
Permission – Tennant Gill Farm.

ROBINSONS' POT   NGR SD 899706   Grade III
Alt. 323m   **Length 2.2km**   **Depth 15m**
Explored 1862; re-discovered 1975, CPC & Ex-BSA; extended 1976, 1984, CDG.

WARNING – The crawl through to MacColl's Rift sumps rapidly in times of flood, as does the Glup Hole crawl to the Worm Series.

A uniquely sited entrance right under the wall of Darnbrook Farm house leading to an interesting and varied system containing the main drainage route from Darnbrook Fell.

At foot of easy 7m entrance pitch is small chamber and choice of four passages. Behind the ladder quickly chokes, while a crawl under the S wall enters a rift and climb down to a further choke. A tight crawl under the N wall splits; left enters a blind chamber in glacial fill, while right continues as a wet crawl to a sump. Last passage is the main route and lies up a short climb

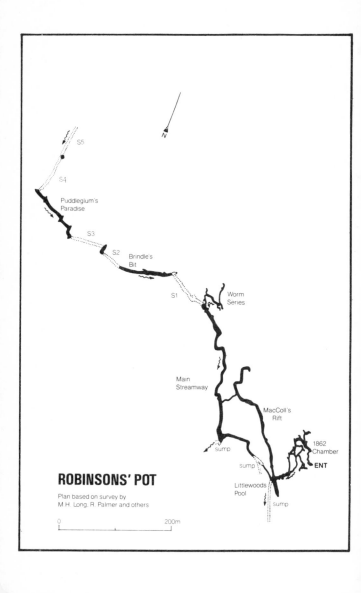

ROBINSONS' POT

Plan based on survey by
M.H. Long, R. Palmer and others

0   200m

N

S5
S4
Puddlegium's
Paradise
S3
S2
Brindle's
Bit
S1
Worm
Series
Main
Streamway
MacColl's
Rift
1862
Chamber
ENT
sump
sump
Littlewoods
Pool
sump

opposite the ladder. Walking and a traverse lead to awkward climb down at start of 1862 Chamber, containing signatures of earlier explorers (unfortunately defaced already), and an inlet sump under the right wall is too small after 4m. Straight across chamber is short passage to further chamber and choke, while way on lies down slope on left into phreatic tube. At a bend to the right, passage splits. The larger right hand passage quickly chokes, while the other low, muddy crawl soon enlarges to walking size and a junction with a stream passage.

The upstream passage is of varying size and leads past several tight inlets and an outlet passage on the right which enters a low, wet bedding complex, to a split, with both routes quickly emerging in Paraffin Pong Passage. Upstream to left, passage lowers over deepening water to where airspace is un-useable. Downstream becomes fine canyon passage ending at a choked bedding on the right, and large breakdown blocks straight ahead.

Downstream in main route passes three other ways into the wet bedding complex, the last being in the floor of a large cross-rift aven, and beyond this a small tube crawl eventually slopes down into a low bedding chamber containing the stream seen earlier. This can be forced upstream through the wet bedding complex in dry weather. The low crawl downstream enlarges gradually and suddenly breaks out into the very large MacColl's Rift, the stream flowing across and under the far wall into Littlewoods Pool which has been dived for 86m, becoming very tight and silted. Also under far wall is further low passage leading through several awkward ducks to the downstream end of the By-Pass Sump, 25m long, which connects through to the main stream passage.

MacColl's Rift is a blind end up slope to left, but in other direction a steep slope leads to main passage with alternating sections of large rift and lower crawls to a chamber with an interesting sludge floor. Concealed under the left wall is the Crossover Passage, leading to the main streamway, while ahead the large passage passes one choke only to encounter another, with a dangerous climb to an upper level and a complete choke.

Crossover Passage starts low and muddy but soon becomes a narrow canyon ending abruptly after 30m at a 3m pitch into a large stream passage containing the Darnbrook water. Downstream rapidly lowers and widens to a large bedding with the stream disappearing into an impossibly tight sump in a rift to the right, while the By-Pass Passage leads off over a cobble bank to a series of crawls and static canals ending at the By-Pass sump. As mentioned this connects through to MacColl's Rift by following the left wall, but there is a diverging route underwater off to the right, dived for 37m in a silt floored phreatic tube. No end was reached.

Upstream is a fine canyon passage which finally lowers and widens at a sweeping bend, and beyond, deepening water and a duck enter a sump chamber with the Glup Hole crawl into the Worm Series on the right hand side. The crawl emerges in a large phreatic passage which splits to the left, both routes choking quickly. Continuing to the right passes a narrow muddy rift leading to a mini-ramp and rift climb to a choke. A small stream usually sinks under the right wall near the start of this, and following up the stream the passage gradually becomes a flat out crawl to a sharp bend and an inaccessible sump.

The main upstream sump has been dived to emerge after 75m in Brindle's Bit, 90m of easy passage ending at another sump. This has been passed by a 36m dive to the Hall of the Archmage, a 20m high aven chamber and short length of passage to the next sump which proved to be 60m long and which is followed by Puddleglum's Paradise, 75m of mainly low canal passage relieved by three unclimbed avens. Beyond is the fourth upstream sump, ending at a large airbell and unstable boulder slope where inlet stream enters through a suicidal choke. The fifth sump, 77m long, passes rift airbells to reach a large underwater chamber, followed by 46m of dry passage ending at a massive boulder choke, from which the stream emerges.

Tackle

Pitch	Ladder	Belay	Lifeline
Entrance	8m	Short spreader	12m
To Main Stream	4.5m	Short bar and sling	8m

Permission – Darnbrook Farm. Access severely restricted owing to position of entrance.

STIRRUP PUMP POT   NGR SD 881702   Grade III
Alt. 465m   **Depth 14m**
Explored 1963, CPC.

To the S of Cherry Tree Hole. Small entrance shaft leads to rift descent and then flat out crawl in water and glutinous mud which becomes too low after the first corner. Was first explored after water was lowered by stirrup pump and bucket.

Permission – Darnbrook House.

TENNANT GILL SHAFTS   Grade II
Nos. 1-3 explored 1965-71, CPC; Nos. 4-7 explored 1965, BSA; No. 8 explored 1977, WRPC.

Small shafts in shakeholes 800m WNW of Tennant Gill Farm.

1. NGR SD 877699   Alt. 495m   Depth 9m
Shaft in large shakehole enters boulder chamber with no obvious way forward.

Tackle – 9m ladder; stake and sling belay; 11m lifeline.

2. NGR SD 877700   Alt. 495m   Depth 6m
Rift which can be descended by chimneying is choked at foot.

3. NGR SD 877700   Alt. 495m   Depth 9m
Scramble down among boulders to small, boulder-choked chamber.

4. NGR SD 874696   Alt. 505m   Depth 20m
Extended 1986, NCC.

Over broken wall 400m SW of Pennine Way, near big silted-up sink. Tight pitch to boulder chamber. Excavated hole through boulders leads to 4.5m climb to small chamber and a further 4.5m climb down to where impassable inlet enters and sinks in the boulder floor.

Tackle – 8m ladder; stake and sling belay; 11m lifeline.

5. NGR SD 875697   **Alt. 500m**   **Depth 11m**

In shallow valley between 4 and Pennine Way. Small opening 3.5m deep to tight sideways crawl beneath loose flakes and further pitch to silt-choked passage. Entrance now blocked by collapsed bank.

Tackle

Pitch	Ladder	Belay	Lifeline
Entrance	4.5m	Stake and sling	9m
2nd	6m	1m	8m

6. NGR SD 877697   **Alt. 485m**   **Depth 9m**

In line of shakeholes at rear of small plateau. Rocky entrance conceals pitch descending in steps to choke.

Tackle – 12m ladder; stake and sling belay; 15m lifeline.

7. NGR SD 877697   **Alt. 485m**   **Depth 7m**

A few metres NE of 6 and covered by an old oil drum. Tight shaft to choke and noise of small stream through cleft at one side.

Tackle – 8m ladder; stake and sling belay; 12m lifeline.

8. NGR SD 878701   **Alt. 495m**   **Depth 11m**

In large shakehole with rock face, just below Pennine Way. Tight squeeze opens out onto 6m pitch into chamber, where a further squeeze on left gains access to 2nd pitch into boulder choked rift.

Tackle

Pitch	Ladder	Belay	Lifeline
1st	8m	Sling and spreader	12m
2nd	5m	3m	8m

Permission – Tennant Gill Farm.

THORAGILL CAVE   NGR SD 889702   Grade I
Alt. 380m   **Length 60m**

Explored 1951, NPC.

Rising for small stream 300m from Malham – Arncliffe road N of Thoragill Beck House. A small entrance leads over fallen boulders into a chamber. At far side passage continues almost straight for 25m to a sump, mainly crawling over large blocks. The sump is about 4.5m long, and involves negotiating a large block underwater. Beyond, the passage is a 3m tall rift some 1m wide for the next 9m to a corner. From here a low crawl for 3m leads to a chamber with a small inlet passage at roof level. The stream emerges from beneath more fallen boulders, and a tight crawl leads to an upward slot and a Y-junction. The left hand passage becomes too tight after 4.5m, while to the right 9m of tight fissure passage leads to a duck, and beyond, the water issues from an impassable bedding plane.

Permission – Darnbrook House; but note that permission is not usually given.

UPSTREAM POT   NGR SD 884710   Grade II
Alt. 465m   **Depth 12m**
Explored 1969, CPC.

Entrance 100m W of Darnbrook Pot. Tight fissure for 12m to boulder floor where stream can be heard.

Tackle – 12m ladder; stake and sling belay; 15m lifeline.

Permission – Darnbrook House.

WALLSIDE POT   NGR SD 885713   Grade II
Alt. 440m   **Depth 9m**
Explored 1974, G.N. Long.

Small opening covered by boulders immediately over wall to S of head of small gorge on Darnbrook Beck. Starting easily, an awkward slide sideways passes a low bedding inlet, water from which sprays one liberally until the foot of the pitch is reached in an enlarged rift. A descent on a sloping shelf leads to a window onto a further small drop, and at the foot the stream flows into a very restricted sump.

Tackle – 9m ladder; stake and sling belay; 12m lifeline.

Permission – Darnbrook House.

YEW COGAR CAVE   NGR SD 908700   Grade IV
Alt. 287m   **Length 1.1km**
Extended 1968-71, CPC; 1973-4, YSS.

WARNING – The whole cave floods quickly in heavy rain.

Low entrance by pool in Cowside Beck leads via a sloping boulder chamber and a series of bedding plane crawls to the main stream in Darnbrook Passage, a wide, low streamway.

Darnbrook Passage
Downstream leads through a short crawl to a circular chamber with a short drop and crawl to a sump which becomes extremely tight after 8m. Upstream is a hands and knees crawl for 90m to Sump 1. This is a 100m low dive and emerges in a pool. Ahead the stream enters through a chaos of boulders in Four Feather Passage, 6m wide, 2m high and 12m long. A climb up several cascades leads to a 15m canal with low airspace to Sump 2, 15m long, which leads to Windermere – a lake 15m long and 6m wide – followed by the 30m long Sump 3. The sump emerges in another, larger chamber ending at two 1m high waterfalls with twin streamways above. Both are easy crawls which rejoin after 45m. Only 15m further on is Sump 4, dived for 189m past an airbell to silt banks where way on seemed to have been lost.

Parishioners' Way
In the initial chamber, 9m in from the cave entrance, a way up on the left at roof level enters Flotsam Crawl, which leads over a rock floor through a pool to a junction with another stream passage at Jetsam Chamber. This independant streamway is presumed to drain the Parson's Pulpit area. Outlet passages to left join, and sump 9m long reaches chamber with daylight

entering through boulders in roof, where floods emerge just down valley.
Continuing sump from chamber is undived. Upstream, a low sandy crawl,
Parishioner's Way, gradually gains height to become a fine, arched passage
which divides after 120m. Stream flows from right branch which continues
for 110m past several squeezes and some fine stalactite bosses before
splitting. Right becomes too narrow and left ends similarly after another
25m. Left at previous junction an inclined tube enters a large passage ending
at the extremely unstable Slurry Dig. This is liable to have collapsed but
beyond is a passage which bends sharply right to choke below an aven.
Permission – The Green Farm, Arncliffe.

YEW COGAR RISING CAVE   NGR SD 910700   Grade II
Alt. 280m   **Length 66m**
Explored 1964, BSA; extended 1977, CUCC.
WARNING – Can only be entered in periods of dry weather.

Entrance under wall at large rising about 250m downstream from Yew
Cogar Cave. Small entrance between boulders gives access to a pool
chamber, and sump after 6m. The sump is 35m long with an airbell after 3m
and ends at a small airbell with two ways on. Left, a sumped continuation
has been followed for 6m to a sharp right bend and narrow descending rift.
Right, 9m of narrow canal passage leads to a chamber with three ways on.
Below water level to the right is a tiny sump, blocked by a boulder almost
immediately; the way left is a body-sized sump which enlarges dramatically
above a deep flooded rift with airbell above. Rift dived to 11m depth and
continued, increasingly awkward. The third way on is a low bedding
providing a dry way to the airbell above the rift.
Permission – The Green Farm, Arncliffe.

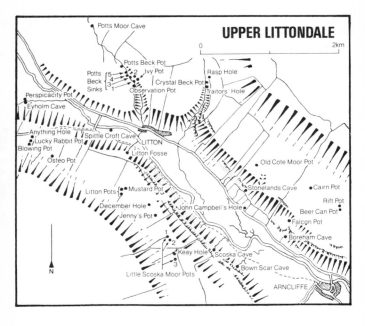

UPPER LITTONDALE

ANYTHING HOLE   NGR SD 889740   **Grade II**
[Frog Pot]
Alt. 394m   **Depth 9m**
Explored 1970, MUSS.

   Very small shaft covered by slabs, just below stream sink higher up small gully containing Blowing Pot. Tight pitch passes through a squeeze to land in a small chamber with a badly choked floor.

Tackle – 9m ladder; stake and sling belay; 12m lifeline.

Permission – Marton Scar Farm, West Marton.

BEER CAN POT   NGR SD 933729   Grade II
Alt. 420m   **Depth 6m**

Below small scar 75m from N boundary wall of Old Cote Low Moor. Entrance fissure covered by large rocks which must be replaced. Easy climb of 2.5m to boulder floor, followed by further awkward climb down of 3.5m into small chamber, the floor of which is covered by empty beer cans. There is no passable way on.

Permission – Old Cotes, Arncliffe.

BLOWING POT   NGR SD 889740   Grade III
Alt. 390m   **Depth 12m**
Explored 1966, BSA.

Entrance in side of dry gully 30m below a tight stream sink, in the field S of track running along S side of Penyghent Gill. A tight squeeze at top of shaft opens out into a large rift, and a landing is made on a floor of boulders 4.5m down. A careful descent can be made through the boulders at one end to a floor of rocks, and a series of small steps can be followed down in a narrowing rift to where the way on is too tight. A strong draught can usually be noticed.

Tackle – 11m ladder; stake and sling belay; 15m lifeline.

Permission – Marton Scar Farm, Marton.

BOREHAM CAVE   NGR SD 925726   Grade III-V
Alt. 251m   **Length 3.1km**
Extended 1959, CPC; 1966, CDG; 1973-75, KCC & CDG; 1986, CDG.

Lengthy dives have confirmed the importance of this cave, by extending the main flooded passage, and with the discovery of an impressive high level series which contains some magnificent formations.

Gated entrance over wall at corner of field midway between Flats and Cross Barns. An easy passage gradually decreases in height until 50m from entrance a canal is met. This can be followed through a series of ducks and airbells for a further 30m to a definite sump. The rest of the cave is only accessible to divers.

First sump is 45m long with airbells 5.5m from either end. Immediately after the sump is crawl on right to 25m aven – bolted to 12m of passage and a choke. Main route is mostly hands and knees until at a sudden right bend it enlarges to a walk. Only 25m further on the main passage is choked, the water emerging from a small sump. In pool at sharp bend a tight underwater slot descends 3m into an enlarging submerged passage; 90m forward a silt slope rises to a short narrow airbell and a similar descent begins Sump 4 which is 25m long to a shattered chamber above water. A slope drops into a further 25m sump to an airbell with a sandbank breaking water. A dive of 37m passes another bell and 15m forward is yet another whose exit is an awkward flooded pot dropping into a meandering tube. After 43m airspace is gained in a large pool with an inlet cascading through boulders. Underwater the tube continues into Sump 9.

Scramble up boulders past flowstone cascade into fine decorated passage

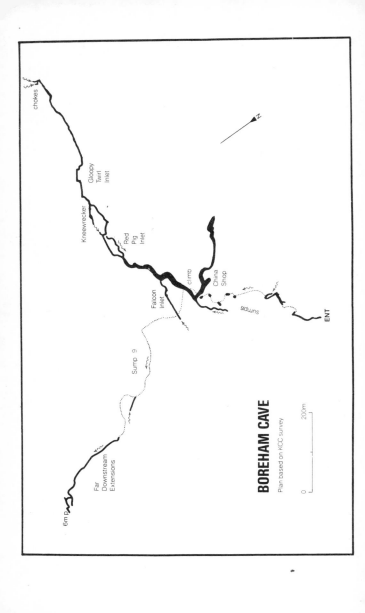

chokes

Gloopy
Twirl
Inlet

Kneewrecker

Red
Pig
Inlet

climb

China
Shop

Falcon
Inlet

sumps

ENT

Sump 9

Far
Downstream
Extensions

6m p.

BOREHAM CAVE

Plan based on KCC survey

0   200m

leading to long chamber with 4.5m waterfall. Above the fall 120m of passage ends in a boulder choke. Continuing along the main tunnel a fork is met. Red Pig Inlet to the right becomes a tight crawl to a choke. Left is a canal and dry oxbow to the active Kneewrecker Series of nasty crawls back to the left.

Upstream swimming leads to a boulder choke; 6m back from end on the right a crawl up through boulders leads to a large and well decorated passage. Stream is regained and 550m of passage with good formations, mainly walking or stooping but eventually crawling, ends at a chamber and junction. Straight on becomes too low in wet bedding after 25m. To right through short duck and crawl ends at choke with stream emerging.

A difficult climb up the flowstone wall near the pool at the start of Sump 9 leads to superb high level passages. Masses of long straws (extreme care) and a unique lake are passed before the route chokes after 250m. To the right an inlet with gours leads into dry chambers and inlets.

Sump 9 has been dived for 460m. There are two small airbells in the first 67m and two more kicking-water bells break the next 260m of sump. Here a large airbell is met, with a 4.5m waterfall from 20m of passage to a roof choke. The sump continues for 110m to canal and shingle bank up into dry passage, stream runs off into very low passage. Ahead a canyon passage suddenly lowers to a crawl to 6m pitch with excessively tight sump at the foot. Permission – Old Cotes, Arncliffe.

BOWN SCAR CAVE   NGR SD 918721   Grade IV
Alt. 260m   **Length 1.2km**   **Vertical range 32m**
Explored 1942, North brothers; extended 1948, NPC; 1967, Preston CC; 1970, ULSA.

WARNING – The cave is liable to total flooding in wet weather.

Large resurgence in Bown Scar Wood; entrance is bedding plane above normal water outlet. **If water is emerging from entrance it is inadvisable to enter.** Low crawl passes under cross joint to join stream, which can be followed up as a nasty crawl for 60m. Way forward is across stream and through shingle crawl to a wide pool. Fossil Crawl is a fine passage giving easy hands and knees progress for 110m until the stream is rejoined. Downstream a 37m crawl becomes too low but upstream the waterway is far more inviting. The first inlet on the left is a 70m long crawl which is finally obstructed by shingle and blocks. Continuing up the main stream, 150m of stooping leads to the main inlet (again on the left), which is a refreshing 60m long crawl through pools separated by gour barriers. The main passage now degenerates into a rocky crawl, until it enters a very extensive canal. At the termination of the canal is a 6m high aven. A continuing short crawl connects with a similar aven, the stream falling from a slot on the right at the base of it. Beyond the last aven the crawl continues at floor level for 100m as Skeleton Passage which ends in a near sump

Scoska Series
The last aven is an exposed 6m climb to a chamber with a 9m waterfall. The fall is overcome by a dry chimney and traverse (exposed) and a further 3.5m fall above is climbed direct to a low passage. The following passage network leads to a high rift and an ascending traverse overcomes a series of

falls to an inlet which is very similar to the crawls in the entrance series. This is the beginning of 250m of canals which contain a low air space, oxbow and water 2m deep for a short distance. The limit of exploration is 5cm air space over a canal 0.7m deep.

Permissison – Ryelands Farm, Arncliffe.

CAIRN POT   NGR SD 930733   Grade II
Alt. 440m   Depth 7.5m
Explored 1968, YURT.

A small hole concealed in a shallow, heathery and insignificant shakehole near a minor stream sink is the entrance to this rift pitch, choked at the foot.

Tackle – 9m ladder; stake and sling belay; 12m lifeline.

CRYSTAL BECK POT   NGR SD 914748   Grade III
Alt. 345m   Length 275m   Depth 27m
Extended 1966, WRPC.

WARNING – Flood water in Crystal Beck flows straight into the cave, flooding it completely within a very short space of time.

Obvious entrance in E bank of Crystal Beck 800m from Litton. An easy 2.5m climb down at the entrance leads to a small chamber with a low wet upstream passage on the left. After 6m a duck is reached, followed quickly by another one, leading to a 2m long sump, which should not be free dived. Beyond, a further section of low wet passage leads through a further duck to a chamber 4.5m diameter and 9m high. Two passages continue, that to the left soon becoming choked, while the other develops into a rift and ends in a choked bedding passage after a 2.5m climb up.

Downstream from the entrance goes over fallen blocks to Sump 1, 1.5m long, followed by a rift passage to a waterfall chamber with a deep pool. An awkward climb up leads to Tatty Passage, and after 30m is Sump 2, 9m long. Beyond, a short length of rift passage leads to yet another sump, which becomes too tight for further progress. Back in the main passage the deep pool is the start of Sump 3, 3m long, and beyond this, 12m of passage leads to a very wet pitch. A traverse over the pitch enters Suicide Passage which can be followed for 64m via a series of very unstable chambers to end in a choke. From foot of the pitch the passage descends sharply round a series of bends to a junction. To the right is choked, while to the left is a further sump, 6m long. Downstream is 45m of high rift to a scramble up over breakdown in a small, boulder-floored rift. Squeeze down regains stream in a narrow rift and 6m of tight crawl leads to a small chamber. Beyond is an awkward duck into a further small, waterlogged chamber and a sump with two ways on underwater. Left has been dived for 6m and right for 3m, both ways being uncompromisingly narrow. The final chamber area is of doubtful stability following the use of explosives to gain entry to the sump.

In severe drought Sumps 1 and 2 dry up and it is possible to get down the pitch.

Tackle – 11m ladder; 6m belay; 20m lifeline.

Permission – West Farm, Litton.

DECEMBER HOLE   NGR SD 905730   Grade II
Alt. 405m   **Depth 11m**
Explored 1970, BSA.

In row of shakeholes, 250m from SE wall of Great Scoska Moor. Entrance is covered by boulders which must be replaced. Top section of shaft is down through unstable blocks, and then it opens out into a large rift 4.5m by 1.5m with fine stalagmite run down one wall. Landing is on choke of boulders.

Tackle – 12m ladder; stake and sling belay; 15m lifeline.

Permission – East Garth Farm, Litton.

EYHOLM CAVE   NGR SD 888746   Grade II
Alt. 270m   **Length 15m**
Explored 1985, UWFRA.

WARNING – Liable to severe flooding in wet weather when entrance may be submerged.

Covered entrance in stream bed a few metres below old ford drops into bedding. In down valley direction all ways on are too tight, while other way leads to an alternative entrance (now blocked) and a crawl off to the left which reaches a total choke just beyond a small drop into a pool. This end point was dug into from surface but failed to produce a continuation.
Permission – Nether Hesleden.

FALCON POT   NGR SD 927729   Grade III
Alt. 340m   **Length 187m**
Explored 1948, CPC; extended 1967, NCC.

Entrance in quarry-like hollow about 250m N of Boreham Cave. Stream, which is public water supply, is met just inside and 6m to right (downstream) is 9m wet pitch, choked at the bottom.

Upstream crawl enters small chamber after 14m, followed by 37m sharp, wet crawl to 8m chimney up rift at waterfall, beyond which is 35m of passage to a 1.5m cascade. Above the cascade 12m of passage leads to a low, wet crawl 20m long, with only 15cm airspace in good weather. This emerges in a chamber of standing height, from which an upper passage runs back over the wet crawl for 20m to a small, calcited chamber.

From the standing chamber the way on is up a 3m waterfall into 12m of crawl to another 1.5m cascade. About 27m ahead is tight fissure sump.

Tackle – 9m ladder; 6m belay; 12m lifeline.

Permission – Old Cotes, Arncliffe.

IVY POT   NGR SD 904749   Grade II
Alt. 370m   **Depth 20m**
Explored 1963, EPC.

In small dry side gill on E side of Potts Beck, 800m upstream from Litton. Climb down over boulders at entrance leads down rift with stepped floor of wedged blocks to head of first pitch. Landing is on rock shelf and second pitch follows immediately—best belayed to first ladder. At foot is series of small interconnected chambers with avens, one reached by short climb up sloping bank of mud and rocks. Outlet passage is too small to follow.

Tackle

Pitch	Ladder	Belay	Lifeline
1st	8m	6m	15m
2nd	8m	–	12m

Permission—West Farm, Litton.

JENNY'S POT　　　　NGR SD 906729　　　Grade III
Alt. 412m　　　　　　　　　　　　　　　　**Depth 23m**
Explored 1980/81, UWFRA.

Excavated entrance in shakehole at end of small stream. Covered oil drum (please replace cover) opening straight onto 21m pitch which is tight and awkward at top. At foot is crawl along rift to enlargement and step up through a squeeze to where passage terminates at a minute floor slot.

Tackle – 30m ladder; stake and sling belay; 30m lifeline.

Permission – East Garth Farm, Litton.

JOHN CAMPBELL'S HOLE　　NGR SD 920729　　Grade II
Alt. 236m　　　　　　　　**Length 12m**　　　　　　　**Depth 4.5m**
Explored 1975, BPC.

Excavated flood rising in field to E of Low Fields Barn and only a few metres from road. Pitch down through oil drums enters low bedding containing stream. Both ways quickly become too low.

Tackle – 6m ladder; stake and sling belay; 9m lifeline.

KEAY HOLE　　　　　　NGR SD 910723　　　　Grade III
[Scoska Moor Pot 4]
Alt. 418m　　　　　　　　**Length 15m**　　　　　　　**Depth 21m**
Explored 1975, BPC.

Excavated entrance in stream bed just above wall leads to climb down to squeeze through to head of 11m pitch which has several tight sections. Landing is in small stream passage which gets too tight upstream immediately, while downstream passes a squeeze and short crawl to a 4.5m pitch with loose boulders. From foot passage continues round bend to end at a large choke. At 2nd pitch, ascending rift leads to squeeze through boulders to emerge in the large Brow Narse Chamber, 12m long and up to 15m tall. Any possible continuation lies concealed beneath the boulder covered floor. Stream needs diverting for a descent.

Tackle

Pitch	Ladder	Belay	Lifeline
1st	12m	3m	15m
2nd	6m	Bar and sling	9m

Permission – The Gatehouse, Arncliffe.

LITTLE SCOSKA MOOR POTS
Explored 1968-69, BSA.

1. NGR SD 909726   **Alt. 405m**   **Depth 10m**   **Grade III**
Tight rift pitch in side of stream bed at sharp bend can only be descended by the slimmest cavers. At bottom is very narrow passage which has been followed for a short way. May be possible to force it further.

Tackle—11m ladder; stake and sling belay; 15m lifeline.

2. NGR SD 909725   **Alt. 405m**   **Depth 9m**   **Grade III**
In shakehole at toe of bank 50m down-valley from 1. Entrance covered by timbers. Climb down in rift leads to unstable chamber. At N end it is possible to crawl beneath dangerous blocks to further short climb to reach stream entering from impassable inlet. At S end of chamber is another climb down to short length of rift passage, quickly becoming too tight.

3. NGR SD 910723   **Alt. 420m**   **Depth 4.5m**   **Grade I**
Over next wall, and beyond small stream is shaft surrounded by wire fence. Awkward climb down over loose debris leads into very unstable chamber with no way out.

Permission—The Gatehouse, Arncliffe.

LITTON FOSSE   **NGR SD 903738**   **Grade I**
Alt. 290m   **Length 30m**
Explored 1962, CPC.

Entrance at obvious rising across river Skirfare from Litton village. The stream is still part of an existing water supply and the cave is closed. A crawl along a bedding cave leads to a drop down into a stream passage 2m high and 1m wide. After about 30m a roof fall blocks the way on.

LITTON POTS   **NGR SD 902732**   **Grade II**
Explored 1939, YRC.

Best reached by footpath from Litton Fosse, over stile, and straight up fell.

Lower Pot   **Alt. 405m**   **Depth 5m**
Large rift in big shakehole with small cave entrance discharging a little stream. Rope descent to choked floor.

Upper Pot   **Alt. 410m**   **Depth 12m**
In small shakehole 60m S of Lower Pot. Pitch broken by sloping shelf halfway down lands in small chamber with way on choked.

Tackle—11m ladder; stake and sling belay; 15m lifeline.

Permission—East Garth Farm, Litton.

LUCKY RABBIT POT   **NGR SD 889740**   **Grade III**
Alt. 393m   **Depth 10m**
Explored 1976, MUSS.

In same gully as, and between, Anything Hole and Blowing Pot. Excavated shakehole gives straight onto a 5m climb down to a partial false floor with a further very tight 5m climb down to a complete choke. Ladder is required to aid return.

Tackle – 11m ladder; stake and sling belay; 15m lifeline.

Permission – Marton Scar Farm, West Marton.

MUSTARD POT   NGR SD 902732   Grade III
Alt. 400m   **Depth 43m**
Explored 1971, MUSS.

Where stream sinks, 50m NE of Lower Litton Pot. Excavated entrance pitch of 11m with belay in stream bed leads to an 8m climb down in a tight fissure. At foot a low crawl of 4.5m opens out at head of 3rd pitch of 20m. There is a large ledge 14m down, and the landing is on boulders in a big chamber. A final climb down of 4.5m leads to a further sloping descent to a draughting bedding plane which is far too low to follow.

Tackle

Pitch	Ladder	Belay	Lifeline
Entrance	11m	3m	15m
2nd	–	–	12m
3rd	25m	No natural belay	30m

Permission – East Garth Farm, Litton.

OBSERVATION POT   NGR SD 903748   Grade II
Alt. 350m   **Length 8m**   **Depth 11m**
Explored 1981, UWFRA.

Obvious open shaft against right bank of gill, a few metres downstream from Potts Beck Sink 1. Careful descent beside wedged boulders reaches boulder floor and silt-filled undercut, with crawl through boulders to north to choked rift.

Tackle – 12m ladder; stake and sling belay; 17m lifeline.

Permission – West Farm, Litton.

OLD COTE MOOR POT   NGR SD 921736   Grade III
Alt. 400m   **Length 40m**   **Depth 26m**
Explored 1963, BPC.

At top of Bracken Gill (dry), 100m SE of sheepfold. Entrance blocked by boulders which must be replaced. Tight entrance straight onto 2.5m climb down into small chamber. Passage doubles back on itself to further easy climb of 3.5m. Below this, rift opens out at a thick shale bed, leading to the top of a rift pitch with a doubtful boulder belay on shelf on left. At foot of 14m pitch is a narrow stream passage which can be followed for 30m to an awkward duck, and just beyond is a sump, too small to dive.

Tackle – 15m ladder; 6m belay; 25m lifeline.

Permission – Old Cotes, Arncliffe.

OSTEO POT   NGR SD 892737   Grade II
Alt. 400m   **Depth 9m**
Explored 1974, MUSS.

Excavated rift in shallow dry valley high on Wilson's Pasture, covered with a variety of girders, timber and rocks which must be replaced. Straight descent to a choked floor with an excessively tight fissure leading off at one end.

Tackle – 9m ladder; stake and sling belay; 12m lifeline.

Permission – Marton Scar Farm, West Marton.

PERSPICACITY POT   NGR SD 888746   Grade III
Alt. 271m   **Length 260m**   **Depth 9m**
Explored 1986-87, UWFRA & MUSS.
WARNING – Liable to severe flooding if gill flows in lower length, when entrance is likely to be completely submerged.

Beneath small scar on left bank of Penyghent Gill, just downstream of footbridge. The covering must be replaced to prevent blocking with flood debris. Easy 3m climb, and feet-first descent of sloping passage, leads to start of crawl. This enlarges slightly after 17m, then after a further 25m encounters a junction with a small streamway. Upstream can be followed for 10m to where stalactites block the way, while downstream quickly reaches a 2m climb down into a small chamber - the only place in the whole cave where one can stand up. An impassable inlet enters beneath the climb, and the continuing outlet crawl is tight for the next few metres. Varied wet crawling encounters a number of impassable inlets, and a unique dam, but 195m from the entrance the water flows off down a ridiculously low passage to the right, leaving only a further inlet to the left, which can be followed for 40m.
Permission – Nether Hesleden.

POTTS BECK POT   NGR SD 902750   Grade III
Alt. 390m   **Length 50m**   **Depth 45m**
Explored 1963, EPC; extended 1970, CPC.

Entrance is a narrow rift in the left hand side of the gill (going up) and is a tight 9m pitch. A climb through boulders leads suddenly to a second pitch of 20m into a very large chamber 30m long, 23m wide and up to 25m high. A 12m boulder slope leads off downwards but ends in a choke. High up on the right, opposite the bottom of the ladder, is a small inlet (scaling pole needed). This is 20m of narrow rift passage ending in a choke. On the left, before the end, running water can be heard.

Tackle

Pitch	Ladder	Belay	Lifeline
Entrance	9m	Stake and sling	9m
2nd	20m	6m	25m

Permission – West Farm, Litton.

POTTS BECK SINKS   Grade I
1. NGR SD 903749   **Alt. 360m**   **Depth 4.5m**
   In left bank of gill below old mine level. Easy 4.5m climb down leads to
short crawl and impossibly tight pitch.
2. NGR SD 903749   **Alt. 365m**   **Length 90m**
Extended 1966, NCC.
   Located up on E bank 50m upstream of 1. Small cave where human
skeleton was found by members of EPC. Cannot be followed downstream,
but the upstream limit has been pushed through a squeeze and tight climb to
a short passage reaching a 6m aven. Above is an awkward, low and winding
passage to a 4.5m aven. The ensuing rift becomes too tight after 6m.
3. NGR SD 903749   **Alt. 370m**   **Depth 11m**
   At top of peculiar rock staircase.A very awkward start leads to a 9m shaft
dropping into a larger rift. Further climb down through boulders leads to top
of too tight cleft down to standing water. To one end of rift is narrow slot
forward to aven. Entrance now blocked.
Tackle – 9m ladder; stake and sling belay; 15m lifeline.
4. NGR SD 903749   **Alt. 370m**   **Length 5m**
   About 30m upstream of 3 is small cave in true right bank. Small chamber
with too low bedding passage leading out.
5. NGR SD 902750   **Alt. 380m**   **Depth 6m**
   Just before gill opens out into an amphitheatre in true right bank. Rift
opening drops down easy climb of 3m and further climb down into small
chamber. Way on is choked and appears too tight. Now blocked part way
down first climb.
Permission – West Farm, Litton.

POTTS MOOR CAVE   NGR SD 898756   Grade III
Alt. 472m   **Length 100m**
Explored 1970, BSA; extended 1977, BPC.

   MdL. Open entrance above rising where Potts Beck plays hide and seek in
the Yoredale beds. Descent to stream is followed by wet crawl and short duck
below wedged blocks. Beyond, aquatic crawling reaches a junction 30m from
entrance. To the left soon becomes too low, while right branch continues as a
wet and tight rift series for a further 50m to where further progress is
impossible.
Permission – West Farm, Litton.

RASP HOLE   NGR SD 914749   Grade I
Alt. 370m   **Depth 6m**
   Obvious entrance in small side gully on true left bank of main gill, just
upstream from Crystal Beck Pot. An awkward descent down a steep boulder
slope in a tight rift with very jagged walls leads to a cross rift and slight
enlargement, beyond which the passage quickly becomes too narrow.
Permission – West Farm, Litton.

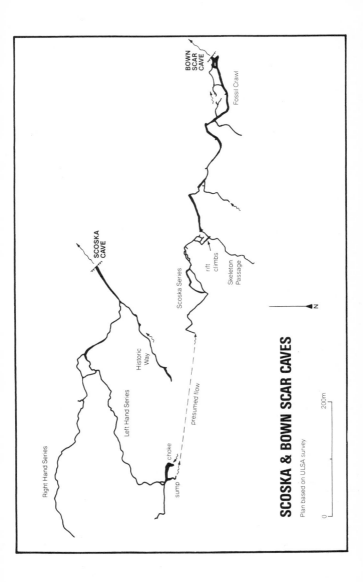

Right Hand Series

SCOSKA CAVE

Left Hand Series

Historic Way

Scoska Series

rift climbs

Skeleton Passage

BOWN SCAR CAVE

Fossil Crawl

choke

sump

presumed flow

N

SCOSKA & BOWN SCAR CAVES

Plan based on ULSA survey

0   200m

RIFT POT   NGR SD 932731   Grade II
Alt. 435m   **Depth 8m**
Explored 1968, BSA.

Above small scar near N boundary wall to Old Cote Low Moor. In side of
shakehole adjacent to stream sink. Rift pitch into narrow fissure which
quickly becomes too tight in either direction. There is a further very tight
shaft covered by boulders beside stream sink, which might be possible for the
slimmest of cavers.

Tackle – 8m ladder; stake and sling belay; 12m lifeline.

Permission – Old Cotes, Arncliffe.

SCOSKA CAVE   NGR SD 915724   Grade III
[Gildersbank Cave]
Alt. 285m   **Length 1.5km**
Explored 1905, YRC.

Entrance is 70m above river Skirfare at the head of Gildersbank Sike. The
imposing entrance is the start of a 3m wide gallery which divides after 70m.
The small stream emerges from the left hand passage, which is gained by a
low crawl, but soon enlarges. Historic Way is easy going at first but finally
becomes too low 200m from the junction. At the end of the passage human
bones 1,500 years old were found during the original exploration. The right
hand passage is easy walking at first but lowers to a wide crawl and divides
after 140m. The right branch is wet at first but the crawl gradually eases until
60m forward is a cross-over to the left hand passage. The right branch
continues as a crawl over mud until static canals are encountered. The
passage ends in a sump, after three ducks have been overcome. Sump has
been dived for 9m to silt blockage.

Left Hand Series
Beyond the junction with the crossover a hands and knees crawl on a rock
floor continues for 290m until a large stream is encountered, which emerges
from a strongly draughting boulder choke. Downstream the water drops
quickly to a fissure sump, dived for 11m to a constriction in a low bedding,
but before the sump a low wet crawl leads via a route through boulders on the
left into the Ancient Way. A climb up over blocks leads to a drop into a
roomy stream passage which continues for 30m to a step down into
deepening water with a soft silt floor. Ahead is a low airspace section which
gradually improves, only to end at a sump. This has been dived for 5m to
where mud banks block the way.

At the junction with the stream a passage on the right contains standing
water and ends after 90m in a sump, dived to a silt bank.
Permission – The Gatehouse, Arncliffe.

SPITTLE CROFT CAVE   NGR SD 900741   Grade III
Alt. 250m   **Length 1.6km**
Explored 1975, BCC & ULSA; extended 1975, CDG.

WARNING – Should only be entered in dry, settled weather as whole of
entrance section fills to roof in flood.

Excavated, climbable entrance rift drops into low bedding passage. This can be followed downstream through a miserable wet crawl to where it splits into several choked rifts after 45m. Main way lies upstream, and short length of crawling enlarges to permit stooping to a junction. Passage on left enters a small chamber with only a choked roof bedding continuation, while to the right emerges past a squeeze in a decent size streamway. Downstream gradually lowers to an impassable crawl, while upstream quickly reaches a chamber with the stream entering down a cascade.

Above cascade, passage becomes a fine vadose canyon with odd oxbows and short lengths of canal to where height drops and crawling eventually leads to a sump – Mud Wibble. This is 170m long, and emerges in a mud coated rift. A small climb up and a traverse enter clean washed abandoned vadose canyon ending in a small chamber with two routes leading on. To the right quickly chokes, but the other, gained by a 3m climb on the left leads to a large chamber, Fat Old Toad Hall, with a powerful stream falling from an unexplored passage 8m up the end wall. The water sinks among boulders in the floor where an unexplored pitch descends, and a further small unexplored passage leads from the chamber on the NE side. A large rift entered from a steep mud and boulder slope near the point of entry to the chamber ends suddenly at a blank wall after 15m.

Permission – East Garth Farm, Litton.

STONELANDS CAVE   NGR SD 919732   Grade III
Alt. 280m   **Length 600m**
Extended 1961-65, BPC and CDG; 1974, NCC; 1986, CDG.

In SE corner of Cave Wood above Cave Barn. Entrance not seen until close at hand. Large entrance chamber 3m high and 8m wide has a small stream flowing across floor and sinking under right wall.

Upstream passage closes in to waterfall which is easily climbed. Above fall passage gradually gets lower to start of canal. This continues as a low wet crawl until, 90m from the entrance, Base Chamber is reached. Beyond, a further 90m of canal with a series of ducks leads to a sump 390m long, in which diving lines very quickly become buried by silt. After 20m of large passage another sump is reached, choked by boulders after 15m. Stream is a public water supply.

Permission – The Gatehouse, Arncliffe.

TRAITORS' HOLE   NGR SD 914748   Grade II
Alt. 335m   **Length 8m**   **Depth 6m**
Explored 1981, UWFRA.

Covered entrance (please replace rocks) in centre of stream bed just above double waterfall, and 75m downstream from Crystal Beck Pot. Tight 5m descent leads to small chamber and slope of debris into short passage ending at a 'hanging death' choke.

Tackle – 8m ladder; stake and sling belay; 10m lifeline.

Permission – West Farm, Litton.

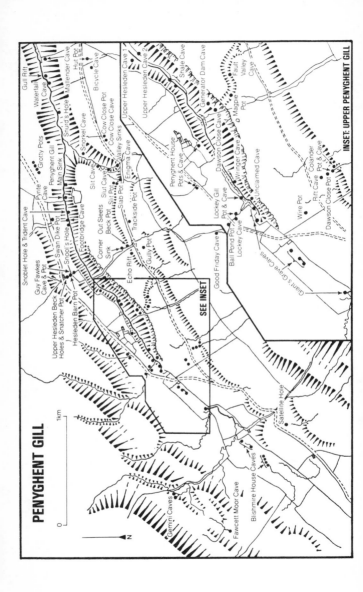

PENYGHENT GILL

0   1km

N

INSET: UPPER PENYGHENT GILL

Gull Rift
Waterfall Cave
Grotty Pots
Hut Pot
Mallender Cave
Bicycle Cave
Snurd's Hole
Pyrite Cave
Penyghent Gill Main Sink
Shale Cave
Cow Close Pot 1
Cow Close Pot 2
Cow Close Cave
Upper Hesleden Cave 1
Upper Hesleden Cave 2
Generation Dam Cave
Snorkel Cave
Slit Cave
Slit Cave
Valley Sinks
Enigma Cave
Penyghent House
Pots & Cave
Dawson Close Cave
Magpie Pot
Fault Valley Cave
Footbridge Cave
Corner Sink
Out Sleets Beck Pot
Slab Pot
Slit Pot
Trackside Pot
Wringer Cave
Unclaimed Cave
Snoblet Hole & Trident Cave
Swan Dike Pot
Snool's Hole
Guy Fawkes Cave & Pot
Echo Rift
Gully Pot
Lockey Gill Pot & Cave
Rift Cave
Colander Cave
Upper Hesleden Beck Holes & Snatcher Pot
Hesleden Barn Pot
Good Friday Cave
Ball Pond Pot
Lockey Cave
Wire Pot
Rift Cave Pot & Cave
Dawson Close Pot
Giant's Grave Caves
SEE INSET
Satellite Hole
Blishmire House Caves
Fawcett Moor Cave
Gemini Caves

PENYGHENT GILL

BALL POND POT   **NGR SD 856735**   **Grade III**
Alt. 405m   **Length 100m**   **Depth 23m**

Small rift entrance on bank near edge of Lockey Gill, covered by boulders which must be replaced. A squeeze down enters stooping height streamway, gradually enlarging to comfortable dimensions before narrowing in at floor level, leaving a traverse along in the roof as the easiest route. At a sharp double bend, passage ends abruptly at the lip of a 17m pitch, with belay up at roof level, or hole for a bolt. An easy but damp climb lands in fine chamber with miserable sumped rift at one end, and a climb and boulder crawl to a further aven chamber at opposite end.

Tackle – 20m ladder; 3m belay, 25m lifeline.

Permission – Penyghent House Farm, Litton.

BICYCLE CAVE   **NGR SD 884740**   **Grade II**
Alt. 410m   **Length 9m**
Explored 1971, MUSS.

Entrance lies in a shallow valley best reached from track along S side of Penyghent Gill via a gate adjacent to a timber hut. A climb down between boulders leads to a junction with the stream passage originating at a sink a few metres further up the gully. A flat-out crawl in the water passes one awkward squeeze to where the way on is too low.

Permission – Nether Hesleden Farm, Litton.

BLISHMIRE HOUSE CAVES   **NGR SD 848723**   **Grade III**
Alt. 410m   **Length 710m**
Explored 1972, MUSS.

A shallow series of passages near the Penyghent Gill watershed. The Launch Entrance is by a small stream sink and the crawl gains height, passing two small inlets, before it reaches Booster Inlet. Upstream is crawling for 45m to tight active and abandoned passages. Downstream past Docking Passage on the right, is easy stooping with roof oxbows to a canal and a 1.5m cascade into the more spacious Moonwalk. Beyond collapse in alcove to right is Orbit Passage but the Moonwalk finally turns left into a wide bedding cave and series of ducks to a dismal canal very close to the waterlogged joint passages at the rear of the flood resurgence cave, which is 40m long.

Orbit Passage is a low crawl which gains in height and leads via squeezes to two entrances and finally Docking Entrance where the continuing crawl drops back to the stream near Booster Inlet.

Downstream of the resurgence is a complex of collapse caves near Blishmire House – the longest being about 12m.

COLANDER CAVE   NGR SD 859730   Grade III
Alt. 420m   **Length 110m**
Extended 1970, CPC.

Small entrance in shakehole scar. A series of sharp corners containing pools lead to a canal. Beyond this is a long crawl and a squeeze into a chamber. Scramble up into a decorated passage which finally chokes under the stream bed.
Permission – Penyghent House Farm, Litton.

COLANDER POT   NGR SD 859730   Grade II
Alt. 420m   **Length 20m**   **Depth 15m**
Explored 1958, CPC.

Rift entrance in large shakehole 100m S of track. Squeeze down through boulders into a long chamber with climb into aven inlet. The stream sinks into boulders to re-appear in Dawson Close Pot.
Permission – Penyghent House Farm, Litton.

CORNER SINK   NGR SD 867737   Grade II
Alt. 402m   **Depth 8m**
Explored 1966, BSA.

In right bank of Out Sleets Beck, 40m downstream from the entrance to Out Sleets Beck Pot. A tight climb down 4.5m leads to a further step of 2.5m. At the foot an impossibly tight inlet enters on the left, while in front the passage quickly becomes too tight.

Further down the beck are two more sinks:

1. In the left bank 30m from Corner Sink is a short tight passage to a 4.5m climb down to a chamber with a choked floor.

2. In the right bank 100m downstream is an awkward climb down to a corner. From here a ladder is best for the remaining drop of 3.5m. At the foot a short crawl leads to a constriction only 15cm wide, and beyond is an unattainable pitch.
Permission – Manor Farm, Halton Gill.

COW CLOSE CAVE   NGR SD 878738   Grade III
Alt. 415m   **Length 55m**   **Depth 5.5m**
Explored 1964, BSA; extended 1966, ULSA.

Entrance at foot of gully shakehole 100m SW of gateway on track along S side of Penyghent Gill. A 1.5m climb down into a rift leads to further climb of 2.7m into a small chamber with an inlet aven 3.5m high and short, tight passage at top. Passage out of chamber is a tight sideways crawl involving several vicious back-breaking bends to where the way on is blocked by shale and peat. There is no room to turn round for the return journey, which is extremely awkward.

Permission – Nether Hesleden Farm, Litton.

COW CLOSE POT   NGR SD 878739   Grade III
Alt. 410m   **Length 53m**   **Depth 35m**

Explored, BCC.

In the clints 30m S of gateway on track is a short climb down into the start of a passage. Another small climb down is followed by a short crawl to The Tube, a tight awkward 3.5m long section which can only be negotiated by slim people. Beyond is junction with stream passage and a flat-out crawl to an aven on the left where it is possible to stand up. A further 9m of low passage leads to the head of the 1st pitch of 27m. There is no obvious belay, and a short bar jammed behind flakes of rock on the floor 4.5m back from the head of the pitch is a possible solution. Lifelining is best carried out from the aven. At foot of ladder is a steep boulder slope to water, best dealt with by extending the 1st pitch ladder. A climb and traverse over bridged blocks leads to a short canal and sump, which closes to an impassable bedding plane almost immediately.

Tackle

Pitch	Ladder	Belay	Lifeline
1st	30m	Short bar and sling	40m
2nd	9m	–	–

Permission – Nether Hesleden Farm, Litton.

DAWSON CLOSE CAVE   NGR SD 862735   Grade III
[Penyghent Gill Cave]

Alt. 380m   **Length 15m**   **Depth 9m**

Explored, St. Thomas Aquinas Caving Club.

Entrance in shallow gully near wall opposite Penyghent House. Climb down between boulders leads into rather unstable chamber with crawl on left to further small chamber. From here a sloping pitch and 2.5m vertical step enter a circular chamber with shower-bath entering from roof. A low wet passage becomes too tight.

Permission – Penyghent House Farm, Litton.

DAWSON CLOSE POT   NGR SD 859730   Grade IV
Alt. 415m   **Length 75m**   **Depth 30m**

Explored 1964, BSA; extended 1970, CPC.

In shallow gully just beyond first gate on track along S side of Penyghent Gill, close to Colander Pot. Entrance pitch of 3.5m leads to rift running back into hill, with top of the 2nd pitch close by. Best belay is a short bar wedged across rift. Climb of 27m down rift with very dangerous, poised blocks leads to boulder floor. Crawl then climb down 4.5m into passage which chokes. Very constricted canal in fissure leads to another, parallel canal, which becomes too narrow. N from pitch leads through boulders to open passage. Crawling for 25m leads to left turn into parallel rift passage, upstream quickly becoming too tight, as are slots in the floor. The way on continues as a crawl, passing a magnificent red beehive stalagmite, to where the passage is completely blocked by stalagmite.

Tackle

Pitch	Ladder	Belay	Lifeline
Entrance	4.5m	Stake and sling	–
2nd	30m	Short bar and sling	40m

Permission – Penyghent House Farm, Litton.

ECHO RIFT   NGR SD 867736   Grade II
Alt. 405m   **Depth 11m**
Explored 1964, BSA.

Over wall W of Out Sleets Beck Pot, at foot of shallow valley. Large rift covered with big slabs of rock which must be replaced. At a depth of 4.5m a landing is made on a ledge of jammed boulders, and a further descent of 6m can be made at end, to the start of a narrow passage which rapidly becomes too tight.

Tackle – 11m ladder; stake and sling belay; 15m lifeline.

Permission – Penyghent House Farm, Litton.

ENIGMA CAVE   NGR SD 874737   Grade I
Alt. 410m   **Length 15m**
Explored 1969, MUSS.

Between track and wall on right bank of small stream that flows down to join large side valley. Low entrance crawl leads to drop into narrow canyon passage which can be traversed by various contortions to where way on becomes too tight.

Permission – Manor Farm, Halton Gill.

FAULT VALLEY CAVE   NGR SD 863735   Grade I
Alt. 390m   **Length 8m**
Explored 1965, BSA.

Part way up the obvious dry valley on opposite side of gill to Penyghent House Farm. A low, wet crawl leads through a deep pool to where the floor steps up a 0.6m fall; the passage above rapidly becomes too tight.

Permission – Penyghent House Farm, Litton.

FAWCETT MOOR CAVE   NGR SD 843727   Grade III
Alt. 455m   **Length 825m**   **Depth 15m**
Explored 1968, WRPC.

WARNING – Flood liable and miserable.

SiL. Beneath an outcrop near a small stream sink. Drop into small chamber and join the stream in a 1m high passage with formations. Uneven going over odd boulders and past oxbows. An inlet at a T-junction soon becomes impassable and the water deepens to a short duck ponded by a pile of boulders. On over blocks is Rumble Hall, 8m wide and 2.5m high, with outlet into a gloomy crawl with a sharp floor. Beyond a small fall is a narrow fissure and the cave ends at a calcited chockstone. The water rises 200m away in Crooke Gill.

FOOTBRIDGE CAVE   NGR SD 870742   Grade IV
Alt. 320m   **Length 45m**
Explored 1972, MUSS and KCC.

Very low bedding with small stream resurging, in true left bank of main gill actually at the footbridge. Extremely wet, flat out crawl with minimum airspace leads to a cross joint where it is possible to sit up. Beyond, the flat out crawl continues with diminishing airspace to where further progress becomes ridiculous.
Permission – Penyghent House Farm, Litton.

GEMINI CAVES   NGR SD 845732   Grade III
Alt. 460m
Explored 1976, MUSS.

MdL. The prominent scar in which these resurgence caves are situated can be seen in one of the main tributaries to Crooke Gill.

1. Length 165m
The entrance is at the top of the most westerly scree slope, from the base of which the stream rises. A tight crawl over blocks drops to the stream, and hands and knees crawling passes a small inlet on the left to where the way on is stooping height. Eventually the passage splits, to the left ending at a boulder choke in a flat out section, while to right also encounters a choke through which daylight can be seen.

2. Length 165m
Above, and slightly to the left of the eastern scree slope is a low crawl which leads to the stream after 10m. Waist deep wading in a canal reaches a short section of breakdown, and beyond, the roof gradually lowers to a crawl and choke. Just before this point is reached a low muddy inlet on the right can be followed a short distance to where it splits into impassable branches.

GENERATOR DAM CAVE   NGR SD 862736   Grade II
Alt. 380m   **Length 34m**
Explored 1965, BSA; extended 1978, CDG.

Part way down S bank of Penyghent Gill, opposite farm, is small pool at inlet to turbine pipe. Upstream is low entrance leading via a duck to a wide bedding passage with floor of small rocks. Hands and knees crawling gives way to flat-out crawling, to where cave ends at a sump. This has been dived for 12m and gets too tight.
Permission – Penyghent House Farm, Litton.

GIANT'S GRAVE CAVES

Main Sink   **NGR SD 853729**   **Grade I**
Alt. 400m   **Length 6m**
    Cave entrance at more southerly of the two sinks. Short bedding plane
choked by flood debris.

Upper Cave   **NGR SD 853730**   **Grade II**
Alt. 402m   **Length 230m**
    Twin entrance slots drop into a stream passage, which is very low
upstream. Downstream enters a 4.5m wide chamber followed by a canal and
rift passage. Final canal has low airspace above 1.2m deep water and can be
followed for 90m to the resurgence, in dry weather.

Main Cave   **NGR SD 855731 Top entrance**   **Grade II**
                        NGR SD 856733 Bottom entrance
Alt. 396m   **Length 460m**
    The whole cave is controlled by one bedding plane. Three top entrances all
connect with an 8m wide and 1m high streamway which forms a series of
oxbows further downstream. In places the coalescence of oxbows has created
open bedding planes 15m wide. Both bottom entrances are dry, part of the
water going to the Main Rising and part flowing via a boulder choke to the
Lower Cave.

Lower Cave   **NGR SD 856733**   **Grade II**
Alt. 390m   **Length 75m**
    Entrance in collapsed area. Downstream, water emerges from boulders
and flows into 1.5m high passage. Waterfalls of 2.5m and 1m provide sport
before the cave reaches daylight in the gorge. At the base of the 1m fall a well
decorated bedding plane runs S to another entrance and narrow streamway,
which mirrors the main one in its direction and waterfalls.
Permission – Penyghent House Farm, Litton.

GOOD FRIDAY CAVE   **NGR SD 869728**   **Grade II**
Alt. 500m   **Length 20m**
Explored 1976, MUSS.
    MdL. Small shattered entrance lies at sink by broken down wall on bench
above Dawson Close. Crawling leads to stooping height passage and small
aven, beyond which, tight sideways crawl ends at a waterlogged rift.
Permission – Penyghent House Farm, Litton.

GROTTY POTS   **NGR SD 875745**   **Grade II**
Alt. 405m   **Depths 6-11m**
    A series of small shafts on bench below the road, all of which are severely
choked. The coverings of corrugated iron must be replaced.
Tackle (all holes) – 11m ladder; stake and sling belay; 15m lifeline.
Permission – Nether Hesleden.

GULL RIFT
Alt. 280m

NGR SD 883744

Length 18m

Grade I

Depth 8m

Explored 1966, BSA; extended 1972, BCC.

Two entrances in long rift up on true right bank of main gill, and a few metres down-valley from the end of the scar containing Waterfall Cave. The entrance nearest the scar is a short climb down into the rift, followed by 12m of crawling. Further progress is impossible without a lot of excavation.

The other entrance is about halfway along the surface rift, and a climb down and squeeze beneath large boulders leads to a further awkward climb down, with a stemple holding back some loose rocks. From the foot a crawl under one wall leads to a drop to a lower bedding passage, and the way on is soon choked completely.

Permission – Nether Hesleden Farm, Litton.

GULLY POT
Alt. 415m

NGR SD 868735

Grade II

Depth 8m

Explored 1965, BSA.

In small shakehole above the track where two drainage gullies sink. Damp 6m pitch leads to boulder floor and complete choke.

Tackle – 8m ladder; stake and sling belay; 12m lifeline.

Permission – Penyghent House Farm, Litton.

GUY FAWKES CAVE
Alt. 373m

NGR SD 865741

Length 40m

Grade II

Explored 1966, MUSS.

Entrance is 30m further downstream than Guy Fawkes Pot, at the foot of a small scar where a small stream resurges. A low crawl for 8m leads to a pool at a sharp bend to the left, and beyond here, flat-out crawling over shingle leads round two bends to an apparent junction. Both ways soon join, however, and 8m of extremely tight crawling brings one to the usual limit of exploration downstream in Guy Fawkes Pot.

Permission – Penyghent House Farm, Litton.

GUY FAWKES POT
Alt. 385m

NGR SD 865741

Length 98m

Grade III

Depth 12m

Explored 1966, MUSS.

Follow small stream at Upper Hesleden down a series of falls. Part way down the third one is a small ledge with a concealed entrance which leads to a climbable descent of 4m. From the foot a small passage leads over boulders to a small chamber and the head of the 2nd pitch which drops into a larger passage below. Downstream it can be followed for 15m to an aven and a choke, while upstream leads round several corners to a large chamber, in the roof of which are several short inlets. At the far end of the chamber a passage leads through two small chambers to a choke. The small stream in the chamber flows back towards the 2nd pitch, then turns off into a tight rift passage at one of the bends. Tight sideways crawling leads to a junction with a small inlet on the right. Beyond here an awkward sinuous passage leads to a vicious bend – the limit for most people. However, the slimmest can continue, to emerge from Guy Fawkes Cave.

Tackle – 6m ladder; sling belay; 8m lifeline.

Permission – Penyghent House Farm, Litton.

HESLEDEN BARN POT   NGR SD 865742   Grade IV
Alt. 400m   **Depth 12m**
Explored 1968, MUSS and BSA.

Entrance is in side fissure to stream channel at the foot of the first large waterfall below the road. A very tight descent ends in a low, impassable bedding outlet, with a small inlet entering part way down.

Tackle – 12m ladder; bar and sling belay; 15m lifeline.

Permission – Penyghent House Farm, Litton.

HUT POT   NGR SD 885740   Grade II
Alt. 405m   **Length 30m**   **Depth 26m**
Explored 1979-85, MUSS.

Large stream sink, enclosed by wall resulting from the massive excavation efforts by MUSS, is covered by timber which must be replaced. Straight pitch leads to large ledge and further descent into start of narrow fissure passage terminating in an over-tight sump.

Tackle – 23m ladder; stake and sling belay; 30m lifeline.

Permission – Marton Scar Farm, West Marton.

LOCKEY CAVE   NGR SD 856734   Grade I
Alt. 395m   **Length 82m**
Entrance is in NE bank of Lockey Gill, 15m downstream of the road bridge, where a small stream emerges. A narrow passage 1.2m high leads to a chamber after 20m. After a further 35m of small passage an enlargement is reached with two small streams entering at roof level on the left. Climb up 1m to more crawling, and the end is reached where the bedding widens and lowers, the way on being blocked by formations.

Permission – Penyghent House Farm, Litton.

LOCKEY GILL CAVE   NGR SD 857733   Grade II
Alt. 380m   **Length 73m**
Explored 1966, BSA.

Entrance at foot of a small scar 30m downstream of the confluence of Lockey Gill and Penyghent Gill. A low sandy crawl leads quickly to the stream flowing from left to right. Upstream is a low wet crawl with two ducks leading to two small avens. A further duck leads to a large chamber with a boulder floor. An inlet up the left wall quickly becomes too tight, and an oxbow leads back into the main passage. The way on from the chamber is a rift passage leading to a deep pool and easy 4.5m climb up a waterfall to a second chamber, the entire floor area of which is a deep plunge pool. The water enters via a 9m aven, and this point can be reached from above by way of Lockey Gill Pot.

Permission – Penyghent House Farm, Litton.

LOCKEY GILL POT   NGR SD 857734   Grade II
Alt. 395m   **Length 50m**   **Depth 15m**
Explored 1966, BSA.

WARNING – Parts of this pot are liable to flooding.

Just downstream from entrance to Lockey Cave in the opposite bank. Entrance is an obvious sink, although it may be blocked by flood debris and gravel. A very tight letter box leads to a tight crawl and a small chamber. Beyond, a further tight crawl gradually enlarges to a small cascade, and from here a well decorated streamway leads to the head of a pitch dropping into Lockey Gill Cave. Original entrance now blocked; new one is 8m out onto bank.

Tackle – 9m ladder; 6m belay; 15m lifeline.

Permission – Penyghent House Farm, Litton.

MAGPIE POT   NGR SD 862735   Grade II
Alt. 390m   **Depth 6m**

Near pool sink at back of scars. Entrance covered by rocks which must be replaced. A straight descent of 6m in a rift, the walls of which are marbled with calcite. The bottom is choked with boulders through which it is possible to descend for a short distance.

Tackle – 8m ladder; stake and sling belay; 12m lifeline.

Permission – Penyghent House Farm, Litton.

MALLENDER CAVE   NGR SD 885744   Grade III
Alt. 297m   **Length 60m**
Explored 1982, MUSS.

Small cave at rising on S bank of gill where pipe and water tank are obvious. Awkward crawling, often in deep water, leads to a junction. To the right rapidly becomes impassable, while to the left continues as a miserable wet crawl.

Entrance now blocked, and permission will not be given as stream is the water supply to Nether Hesleden.

OUT SLEETS BECK POT   NGR SD 868737   Grade III
Alt. 405m   **Length 975m**   **Depth 67m**
Explored 1966, BSA.

WARNING – As the entrance lies below beck level, care should be taken to ensure that the dam is in good condition and weather is settled.

Entrance is 60m downstream of track along S side of Penyghent Gill, in side of beck. Short climb followed by walking size passage leads to further

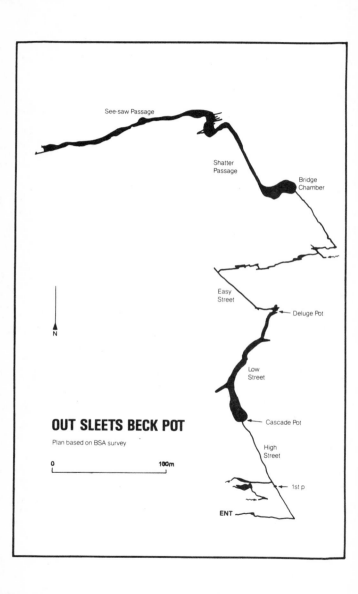

See-saw Passage

Shatter
Passage

Bridge
Chamber

Easy
Street

Deluge Pot

Low
Street

Cascade Pot

High
Street

1st p

N

ENT

OUT SLEETS BECK POT

Plan based on BSA survey

0   100m

awkward climb down and crawl. Beyond crawl, more climbs lead to 1st pitch, with belay at head on left, into chamber and junction with large inlet on left. This subdivides and becomes too narrow. The main passage continues as a clean washed rift to head of 2nd pitch, with Rawlbolt hole on shelf on right. At foot of pitch, Cascade Pot, is chamber with low crawl leading on to junction with low, wet inlet on left. Beyond, further crawling gives way to upright going to top of 3rd pitch with thread belay in roof bedding on left. (The obvious spike should only be used for a pulley belay point.) The pitch, Deluge Pot, is usually very wet, and requires care at the top. From the bottom an easy walking size passage continues to a canal, with deep water and an awkward, tight squeeze to a duck with 0.3m airspace. At far side the way continues walking size in a much cockled rift passage to double climb down into Bridge Chamber, followed by climb down at start of Shatter Passage. Caution is required here with loose blocks, contrasting with the rest of the pot which is in good sound rock. A final climb up over a big block at a sharp corner to the left leads to the start of See-saw Passage which consists of alternating stretches of crawling and walking until the end is reached where the water flows into a impenetrable bedding and the upper level closes down, very close to the resurgence.

Tackle

Pitch	Ladder	Belay	Lifeline
1st	3.5m	Sling	–
2nd	14m	Rawlbolt and karabiners	20m
3rd	12m	2m	20m

Permission – Manor Farm, Halton Gill.

PENYGHENT GILL MAIN SINK
NGR SD 873742
Alt. 308m   **Length 110m**
Explored 1966, BSA.

Grade IV
Depth 5.2m

WARNING – The whole of this cave lies below water level in the pool at the entrance, and is liable to complete flooding in times of wet weather.

If Penyghent Gill is followed upstream for 400m from the junction with the large side valley entering from the S side, a large deep pool is reached with obvious signs of excavation on the S bank at the end of a small scar. A small climb down against loose blocks leads into the first chamber, with water spurting into it through the boulders all the way round the left side. There are two ways on, which unite in a further low chamber with an unstable roof, and from here the combined waters enter a low bedding passage beside a tremendous fallen block. The way on is a flat-out crawl in the stream until the majority of the water disappears to the right. More flat-out crawling down a water slide leads to a large chamber with a floor of collapsed boulders, and a large inlet entering on the right. This can be followed up a small cascade to a wide but low bedding which becomes too low to follow after some 25m of flat-out crawling.

On the opposite side of the chamber is a small hole leading down to a bedding cave at a slightly lower level, and the stream is again encountered. This can be followed through a low section with an unstable roof to a further cascade and chamber, the water entering a miserable low canal passage on the left. The canal can be forced for 33m to a very awkward duck beyond which a sump is reached in a further 6m. Entrance blocked at present by collapse and flood debris. Stream tested to Skirfare Risings, 5km away and 60m lower.

Permission – Manor Farm, Halton Gill.

PENYGHENT HOUSE CAVE   NGR SD 860736   Grade III
Alt. 375m   **Length 100m**
Explored 1922, YRC.

Entrance is in corner of field S of Penyghent House Farm, and leads straight into an impressive streamway. Upstream the water deepens considerably, the roof lowering at the same time, until the way on is almost a swim for 12m to where the roof lifts and a sandy floored passage leads via a low, wide chamber to the streamway again, here a narrow, meandering passage. Following this leads to a short crawl into a chamber 3m wide by 6m long, with the stream entering via a 6m waterfall at the far end. This has been scaled, but the very narrow passage at the top could not be entered.

Permission – Penyghent House Farm, Litton.

PENYGHENT HOUSE POTS   NGR SD 858736   Grade II
Alt. 395m   **Length 90m**   **Depth 14m**
Explored 1970, BSA.

Both entrances lie close to the blind-ended sink of Penyghent House Gill at the roadside.

1. Entrance is the main sink, and easy passage leads to a small chamber where two inlets enter. One of these 2.5m up in the wall, leads to an alternate entrance via a tight crawl, while the other quickly splits, both ways being choked. Downstream from the chamber a lofty but narrow passage leads via several cascades to another chamber, the exit being a low crawl which soon develops into a tall passage terminating at the top of a pitch. At the foot the water sinks into a choked bedding passage, while in the opposite wall is a fissure passage which connects with 2.

Tackle – 8m ladder; 3m belay; 12m lifeline.

2. Entrance in the SW bank of the gill; a short crawl leads into a 1m high streamway. Upstream can be followed for 20m to near a choked sink, while downstream the passage rapidly enlarges to a 3m cascade into a roomy chamber. From here a short crawl reaches a passage bridged in places by large collapsed boulders, and beyond these, a further crawl on fill and climb down leads to a 3m high passage. More crawling on fill leads to an impenetrable bedding taking the stream, while straight ahead is the fissure passage connecting with 1.

Permission – Penyghent House Farm, Litton.

PYRITE CAVE   NGR SD 872742   Grade I
Alt. 315m   **Length 8m**
Explored 1973, BCC.

Excavated entrance at large rising immediately over wall from main stream, and just down valley from triple resurgence. Very wet crawl leads upstream to where way on becomes too tight without further digging. Pyrite crystals may be found in the shale bed in which the cave is formed.
Permission – Penyghent House Farm, Litton.

RIFT CAVE   NGR SD 859731   Grade I
Alt. 415m   **Length 9m**   **Depth 6m**

Just beyond first gate on track along S side of Penyghent Gill, in shallow valley leading up to Colander Pot. Easy walk down mud slope into long rift, choked completely at far end. May have once been an inlet into the downstream section of Dawson Close Pot.
Permission – Penyghent House Farm, Litton.

SATELLITE HOLE   NGR SD 852721   Grade II
Alt. 436m   **Length 15m**
Explored 1972, MUSS.

Entrance in second shakehole N of sink 100m S of cattle grid. Water sinks into fissure but an upstream crawl can be followed to a point close to the next shakehole.

SHALE CAVE   NGR SD 863739   Grade I
Alt. 340m   **Length 37m**

A short through cave formed in a washed out shale bed, situated in the NW bank about 200m down-valley from Penyghent House Farm. A low crawl over boulders at the top entrance leads into a wide bedding passage taking a considerable proportion of the main stream. After two lower sections an exit may be made beneath a large waterfall that is extensively undercut. The route through may be blocked by inwashed boulders.
Permission – Penyghent House Farm, Litton.

SLAB POT   NGR SD 874737   Grade II
Alt. 408m   **Depth 15m**

Entrance is 50m below the track running along side of Penyghent Gill near the small stream W of the large side valley. A small stream rises from an impenetrable bedding plane and falls into the pot. Entry is best effected by removing the smaller slabs at E end of the rift, and an easy pitch of 8m leads to a large sloping ledge. From here a further easy climb lands on a boulder floor. Water can be followed down into a side rift; way on narrows and becomes choked.

Tackle – 15m ladder; stake and sling belay; 25m lifeline.

Permission – Manor Farm, Halton Gill.

SLIT CAVE   NGR SD 876740   Grade III
Alt. 355m   **Length 140m**   **Vertical range 14m**
Explored 1952, CPC; extended ULSA.

Entrance rift 2m high discharges a stream 230m upstream of Snorkel Cave. The rift ends in a 5m waterfall which can be climbed to a 6m wide chamber. Further cascades of 3.5m and 1.5m ascend to a low crawl in a shale band and through a boulder choke into a chamber. A passage above a 1.5m waterfall passes through another tortuous boulder choke to a cascade emerging from a narrow fissure.

Permission – Marton Scar Farm, West Marton.

SLIT POT   NGR SD 874737   Grade III
Alt. 405m   **Length 140m**   **Depth 18m**
Explored 1972, BCC.

Boulders cover the top of the entrance pitch which lies a few metres down the gully from the more obvious entrance to Slab Pot where a small stream sinks. At the foot of the 15m shaft is a long rift, and at the upstream end can be followed in a passage of decreasing dimensions round two corners to where it becomes too tight. The other end of the entrance rift descends a slope of loose boulders to a low streamway. Upstream, a hands and knees crawl develops into a narrow fissure involving traversing to an acute bend, beyond which the passage soon terminates at a stalagmite blockage.

Downstream is a low crawl to a small chamber from which a flat-out crawl in the water leads to a further chamber and a hands and knees crawl to a junction with an inlet. This can be followed for 25m to a silted constriction preventing further progress. On downstream in the main passage continues as a wet crawl for only another 25m to a restricted sump.

Tackle – 17m ladder; stake and sling belay; 25m lifeline.

Permission – Manor Farm, Halton Gill.

SLUT CAVE   NGR SD 875738   Grade II
Alt. 380m   **Length 186m**
Explored 1977, MUSS.

Superbly quarried entrance crawl at rear of large rock filled shakehole 90m upstream of obvious entrance to Slit Cave. Squeeze over block at end of crawl lands on boulder slope in rift chamber with easy climb down to the stream. Downstream sumps almost immediately; water reappears in Slit Cave. Upstream, a narrow rift passage leads off either as a traverse, or a crawl in the stream for 50m to a circular chamber. The narrow inlet entering on the right can be followed for about 30m of grovelling size passage, including a bad duck, to end at a slight enlargement and sudden narrowing of the rift.

The main passage continues as a fine vadose canyon with odd traverses on wide ledges until the way gradually lowers and ends at a sump which descends to a scree slope and constriction. The sump is believed to be the downstream side of the sump at the end of Slit Pot.

Permission – Marton Scar Farm, West Marton.

SNATCHER POT   NGR SD 865742   Grade III
[Upper Hesleden Beck Hole 1]
Alt. 402m   **Length 470m**   **Depth 66m**
Explored 1979, MUSS.

WARNING – Parts of entrance series, and pitches, may become impassable in wet weather.

This pot – formerly known as No. 1 of the Upper Hesleden Beck Holes – now offers a fine sporting trip. Digging may give a through route to Snool's Hole.

Entrance covered with corrugated iron sheet is on right bank of small gill some 50m below road. Drop enters rift and further short step into small chamber with steeply descending rift to 3m climb down into another small chamber. Beyond a sharp corner a junction is reached, with an over-tight stream inlet straight ahead; the way on is a wet tubular crawl to the right. Where stream falls into narrow slot, traversing leads to a climb down at jammed boulders into tall rift passage. After a few metres the water route gets too tight, but interesting climb down over flake to right (line may be useful) leads to a chamber and continuing hands and knees crawl.

Maypole Inlet enters crawl on left and can be explored to an 8m aven. Above, the passage becomes too tight after only 10m. Beyond crawl is large passage to head of 4m first pitch into chamber and meandering passage on to junction with Iron Maiden Inlet on the right. This is a tortuous rift to a squeeze up into a bedding, and crawl to more tight rift and very short free-diveable sump. Only 50m further the narrow rift breaks out into a chamber with the stream showering down over boulders from an over-tight rift 5m above.

Main passage continues to short crawl and several small drops to enlargement at head of the 14m second pitch. A climb up through boulders to left leads to a small ledge and better ladder hang than direct route. Below, rift passage can be followed to where two parallel routes re-unite in a chamber below short climbs, and the continuing hands and knees crawl quickly reaches the head of last 8m pitch, with a bolt belay. The landing is a chest deep pool with a narrow canyon passage leading onward to a chamber, with the stream filtering away through boulders just before this is reached. The pool in the chamber appears to be static, and marks the present end of the cave, although the upstream end of Snool's Hole is believed to lie only some 30m away.

Tackle

Pitch	Ladder	Belay	Lifeline
Flake Climb – 6m handline			
1st	8m	3m	12m
2nd	18m	2m	23m
3rd	8m	spreader	12m

Permission – Penyghent House Farm, Litton.

SNOBLET HOLE   NGR SD 871742   Grade III
Alt. 314m   **Length 64m**
Explored 1979, MUSS.

WARNING – Entrance completely submerged when stream flows along this part of the gill.

Entrance, blocked at present, lies in miniature gorge just above deep pool by Trident Cave. Sloping descent and 6m flat-out squeeze crawl lead to T-junction. To left can be followed for 30m through comfortable height crawl to a sump, with daylight visible through a narrow crack 6m before end is reached. The right, upstream, passage is 15m of lowering crawl to a further junction. Left here gets too low after 6m, while the flat-out right branch has only been pushed for 6m at present.
Permission – Penyghent House Farm, Litton.

SNOOL'S HOLE   NGR SD 869742   Grade III
Alt. 323m   **Length 268m**   **Vertical range 20m**
Explored 1973, MUSS and KCC.

WARNING – Liable to become impassable in flood, when the Grimbit sumps.

An interesting cave which carries drainage from the Hesleden Barn area to Penyghent Gill. The entrance is 100m above the footbridge and just downstream of a waterfall. Shaft in left bank is a scramble down to a very tight rift dropping into a pool. The water sinks into a sump which has been dived for 12m but the resurgence is only a short distance away. Upstream is a roomy chamber 6m square, where cascades rise to a bedding plane with two inlets from the main gill. The continuing Catamite Crawl lowers to a 3m long duck (the Grimbit) and a walking passage. Brilliant white walls characterise Omo Way leading to a fine chamber succeeded by 4.5m and 1.5m waterfalls. Above is a beckoning passage opening into a flat roofed chamber which is best left by climbing into a shale crawl. More cascades rise to a well decorated streamway lowering to a flat crawl becoming choked by cobbles and shingle. Entrance currently blocked by boulders and inwashed debris.

SNORKEL CAVE   NGR SD 876740   Grade IV
Alt. 338m   **Length 792m**   **Vertical range 40m**
Explored 1959, NPC; extended 1966, MUSS.

WARNING – Parts of this cave are liable to serious flooding.

Low resurgence cave above the main S tributary to Penyghent Gill. Entrance crawl is a dismal introduction to the cave since for much of its 90m the air space is only 15cm. The first waterfall of 6m requires scaling to a short passage and a second waterfall chamber. Here, scaling a dry aven of 11m or taking a crawl on the right to a high climbable rift, unite below a 3.5m climb to a bedding plane. A crawl enters White Chamber and, shortly beyond, the stream is rejoined in a rift passage with several small waterfalls up to a chamber formed in a shale bed. A further small fall leads to City Series – a long angular streamway to a junction of two inlets. Straight ahead the main stream comes from a deep sump in a bedding plane. To the right Unhappy Passage is 180m of mostly awkward traversing and crawling, relieved by one welcome cavern, Happy Chamber. The inlet ends in a roomy sump, which has been free-dived to an airbell, as have the next two short sumps, although this is not recommended.

Tackle – 6m scaling pole; 8m ladder.

Permission – Marton Scar Farm, West Marton.

SNURD'S HOLE NGR SD 880743 Grade III
Alt. 288m **Length 110m** **Depth 11m**
Explored 1973, BSA, MUSS and BCC.

WARNING – When gill is in flood entrance is completely submerged.

Small entrance covered by boulders on rock shelf against true right bank of main gill, just where stream bed changes from bed rock to boulders. A climb down leads to involved squeeze over fallen slabs into open bedding passage. Low crawl gradually gains height to where it is possible to walk down a steep slope to the head of a spacious pitch. At the bottom is a circular chamber, and a rift at one end with muddy climb down brings one to the main underground stream. Upstream, the roof drops close to the water, and the way on can only be followed for about 6m to a gravel bank blocking the passage.

Downstream is a deep canal with limited airspace, but this is only short and ends after a bend to the left. A muddy crawl off to the right here goes for about 15m to a blockage, while the main way continues as a comfortable crawl. At a widening of the passage to the left an excavated route leads up through boulders to the chamber at the foot of the pitch, but this may now be blocked again. On downstream the passage narrows in to become a small tube, and on the right at the start is a further muddy side passage which can be followed for about 20m. The far end of the tube encounters a wide, low section, and it is possible to push on along the right hand side, through a duck to where further progress is impossible. This area has been examined by members of the CDG but there seems to be little hope for a negotiable route underwater. Entrance now blocked by rocks and flood debris.

Tackle – 8m ladder; 3m belay; 12m lifeline.

Permission – Marton Scar Farm, West Marton.

SWAN DIKE POT NGR SD 870743 Grade III
Alt. 390m **Length 335m** **Depth 47m**
Explored 1984, Airedale Caving Club.

WARNING – All the boulders in the entrance pitch, including those that are shored (!), should be treated with the utmost caution.

Entrance immediately over fenced gap in wall below road. Top part of pitch is free-climbable, but ladder needed lower down to avoid standing on loose rocks. At foot is squeeze down rift to stream and a 2m climb down to an enlargement. Bouldery rifts to either side close in, but way on lowers to a short canal followed by good going to a series of cascades and a 4m climb. Two further short climbs lead to a chamber and bottom end of an oxbow which starts above the 4m climb. On downstream quickly reaches an 8m pitch dropping to a sump, and the passage over the head of the pitch also ends in an 8m dry pitch to a short rift passage and further sump. Diving has failed to produce an extension.

Upstream from foot of entrance pitch leads to passage ending at 11m aven, and above this, route continues to a junction. Main way, straight ahead, finally splits into two impassable passages. Right at junction encounters another wet aven, 8m up which is very narrow traverse to passage which ends in deep canal after 87m.

Tackle –

Pitch	Ladder	Belay	Lifeline
Entrance	7m	Bar and spreader	Inadvisable
Climb	5m handline may be useful		
Either bottom pitch	10m	3m	12m

Upstream avens require scaling or bolting equipment

Permission – Penyghent House Farm, Litton.

TRACKSIDE POT   NGR SD 870737   Grade II
Alt. 418m   **Length 11m**   **Depth 8m**
Explored 1964, BSA.

Close to track running along S side of Penyghent Gill, almost below limekiln. Entrance is covered by large slabs which must be replaced. At a depth of 3m it is possible to step off the ladder into a rift floored with boulders, and follow it upstream to where a small stream enters through the roof. Beyond this point the rift narrows and is choked. If the ladder is descended for a further 1.5m it is possible to traverse round at the opposite end of the rift and squeeze through a small opening into a chamber, the walls and floor of which are completely covered in stalagmite; no passable way on. At the foot of the ladder a narrow rift closes in. Water can be seen flowing off down a passage of minute proportions.

Tackle – 8m ladder; stake and sling belay; 12m lifeline.

Permission – Manor Farm, Halton Gill.

TRIDENT CAVE   NGR SD 871742   Grade I
Alt. 317m   **Length 18m**
Explored 1972, MUSS.

Small entrance amongst boulders at water level in the true right bank at the first large pool downstream from the footbridge. Awkward squeeze leads to flat-out crawl ending at a pool to the left and a very tight crawl over a fallen block straight ahead. More comfortable hands and knees crawling encounters the main stream emerging from a sump upstream, and sinking through boulders downstream. Just before the stream is reached a low crawl off to the right ends at a small chamber.

Between the entrance, and the waterfall into the pool is another cave entrance under an overhang. This excavated passage can be followed for 15m as a flat-out crawl to where there is no passable way on.

Permission – Penyghent House Farm, Litton.

UNCLAIMED CAVE   NGR SD 857734   Grade III
Alt. 375m   **Length 245m**
Extended 1978, CDG.

Excavated entrance at foot of scar on opposite side of gill from confluence with Lockey Gill. Small slope down over loose rocks leads to streamway, too tight downstream, and passing through a duck upstream. Beyond, crawling in water, sometimes deep with the occasional boulder obstruction, leads to a constricted sump just past where the passage splits. The sump is 12m long and should not be free-dived as it is tight in places. At far end it emerges in a tall rift passage which can be followed for 200m to a complete choke.

Permission – Penyghent House Farm, Litton.

UPPER HESLEDEN BECK HOLES
NGR SD 865742   Grade I
Alt. 402m – 373m
Explored 1966-72, MUSS.

All the following holes are in, or on the sides of the small stream, and are numbered in order going downstream from the road.

1. Snatcher Pot – see separate description.

2. Small cave over the wall on left bank almost opposite the above. Descent through boulders for 3m ends in choke.

3. Hole in right bank descending for 18m to a boulder floored chamber with no way out. Climbable, but a ladder and line helpful on the return.

4. Downstream of above near top of waterfall, in left bank. Small rift descent of 4.5m to where it is too tight.

5. Hesleden Barn Pot – see separate description.

6. Small cave entrance at foot of waterfall. Very low bedding to a cross rift, after which better going ends after 6m where it gets too tight.

7. Guy Fawkes Pot – see separate description.

8. Low cave in left bank directly below Guy Fawkes Pot. Short crawl leads to small chamber with no way on.

9. In scar on left bank. Short drop enters low chamber with undescendable pitch to one side.

10. Guy Fawkes Cave – see separate description.

Permission – Penyghent House Farm, Litton.

UPPER HESLEDEN CAVE 1   NGR SD 864739   Grade II
Alt. 344m   Length 130m
Explored 1932, YRC; extended 1964, BSA.

Entrance is 400m down-valley from Penyghent House Farm, 15m up the N bank, where a small stream resurges. The passage is a hands and knees crawl, and just inside is a junction with a small inlet on the right which becomes too tight after 11m of awkward crawling. The main passage continues as a crawl for 30m in a winding streamway, until a low section leads to a small chamber with a 3.5m waterfall entering. Above the fall a high canyon passage leads up several cascades to Relief Chamber, with a floor of collapsed blocks. Beyond, the passage is a flat-out crawl in water for 27m to where the floor lifts slightly. The floor is now fine gravel and silt, and by pushing through this it is possible to proceed for a further 23m to where it becomes too low. All this last section of passage is extremely well decorated with straw stalactites.

Tackle – 4.5m scaling pole; 4.5 ladder.

Permission – Penyghent House Farm, Litton.

UPPER HESLEDEN CAVE 2   NGR SD 864739   Grade IV
Alt. 337m   Length 600m   Vertical range 60m
Explored 1932, YRC; extended 1951, NPC; 1970-71, BSA; 1979, NCC & WRPC.

S bank of Penyghent Gill 400m down-valley from Penyghent House Farm. An obvious entrance with stream emerging, below wall. Hands and knees crawling in water for 45m in a clean washed passage leads to the first aven of 5m, now rigged with a permanent steel ladder. From the top easy walking in a well decorated passage leads to a junction with an inlet on the left. This can be followed to a further junction, both ways soon becoming too low. The main passage continues as a meandering canyon passage until, 140m from the 1st aven, the 2nd aven is reached at a reasonable sized chamber. This one is 9.5m to the lip above, and is followed by a couple of small cascades to a lowering of the roof at a pool. At the far side of this is the 3rd aven, 8.2m to the lip above. From the top, easy walking in a further length of meandering canyon passage leads after 90m to the 4th aven, Thunderstorm Aven, and the largest chamber in the cave. The aven is 17.5m to the passage above, Good Friday Passage, which can be followed as a hands and knees crawl for 67m to a sump. This has been passed after a 4m dive to a short canal and second sump of 6m, which leads to an aven chamber. Above the 5m waterfall 30m of well decorated hands and knees crawling eventually lowers to a flat-out crawl ending too low after a further 20m.

At the point of entry to Thunderstorm Aven, a low passage on the left can be followed through a low crawl to a pool and further aven 4.3m high leading to '70 Passage. A short length of walking passage gives way to hands and knees crawling in a well decorated section, and just beyond some breakdown the way steps to the right into a rift. Short climbs and traverses leads to three cascades and a further length of open passage. Finally, at the foot of a small aven, the roof drops to a nasty flooded section 4.5m long. Beyond is a chamber with an aven, and the passage ends at a choke.

Tackle

Pitch	Ladder	Belay	Lifeline
Waterspout Aven	Rigged with permanent steel ladder		
Scaffold Aven	12m	Short spreader	20m
Shower Aven	11m	Short spreader	20m
Thunderstorm			
Aven	20m	Sling	30m

A minimum of 11m of scaling pole is needed to reach the foot of Thunderstorm Aven. To ascend it needs more elaborate climbing aids.

Permission – Penyghent House Farm, Litton.

VALLEY SINKS   NGR SD 875737   Grade II
Alt. 408m   **Depth 6m**

Two open sinks in steep valley, just below track. Both are severely choked, but water flows to Snorkel Cave.

Tackle – 8m ladder; bar and spreader; 10m lifeline.

WATERFALL CAVE   NGR SD 883744   Grade III
[Lower Hesleden Cave]
Alt. 290m   **Length 140m**
Extended 1971, ULSA.

Twin dry entrances are located on the S bank of Penyghent Gill by a waterfall. They both enter a low chamber 9m long. Low crawl leads to a very wide bedding plane which chokes to the E after 20m. To the W the wide crawl opens out within 30m to a collapsed chamber, 12m long and 2m high. In the floor a pit 3.5m deep contains a tortuous streamway which eventually becomes low over thick mud.

Permission – Marton Scar Farm, West Marton.

WIRE POT   NGR SD 857731   Grade II
Alt. 407m   **Depth 6m**
Explored 1966, BSA.

Below track along S side of Penyghent Gill just E of first fence. A tight pitch with choke at bottom. The sound of flowing water can be heard through a very tight slot in the wall.

Tackle – 8m ladder; stake and sling belay; 9m lifeline.

Permission – Penyghent House Farm, Litton.

WRINGER CAVE   NGR SD 858734   Grade III
Alt. 370m   **Length 37m**
Explored 1966, BSA.

About 150m downstream of the confluence of Lockey Gill and Penyghent Gill is a small rising on the S bank. Entrance is gained by climb over collapsed blocks, into a low wet bedding plane which can be followed for about 6m to where it is under 20cm high. After a further 20m of slightly better going daylight can be seen, and a second entrance is reached – blocked at present. To the left of the collapse at this entrance the bedding can be followed for about 12m to where it becomes too low at a small step up in the floor. This cave is the rising for Dawson Close and Colander Pots.

Permission – Penyghent House Farm, Litton.

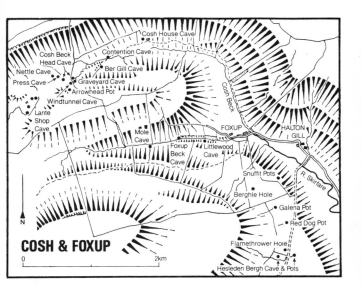

COSH & FOXUP

0   2km

COSH AND FOXUP

ARROWHEAD POT   **NGR SD 845774**   **Grade I**
Alt. 477m   **Length 18m**   **Depth 6m**

MdL. Obvious "walk-down" pot 100m SSW of Windtunnel Cave. Passage behind boulder at foot quickly becomes too tight.

BERGHLE HOLE   **NGR SD 873758**   **Grade I**
Alt. 410m   **Length 9m**   **Depth 8m**
Explored 1972, ULSA.

Entrance 50m from stream sink in large triangular field. Drop of 2.5m with a further descent down rift to left past stacked boulders. Forward under nasty dribble is a tight low canal for 4.5m. A bend can be seen ahead but further digging is needed.
Permission – Foxup.

BER GILL CAVE   NGR SD 850777   Grade II
[Cosh Beck Cave]
Alt. 445m   **Length 210m**   **Depth 12.5m**
Explored 1967, MUSS; extended 1968, YURT.

SiL. At head of shallow valley where track W of Cosh House fords beck.
Main entrance in large shakehole with smaller entrance nearer sink. Latter
entrance leads round sharp bend into small chamber after 15m with
excessively tight crawl continuing. From main entrance, passage becomes
higher to junction with Crinoid Passage on right, which ends in narrow rift
and crawl on left, connecting with passage from small entrance. Continuing
downstream passage lowers to short crawl into larger passage. Walking down
to cascade where upper and lower passages diverge and shortly rejoin to
continue low and muddy to sump. Stream tested to rising on S bank of beck
below ford, at same level as sump.

CONTENTION CAVE   NGR SD 851778   Grade II
Alt. 432m   **Length 9m**
Explored 1977, ULSA.
WARNING – Floods completely.

SiL. In N bank of Cosh Beck below waterfall at ford W of Cosh House,
opposite rising from Ber Gill Cave, is low bedding. Crawl and squeeze enter
narrow stream passage. Left is joint open to stream bed above waterfall; right
leads past blind muddy rift on right to end at narrow triangular fissure.
Water rises a short distance to E.

COSH BECK HEAD CAVE   NGR SD 846775   Grade III
Alt. 470m   **Length 280m**
Explored 1968, YURT.

MdL. Low entrance below wall at head of Cosh Beck, right of ruined hut.
Wet crawling via either entrance to junction. Oxbow to left, main passage to
right with muddy inlet ahead, choking after 60m. Main passage to left is
sharp crawl for some distance, ending in wide bedding plane which divides
and lowers beyond boulder choke. Several short wet caves ending in sumps
between end of main cave and sink also connect with streamway.

COSH HOUSE CAVE   NGR SD 856781   Grade III
Alt. 430m   **Length 60m**
Explored 1967, MUSS.

SiL. Entrance over wall behind Cosh House. Hole above rising drops into
streamway which is roomy crawl in canal, becoming very narrow with
awkward bends. Inlet on right a short way from entrance becomes
increasingly choked with mud.

FLAMETHROWER HOLE   NGR SD 877750   Grade II
Alt. 405m   **Length 37m**
Explored 1972, MUSS.

Only entered after the initial opening was enlarged by heating the rock with a flamethrower, and cracking it by rapid cooling. The small entrance lies a few metres away from the stream sink just above the road, and a 1.5m drop enters a low stream passage. Tight crawling downstream leads to a small aven where it is possible to sit up, and beyond the way develops into a narrow rift which gets too tight for further progress.

FOXUP BECK CAVE   NGR SD 862766   Grade IV
Alt. 350m   **Length 370m**
Explored 1967, MUSS.

WARNING – Many low sections of cave are liable to sudden and complete flooding.

Entrance is rising at base of small scar 400m upstream of Littlewood Cave on N bank of Foxup Beck. Low airspace passage to climb up boulders into small chamber, followed immediately by drop back to stream and squeeze on left into drier going. On through rift with deep water into pleasant going to the Deadly Duck, series of small airbells followed by very low airspace for about 12m. Crawl then drops into deeper water and higher passage ensues, lowering to sump with bypass via tight tube on right. Crawling through low chambers is succeeded by dry walking. Climb of 2.4m on right into The World of Oz chamber, with straws and short passages. Main streamway continues to 3.5m climb and crawl to junction. Left is stream route, avoided by tight crawl on right into Crystal Chamber, wide cavern with excellent formation. This continues as sizeable tunnel for short distance to mud passage, crawl to sump and narrow passage on left.
Permission – Foxup Bridge Farm.

GALENA POT   NGR SD 876756   Grade II
Alt. 395m   **Length 18m**   **Depth 17m**
Explored 1972, MUSS.

Small entrance below stream sink, about 190m from boundary wall to N. Steeply sloping passage enters small chamber where surface stream is met. A short, low passage ends at the top of a pitch, with a large ledge a short way down. Immediately at the foot of the shaft the water flows into an impossibly tight sump.

Tackle – 9m ladder; 3m belay; 15m lifeline.

GRAVEYARD CAVE   NGR SD 846775   Grade II
Alt. 470m   **Length 45m**
Explored 1968, YURT.

MdL. Entrance in small scar S of Windtunnel Cave. Crawl to point where streamway becomes too low and oxbow to right is very narrow.

HESLEDEN BERGH CAVE   NGR SD 876749   Grade II
Alt. 410m   **Length 21m**

Entrance in end shakehole of row, situated above the road. Small drop leads into low passage and junction with stream. Further crawling leads to sharp corner and tight sideways crawling. A cross rift followed by a tight squeeze reaches a boulder pile, and beyond is a chamber, with impassable outlet, and very tight rift inlet on the left.

Permission – Penyghent House Farm, Litton.

HESLEDEN BERGH POTS   NGR SD 878749   Grade II
Alt. 395m

1. Depth 11m

Excavated 1969, MUSS; 1970-73, BUSS.

Normally dry rift at end of watercourse E of Stainforth-Halton Gill road. Shoring in dig should be avoided. Ends in choke of boulders and gravel.

Tackle – 12m ladder; spreader belay; 18m lifeline.

2. Depth 6m

Small hole on bank to S of main pot is covered by large rocks which must be replaced. Straight shaft narrows to choke floor.

Tackle – 8m ladder; stake and sling belay; 12m lifeline.

LANTE SHOP CAVE   NGR SD 839770   Grade III
Alt. 470m   **Length 370m**

Explored 1939, BSA and others subsequently.

WARNING – Liable to flooding.

MdL. Several entrances on Cosh Outside, a broad shallow valley between headwaters of Cosh Beck and Hull Pot Beck. The cave is generally low, wet and after the long walk necessary to reach it, rather uninspiring.

Goodly Bottom Sike flows out of Main Entrance, the southernmost of the four and noted for its porch-like appearance. Middle Entrance is N of Main Entrance, 60m SSE of a sheepfold, in a small slump on side of a knoll. Between the two a hole was dug out in 1939 giving access to a short section of passage, choked in both directions. Upper Entrances 1 and 2 are 150m ENE of sheepfold and are holes in grassy area pocked with shakeholes.

Cave at Main Entrance is roomy boulder-strewn passage to blank wall pierced by slit which is squeeze into small aven with straws. Low upstream crawl has not been followed as far as choke met in dug hole. Middle Entrance is slot down through blocks into passage with unstable choke downstream. Upstream through collapse chambers into complex of narrow wet rifts with roomier sections. This point is presumed to be the same as that reached downstream from Upper Entrance 1, where low bedding crawl continues for 140m to section with deepening water. Upstream from Upper Entrance 1, bedding plane crawl to Upper Entrance 2, further E, beyond which is crawl in canal passage to abrupt right bend and short walk to choke where daylight can be seen.

Permission – High Birkwith Farm, Horton-in-Ribblesdale.

LITTLEWOOD CAVE   NGR SD 866766   Grade III
Alt. 345m   **Length 305m**
Explored 1967, MUSS.

Entrance above S bank of Foxup Beck opposite W end of small wood, 650m above junction of Cosh and Foxup Becks. Crawl to 2.5m climb followed by further low passage with short branch on right becoming very muddy. Wide, low crawl, The Canal, to junction, with side passage to left becoming too low after 15m. Varied going to 8m aven, and passage beyond develops into boulder-filled rifts with excellent straws. Crawl by-passes choke and emerges in Straws Chamber, which has more fine formations, and a 1.5m wet climb to base of 6m fall. This has been scaled to 120m of passage and 11m waterfall. Below 6m fall, main passage continues past fine helicities which must be traversed over. Above small cascade is Prospect Chamber, where stream enters as 12m waterfall. Flat out crawl 1.2m above floor is 20m long to 6m climb up to tight rift.

MOLE CAVE   NGR SD 857765   Grade I
Alt. 375m   **Length 8m**
Explored 1967, MUSS.

Entrance in small sink over wall on S side of beck, 450m upstream of Foxup Beck Cave. Entrance drops 1.5m into small chamber and short crawl reaches chamber where water sinks in tight rift. Stream emerges from 9m long tight bedding plane over wall on N bank of Foxup Beck. There is a 6m long bedding plane under a 3m dry waterfall in the beck at this point.

NETTLE CAVE   NGR SD 843775·   Grade II
Alt. 478m   **Length 60m**
Explored 1969, YURT.

MdL. Entrance in insignificant shakehole full of nettles near N side of broad valley between Cosh and Lante Shop, about 80m W of Cosh Beck Head Cave sink. Upstream too low after 6m. Downstream becomes higher and narrower and ends in mud choke.

PRESS CAVE   NGR SD 844776   Grade I
Alt. 478m   **Length 12m**
Explored 1969, YURT.

MdL. Entrance is 1m high and lies in shakehole 50m W of Cosh Beck Head Cave sink. Becomes increasingly shingled up and soon gets too low for further progress.

RED DOG POT   NGR SD 878754   Grade III
Alt. 385m   **Length 290m**   **Depth 20m**
Explored 1972, MUSS.

Insignificant entrance in cross joint in small exposed area of rock about 30m below small stream sink. An awkward descent down a rift and past a tight section leads to the head of a pitch which is split by a large flake part way down. One side leads to an impassably tight section of streamway, while the other is the main way on. A hole about 3m above the floor enters a small chamber with a climb down on loose boulders to a separate streamway. Upstream is a long, low wet crawl getting gradually lower and wetter which has been followed for about 200m, and could possibly be pushed further.

Downstream from the bottom of the climb is also a low bedding passage, but with a narrow rift going up to unknown heights. At times along its length a yellow shale bed can be observed, and the passage meanders occasionally in the next 90m, until suddenly a sump is encountered, with a blank wall straight ahead.

Tackle – 12m ladder; 3m belay; 15m lifeline.

SNUFFIT POT 1   NGR SD 876761   Grade III
Alt. 335m   **Length 138m**   **Depth 9m**
Explored 1980, MUSS.

WARNING – **Floods severely in times of wet weather.**

A shored 9m entrance pitch, at uphill side of large shakehole, leads to a walking size stream passage with waist-deep water. Upstream the roof lifts beyond a dog-leg, and easy going reaches a junction with a passage on left carrying the main flow. This can be followed by awkward sideways traversing round several nasty bends to where stream emerges from an impassable slot. The main route continues either as floor-level crawl or traverse on blocks at roof level, to short length of larger passage and further unpleasant crawl over boulders to a chamber, which marks end of cave.

Tackle – 9m ladder; sling and spreader belay; 12m lifeline.

SNUFFIT POT 2   NGR SD 876761   Grade III
Alt. 335m   **Length 130m**   **Depth 28m**
Explored 1980, Derbyshire Cave Club.

WARNING – **Entrance shaft passes beneath and through highly unstable boulders.**

Excavated entrance on down hill side of same shakehole as Snuffit Pot 1. From foot of entrance pitch the water, which enters via an impassable slot, quickly drops down a narrow slot and the way on is an abandoned rift for about 15m to a 5m climb down into a small chamber where an inlet enters, and the main stream is regained. Walking continues to a further chamber and a wet crawl, to a 2m drop. From the chamber below more crawling leads to a traverse and a 3m climb down to a right-hand bend. The end of the cave is reached as the stream drops down a chute containing two deep plunge pools and a final 5m climb to a sump.

Entrance blocked by large collapse.

Tackle – 13m ladder; bar and spreader belay; 18m lifeline.

WINDTUNNEL CAVE   NGR SD 846775   Grade III
Alt. 470m   **Length 275m**

MdL. Entrance at head of Cosh Beck over wall to left of ruined hut. Low canal passage to drier going and junction. Passage on left becomes too low almost immediately. Going ahead varies considerably, with much crawling, but after low section improves somewhat to awkward walking, succeeded by crawling to wide bedding chamber, with water emerging from choked bedding plane.

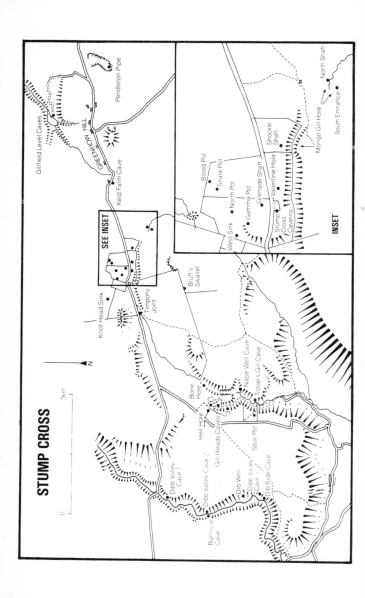

STUMP CROSS

0   2km

▲ N

Gillfield Level Caves

GREENHOW HILL

Pendleton Pipe

Keld Farm Cave

SEE INSET

Knot Head Sink

Timpony Joint

Bruff's Swaller

Bone Hole

Hell Hole

Gill Heads Caves

Nape Well Cave

Tollers Gill Cave

Spar Pot

Dibb Valley Cave 1

Barnicar Cave

Dibb Valley Cave 2

Dibb Well

Dibb Valley Cave 3

Dibb Side Cave

INSET

West Sink

Blood Pot

Snare Pot

North Pot

Gamma Pot

Grenade Shaft

Valentine Hole

Stump Cross Caverns

Shockle Shaft

Mongo Gill Hole

South Entrance

North Shaft

STUMP CROSS

BARNSCAR CAVE NGR SE 048619 Grade I
Alt. 185m Length 12m
Explored 1968, YURT.

On W side of gorge 1.2km below Dibbles Bridge is small entrance half way up cliff. Narrow crawl becomes too tight.

BLOOD POT NGR SE 090639 Grade II
Alt. 370m Length 9m Depth 25m

Entrance is small hole in large shakehole with limestone pillar, 275m NE of Stump Cross. Ledge followed by 2m drop and then under poised boulders into top of 9m climbable pitch. Crawl into small chamber and muddy crawl opens directly into ladder pitch with very narrow fissure at foot.

Tackle – 15m ladder; 1.5m belay; 20m lifeline.

BONE HOLE NGR SE 069622 Grade I
Alt. 250m Length 12m

Above sink at head of Jackdaw Nick in Trollers Gill. Entrance in scar on W side of stream 400m below New Dam. Crawl in tube is joined by passage from alternative entrance to left just before pool is encountered. This is sump in wet weather and beyond is short narrow crawl to abrupt left bend and partial calcite blockage with very narrow passage beyond.

BRUFF'S SWALLET NGR SE 086626 Grade I
Alt. 390m Depth 4.5m
Excavated 1942/3, BSA.

Climbable pot at bend in wall near old mine dam. Shingle floor and narrow fissure which draughts on occasions.

DIBB VALLEY CAVES

1. NGR SE 050628 Alt. 210m Grade I
About 200m down valley of river Dibb below main road bridge. Small entrance part way up bank. Crawl into low chamber 3m long. Possibly partially mined.

2. NGR SE 048620 Alt. 180m Grade I
Obvious entrance just above river level in E side of gorge a short way upstream of Barnscar Cave. Opens immediately into chamber with slope down to left to pool and dead end.

3. NGR SE 051613   **Alt. 200m**   **Grade I**
   Mine level about 30m long connecting with natural aven.

DIB SIDE CAVE   NGR SE 050612   Grade I
Alt. 165m   **Length 3.5m**

   Close to river Dibb just downstream of mine workings is obvious, arched
entrance on E bank. Immediately inside is a large bank of stalagmite flow,
above which a narrow, rising passage quickly closes in.

DIB WELL   NGR SE 051615   Grade I
Alt. 185m   **Length 4.5m**

   Prominent rising 275m N of old mine. Passage rises, then lowers to fissure
sump which becomes too tight almost immediately.

GAMMA POT   NGR SE 088636   Grade II
Alt. 351m   **Depth 6m**

   Climbable excavated pot in small shakehole 90m W of Grenade Shaft.

GILLFIELD LEVEL CAVES   NGR SE 115648   Grade I
Alt. 290m

   Gillfield Level is now gated and used by Leeds University Mining
Department. About 283m into the adit is a natural fissure in the roof at the
unconformable junction between the Millstone Grit and Carboniferous
Limestone. Water falls down the fissure which hades southwards and has
been climbed for about 20m to where it becomes uncomfortably wide, but
continues upwards.
   Further into the mine, about 60m S of the sump on Waterhole Vein East a
muddy natural cave on the E side of the Level rises quickly and closes in after
20m.
Permission – Leeds University Mining Department.

GILL HEADS CAVES
1. NGR SE 067621   **Alt. 270m**   **Length 4.5m**   **Grade I**
   Small hole in shakehole SE of Hell Hole leads to a square chamber littered
with boulders. In the chamber floor is a peculiar oblong hole reminiscent of
a shallow grave.
2. NGR SE 067620   **Alt. 250m**   **Depth 20m**   **Grade III**
   Open rift at east side of valley is part mined and part natural. There is a
ledge at 8m; the rest of the shaft is extremely shattered and dangerous, and
choked at the foot.
Tackle – 15m ladder; 1.5m belay; 20m lifeline.
3. NGR SE 065619   **Alt. 245m**   **Grade I**
   Level 140m S of Gill Heads Mine is 45m long to a natural chimney and
short section of passage.

GRENADE SHAFT
NGR SE 089636
Grade II

Alt. 362m
Length 120m
Depth 16m

Explored 1970, YURT.

Artificial entrance shaft in field N of Stump Cross, 55m from road. A short cave with superb formations which should be treated with utmost care. Pitch in narrow shaft connects with boulder-filled rift and wriggle into The Barbican, a low passage with formations. Careful crawling over fragile calcite floor with low crawl between straws on right into The Treasury, small chamber terminated by block fall. Main way continues delicately round edge of large crystal pool to crawl between formations into The Keep, large but low chamber with magnificent stalagmite columns and flows. Short crawls leading off are all choked quickly. Shaft is blocked by debris.

Tackle – 12m ladder; stake and sling belay; 20m lifeline.

Permission – Stump Cross Caverns, Greenhow Hill.

HELL HOLE
NGR SE 065622
Grade III

Alt. 280m
Length 210m
Depth 55m

Explored 1896, YRC; extended 1976, CPC; 1980, CUCC.

Entrance is large rift in obvious stream sink 400m NE of first sharp bend on Appletreewick road after leaving main Pateley-Grassington road. An interesting and varied pot with some sizeable passages, unfortunately of no great length. Walk down boulder slope to T-junction where stream can be followed up cascades to left, ending in short choked crawl at top of 3.3m climb just below surface stream bed. Right from T-junction passage lowers to crawl followed by 3.5m climb and 1st Pitch, belayed to wedged rail and broken by small ledge half-way down. A traverse and short awkward climb here lead to a tight passage which becomes impassable after 9m. Boulder slope near foot of pitch leads to two high avens. Large passage is main way and ends in long muddy slope up to calcite choke. Near foot of slope are crawls on left and right of passage.

Left crawl passes below 15m aven and becomes narrower and tighter before ending at excessively tight drop. Right crawl leads through duck and low going to junction. Straight ahead, crawl splits and becomes too low. Right through very tight squeeze quickly reaches slot in floor, Limbo Pitch, with no good belay nearby – bolt needed. Across slot leads to unclimbed aven. Down pitch is chamber and climb up through series of chambers for 30m to choke. Water sinks at foot of pitch in narrow rift which has not been followed for any distance.

Tackle

Pitch	Ladder	Belay	Lifeline
1st	21m	0.6m	25m
Limbo	20m	2m	30m

Permission – High Hall, Appletreewick.

KELD FARM CAVE   NGR SE 103638   Grade I
Alt. 395m   **Length 20m**
Explored c. 1975.

   Cockhill Limestone. Small cave, unusual in that it is in limestone only some 2.5m thick, within Millstone Grit series. Found when inspection pit was excavated in garage behind Keld Farm. Short dry passage from pit enters streamway heading N, which becomes too low. Water sinks adjacent to garage and probably rises at Craven Keld, about 100m to N and at same approximate level as end of cave. Limestone is very thinly bedded and cave is now completely blocked by unstable collapse 3m in.
Permission – Keld Farm, Greenhow Hill.

KNOT HEAD SINK   NGR SE 084639   Grade I
Alt. 363m   **Length 9m**   **Depth 6m**
   Entrance in large shakehole 500m NW of bend on road W of Stump Cross Caverns. Small stream sink 90m N of gate in moor wall. Series of boulder chambers connected by two short climbs. Stream is heard but not seen in cave.

MONGO GILL HOLE   NGR SE 092635   Grade III
Alt. 370m   **Length 2.5km**   **Depth 37m**
   Discovered in part by lead miners. Explored and extended 1957, 1959 and 1964, CPC; subsequent small extensions by others, including NCC & YURT.

WARNING – Liable to severe flooding in lower sections. Great care should be taken in mine workings which are unstable.

   Three entrances, principal one being Shockle Shaft (NGR SE 092635), in second field, 400m on Greenhow side of Stump Cross. On top edge of N slope of Dry Gill, it is an old mine shaft with steel lid. Others are North Shaft, (NGR SE 096632) 150m S of old mine building 800m up gill from Stump Cross, which is excavated natural pot in flood sink close to active sink. South Entrance (NGR SE 096631) is in large shakehole 70m away on S side of gill. A cave associated with the Stump Cross system and containing some of the largest chambers in Greenhow. Many fine formations were smashed by visitors when the cave was opened as a lead mine in the early 19th century but many remain untouched.

Mongo Gill South (1957 Series)   ·
   Crawl behind boulder drops into small chamber and further slides emerge in chamber. To left (S) a cratered gallery leads to a stream inlet aven and several fissures, all rapidly ending. To right from chamber crawl over slab enters Platt's Passage and past hole in floor the way ends at the choked Black Cavern. Hole in floor leads to crawl and boulder fall, followed by further crawl ascending to climb up blocks into Cavern 322. At upper end of this, hole down leads to crawl into climbable choked inlet aven, while to right crawl rises to step up into bedding plane. Down to left into easier going to reach foot of North Shaft against left wall of low, flat-roofed cavern. To right

in bedding plane leads down into Cavern 152, a pleasantly roomy chamber with routes to North Shaft on left and Dunstone Incline, slope down to tight tubes, on right.

North Shaft is broken pitch, last 4.5m of which are down narrow rift, into low cavern. To S leads back to Cavern 152 while to N, route down against left wall lowers to hole and slope into transverse bedding plane which becomes low to right. Left is a fallen boulder—Luckstone Gate—and the start of Mongo Gill North.

All the cave so far described lies close to the North Craven Fault zone and there are many unstable sections which should be treated with care. The area is extremely confusing and cannot be adequately described in a guide of this sort.

Mongo Gill North (1959 Series)

From Luckstone Gate a single passage, Luckstone Level, gives varied crawling to chamber, Bottomley's Basin, with muddy tubes down pot and way on to right into Cavern 358. After calcite boss, passage diverges to right and becomes low before opening into Freezeland, chamber with mine debris forming floor. Excavated sandy crawl pops up through floor of natural passage which undulates its way to a boulder choke. Avoid damaging disintegrating remnants of wooden channel, constructed by lead miners to carry trickle of water over a hole they were digging. Uphill from entry into natural passages is a series of small mine workings ending in short choked sections of cave.

Ahead from Cavern 358 is The Forest, a fragile and exotic barrier of stalagmites and helictites with way round on right. Series of crawls on left connect to Bear Pit, where muddy descent encounters stream which quickly sumps in both directions. Cavern 324 is the continuation of the main way and has some short crawls on its right. Walking gives way to flat crawl, then way over boulders on left to hole in floor and massive breakdown—East Hade—ahead.

January Series and Miners' Series

Down hole in floor is crawl into January Series. Pool Chamber is succeeded by crawling to J.J. Cavern, where route over boulder choke emerges in boulder-floored passage continuing to Judson's Cavern. Oxbow connecting with Judson's has branch ending in mud choke. Initials Passage runs S from Judson's Cavern as crawl ending too low; various worked lead veins end in calcite chokes. Numerous smoked initials on walls and roof from here on are left from mining days. In floor of Judson's Cavern is hole into Dodge Deads Passage, which descends past squeeze to sandy crawl. From small chamber 15m ahead, 4.5m high rift with unstable mine debris and rotten timbers ascends to 18m long choked mine level. Squeeze down below rift enters sandy passages; one way chokes and the other ends at a small, draughting chamber, sumped in wet weather.

North from Judson's Cavern is low passage to drop into mine level on left and walking to fall where hole up gives access to small chamber connected with New Cavern, massive chamber with good formations. On past falls in mine level into aven with choked mine levels above and then into 1792

Cavern. Crawl traverse on left wall to drop down into Ladder Cavern, then over pots in floor, past rift on left and passage on right to pack-walled section ending at fall where short passage from Shockle Shaft enters on right. Over fall is South Passage, ending in massive collapse.

Shockle Shaft is old, twisting mine shaft to landing on timbers wedged across. Short mine working goes off in one direction while climb down pack-wall at opposite end reaches muddy slide emerging at the beginning of South Passage.

Passage leading off Ladder Cavern is Bell & Pratt's Passage, crawl to top of Vein Cavern. This is a high rift with steep descent to normally dry stream passage. Downstream is wide passage with inlet crawl on left about 45m long, low and tight, becoming more severe. From Boulder Chamber, stream takes separate route to right of dry sandy high level and can be entered down various holes and followed down through pools to flooded pot sump. Upper passage is easy going to 17m aven, where short choked crawl diverges, and beyond to clay choke corresponding with end of 1949 Series in Stump Cross Caverns.

Upstream Passage

From foot of Vein Cavern upstream crawl leads through Sump 1, which exists only in floods, then walking to Sump 2, also normally dry and with fissure descent from Ladder Cavern at its downstream end. Crawl through sump to walking passage with muddy crawl on left connecting with Ladder Cavern near pots. Onwards past barytes and lead veins to Sump 3, which dries up after short periods of dry weather. In chamber on other side 4m climb up on left into Giraffe Passage, crawl which becomes too low. Streamway continues to blocks where crawl goes off on left and nearby climb up gives access to Roof Cavern, calcite choked one way and the other way opening into streamway further upstream. Next feature of passage is long inlet on right to constricted descending muddy tube. Sump 4 is about 60m away and only dries up in very dry conditions. Crawling beyond to bedding plane which becomes too low. On left just past Sump 4 a series of low level tubes can be entered. These are prone to very rapid flooding.

Tackle

Pitch	Ladder	Belay	Lifeline
North Shaft	15m	1m	20m
Shockle Shaft	20m	3m	25m

Permission – CNCC.

NAPE WELL CAVE   NGR SE 068616   Grade I
Alt. 210m   Length 27m
Explored 1967/68, CPC; extended 1976, CDG.

Below Nape Scar on E side of Trollers Gill where small stream emerges. Crawl enters an L-shaped passage with water flowing under right wall, and can be followed to a sump. This has been dived in a low bedding for 4.5m to an enlargement of the rift where it was possible to turn round; beyond continues very low. Blasting here has failed to open up the continuation.

NORTH POT   NGR SE 088637   Grade II
Alt. 360m   **Length 12m**   **Depth 27m**
Explored 1958/59, BSA/CPC.

Open shaft 300m N of Stump Cross Caverns. A 3m shaft and tight passage lead to 6m pitch. A 4.5m crawl leads to boulders and 2.5m drop into choked shaft. Down slope with avens above to final 4.5m climb down narrow slit. Rope useful for climbing pitches.
Permission – Stump Cross Caverns, Greenhow Hill.

PENDLETON PIPE   NGR SE 123640
Alt. 420m

A pre-mineralisation solution cavern 200m long, which was divided into two parts by an opencast for lead and fluorspar on Garnet Vein. Contained a large chamber 36m long but has now been quarried away.

SNARE POT   NGR SE 091638   Grade II
Alt. 366m   **Depth 8m**

In shakehole about 50m SW of Blood Pot. Entrance now collapsed but hole beneath boulder pile was formerly head of 8m fluted pot choked with shingle.

SPAR POT   NGR SE 065614   Grade II
Alt. 267m   **Depth 9m**
Explored 1974, WRPC.

WARNING – The whole pot is unstable, with loose boulders throughout.

Open rift sink with small stream, and an excavated entrance at opposite end. Climb down through boulders onto chocked blocks, followed by a second dangerous climb leads to short crawl into aven chamber. Piles of loose rocks block any possible continuation.

STUMP CROSS CAVERNS   NGR SE 089635   Grade II-IV
Alt. 360m   **Length 3.3km**   **Depth 43m**
Discovered by lead miners 1860; extended 1922, C.F.D. Long and others; 1949, 1955, CPC; 1967, 1971, YURT; 1977-80, CDG; and others at various dates.

WARNING – Virtually all the cave below Heartbeat is subject to flooding in severe conditions and this danger is even greater in Hell and the active parts of the cave, which can flood without warning.

Entrance midway between Pateley Bridge and Grassington, adjacent to S side of main road, unmistakably marked by the visitor centre and car park for the show cave. A fascinating and complex system showing numerous levels of development, the uppermost of which is partially used as a show cave. Formations have suffered from the passage of generations of visitors but those which have been preserved are particularly fine. A great deal of digging has been done in attempts to extend the cave.

Show Cave Level

Cave is entered down steps in visitor centre, via artificially widened fissure. Show cave is electrically lit and consists of a single passage which breaks into a larger cavern and finally ends at a boulder choke which was by-passed by sinking Grenade Shaft, together with a branch passage, Wolverine Cave. Show Cave is adequately described in the guide book to the Caverns, in more detail than is possible here, but its branches deserve further comment. Straight on from foot of steps a low gallery soon meets a T-junction with several short, muddy and boulder-choked crawls going off to the right. Main cavern continues left and then swings right to a large collapse. Short crawl back on left before collapse closes down to join. Over collapse, slide down into Circular Cavern, from which crawl diverges at NE corner, quickly becoming too tight, and narrow choked fissure runs N. Way out is at NW corner where easy passage emerges in show cave near Sentinel, large stalagmite column.

Passages on left going inwards are more numerous in show cave and are now described. From bottom of steps first opening, blocked by wooden door, leads along passage of varying height to squeeze into Susilk Gallery, crawl into chamber with tight outlet on right side into short blind crawls. A few metres inside wooden door is opening on left again, leading to boulder choke, with second wooden door on left giving access to lower levels, described later.

Second passage from show cave is blind crawl about 25m long at rear of Butcher's Shop. Third opening is Wolverine Cave, ending at a barrier beyond which is the Bowling Alley, low passage with stalagmites, on the right. An oxbow by-pass rejoins beyond Bowling Alley and cave then turns sharp left, becoming a flat crawl to final boulder choke. Fourth opening is adjacent to Sentinel, where very short crawl opens into Fairy Palace, rift aven with short boulder-choked crawl at lower end.

Fifth opening is at back of Chamber of Pillars where hole up emerges in blockfall chamber. To left is fissure where reindeer bones were found and to right obvious way over boulders leads into Reindeer Cavern, long chamber with fine formations. At far side of final boulder fall short crawl leads to aven with excellent stalagmite cascade. Excavated route through fall into Link Chamber with fine formations and massive strata collapse at far side. Hole down to right of entry point drops into inclined bedding planes ending in boulder fall close to 3m pot in lower levels.

Lower levels down to stream passage

Behind second wooden door is Coal Shute, easy climb down of about 2.7m. At bottom of this Parallel Gallery leads off on left, mostly low going with various short crawls on right, one of which emerges in roof of Clay Level. Main way is to right and down through short low section into side of Clay Level, collapsed to right. Left, walking followed by crawling over fall to series of muddy caverns with one arduous choked crawl branching off on right.

Clay Level ends at sudden lowering of roof followed by crawl diverging on left. This is The Cut – about 30m long and dug out by Long, Barton and others in a continuous seven-day effort in 1922 – which emerges in Barton's

Cavern (also known as the Skittle Alley). Left over mound of clay is Long's Gallery, high fissure choked with calcite. Right is aven climb into Sawdust Gallery, short crawls which choke. Ahead, main route leads over dug hole in floor and round into Sand Cavern, roomy walk ending in chamber with stalagmite known as Astor Column. At commencement of Sand Cavern climb up to left and short passage to junction. Left is crawl into Long's Gallery; right is Jericho, crawl along gours into small cavern. Ahead is Driffield Gallery, becoming too low. Down to left into passage and straight ahead into Dickinson's Gallery, crawl into aven choked with calcite flow where draught emerges from floor. Left, instead of going into Dickinson's, is crawl into rift which emerges near Astor Column.

On same alignment as Sand Cavern, way on to W is descending crawl to Heartbeat, 2m long inclined tube followed by 1.2m drop. Low muddy passage and shallow canal to pile of mud. Rails and wagon in Cook's Dig on left date from 1964 when dig through clay ended at solid wall. Main cave continues with only short branches, as series of small caverns connected by crawls, until Putrell's Cavern is met. Hole in floor crossed on unsafe plank and walk to hole down on left where stream heard. This is climb down to Dissected Area, complex of crawls and stream passage with sumps both up and down stream. From downstream sump pool a duck on left gives access to an airbell and flooded shaft. A 4m tight descent enlarges to a flooded tube, and the sump is passed after 33m, following a low section. About 45m of crawling passage ensues, with three static sumps, and one active sump – too small after 9m. The furthest static sump is 15m to an airbell with muddy aven above, rock bridge 1m above water, and no obvious way on.

Further along main cavern above climb down into Dissected Area is crawl on left to boulder choke under floor of Raistrick's Cavern, which is reached by following main route and is one of largest caverns in system. Crawl at end into larger passage ending at 3m pot. Passage on left at top of pot is Gothic Gallery, ending in crawls and boulder chokes. Easy climb down pot and crawls to slope down into stream. Downstream, water up to waist deep and waterfall and climb down into sump, with dry passage continuing to deep flooded pot sump.

Heaven and Hell

Upstream, steep slope up on left out of water and into Heaven leads under boulders into high chamber. Climb down boulders into continuation, which passes fissure on right, to crawl ending at drop into Rat-trap, a series of flooded fissures. A 4.5m ladder is **essential** for ascending this drop. Fissure on right before crawl to Rat-trap is main route along zig-zag rifts with hole in floor connecting with Rat-trap. Short crawl into higher fissure, with old dig on left, usually entered by mistake on way out, and winding passage to another high rift, where passage to Cook's Pot diverges on right.

Pot is short climb into streamway which is normally occupied only by standing pools. Downstream leads to sump. Upstream is Hell, very sharp crawl to Cook's Caution Pot, 3m climb and normally flooded. Passage beyond has only been entered in drought conditions and continues for undetermined distance as sharp crawl, prone to **extremely rapid flooding.**

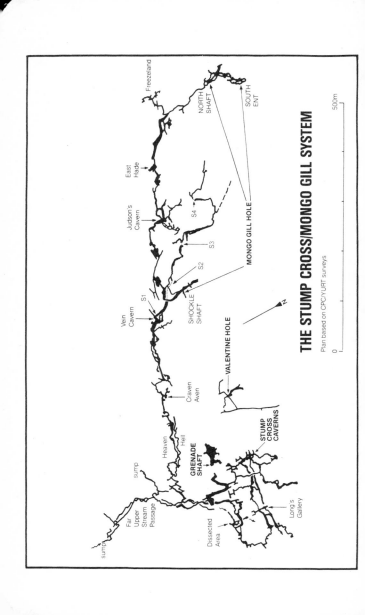

THE STUMP CROSS/MONGO GILL SYSTEM

Plan based on CPC/YURT surveys

0   500m

Freezeland

NORTH SHAFT

SOUTH ENT

East Hade

Judson's Cavern

S4

S3

MONGO GILL HOLE

S2

SHOCKLE SHAFT

S1

Vein Cavern

VALENTINE HOLE

N

Craven Aven

Heaven

Hell

sump

Far Upper Stream Passage

sump

GRENADE SHAFT

STUMP CROSS CAVERNS

Dissected Area

Long's Gallery

Varied going beyond entrance to Cook's Pot as far as Bradley's Boulders, where crawl through collapse opens into Miners' Chamber, crossed by worked vein in roof. Continuing crawl into November Series and high level bedding and fissure on right to roomier passage with avens. Largest and final one is Craven Aven, with small choked crawls leading off from ledge on left. Main passage to left ends in unstable clay choke which was briefly connected with Mongo Gill Hole, but soon fell in again.

Far Upper Stream Passage

From entry point into streamway, water can be followed through low section into higher going. Where passage lowers again and continues to sump are holes up to left into fissure and cross over into passage, followed by climb and crawling through chamber, with blind pot in floor, to further crawling to traverse over stream.

Drop down to water level and sideways crawl to E followed by series of narrow crawls into another streamway–Runestream. Downstream ends in tight rifts after very deep sections. Upstream mostly crawling for some distance to duck and sump.

Along at traverse level two routes are met. Wet route is easiest and connects with dry route at several points. Upper route stops at 4.5m ladder pitch down into stream, avoidable by slope into water some metres back. Way divides again, right being dry crawls to choke which is other side of calcite choke met by following water along canal and taking passage up to right where going gets lower towards sump. Calcite choke is on right of cross fissure and way is to left where T-junction is met immediately. Right is 'CPC 1939' passage, ending in mud filled tube. Left is crawl and squeeze into Caleb's Cringes, aptly-named muddy rift ending where crawl turns left. Slide down in front to low sumped section of streamway. Crawl to left leads into fissure with wet or dry routes into final sump pool.

Permission–Stump Cross Caverns, Greenhow Hill. Potholers only allowed into lower levels November-March.

TIMPONY JOINT   NGR SE 081633   Grade I
Alt. 310m

Through gate and in right hand side of dry valley opposite Dry Gill House. Three entrances close together, numbered going down valley.

1. Length 8m

Small tube descends to constricted sump.

2 & 3. Length 20m

Both entrances join and lead to 3m sump into small, rock-filled aven; way on is choked.

Permission–Dry Gill, Hebden.

TROLLERS GILL CAVE   NGR SE 067613   Grade II
Alt. 200m   Length 60m

Located by breach in lower dam. A mine level which has intersected a cave system. Entrance passages are a mine working on two levels but muddy rift opens on to steep slope down to water. Short canal soon sumps; water level is variable and sump dries up to reveal a mud choke. Up the slope a steep up-dip passage ascends past constrictions as a switchback ending at a flowstone blockage.

VALENTINE HOLE   NGR SE 090635   Grade III
Alt. 359m   **Length: Cave 60m; Mine 282m**   **Depth 23m**
Discovered by lead miners; re-opened 1965, YURT.

Entrance on shaft hillock 90m E of Stump Cross Caverns. A series of mine levels which encountered a natural cave, probably associated with the Stump Cross system, although extensive boulder falls block any connection. Beneath steel lid is mine shaft, narrow and brick lined for top 5m. Four mine levels in shaft all end at solid walls in short distances. From small chamber at shaft foot, four routes diverge. Opposite the shaft is East Level, walking to clay fall with way on to right ending where working ceased in low flatting bed. Left from shaft foot is North Level, driven through fill below natural roof. Narrow aven on left halfway to end, where working stopped after 30m. Hole in roof at shaft foot gives access to crawl in cave passage, becoming flat-out before entering Dog Cavern, chamber with dog's skeleton on floor, ending in a large choke. Crawl over boulders on right into South-west Cavern which ends abruptly at a calcited boulder fall. Formations in both caverns have been smashed by the miners. Fourth way from shaft is slide down into West Level where crawl over backfilled rocks leads into slope and further crawl under dangerous poised boulders to junction. Left is South Cross Vein, stooping and crawling for some distance to solid collapse of calcite vein. Choked drift on W side before end. Right at junction is North Cross Vein; very muddy crawl up and over clay fall to glutinous continuation of level, ending in choke of large gritstone boulders.

Tackle – 25m ladder; 3m belay; 25m lifeline.

Permission – Stump Cross Caverns, Greenhow Hill.

WEST SINK   NGR SE 087637   Grade I
Alt. 350m   **Length 6m**   **Depth 3m**
Stream sink in large shakehole against W wall in field N of Stump Cross Caverns. Water sinks into fissure which divides about 3m in and becomes impenetrable. To left is longer fissure, also becoming too narrow where stream sinks in shingle floor of narrowing rift. All now blocked by large boulders.

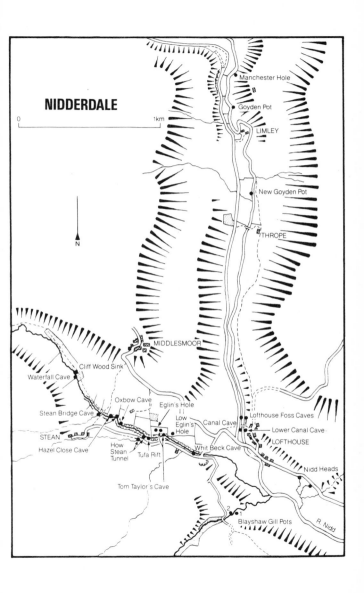

NIDDERDALE

0   1km

N

Manchester Hole

Goyden Pot

LIMLEY

New Goyden Pot

THROPE

MIDDLESMOOR

Cliff Wood Sink

Waterfall Cave

Oxbow Cave

Eglin's Hole

Stean Bridge Cave

Low
Eglin's
Hole

Canal Cave

Lofthouse Foss Caves

STEAN

Hazel Close Cave

How Stean
Tunnel

Tufa Rift

Whit Beck Cave

Lower Canal Cave

LOFTHOUSE

Nidd Heads

Tom Taylor's Cave

Blayshaw Gill Pots

R. Nidd

NIDDERDALE

ANGRAM CAVE   NGR SE 046766   Grade I
Alt. 350m   Length 9m
Explored 1970, YURT.

UnL. Small entrance near gully at SW end of limestone scar, 200m NE of Angram Dam. Small dry cave formed on cross-joints. After wriggle under boulder at entrance, crawl continues past small collapsed chamber to end in gravelly choke close to surface.

(For location see Wharfedale Area map on back endpaper).

BLAYSHAW GILL POTS   NGR SE 099728   Grade III
Alt. 177m

A fascinating pair of small potholes close to a major fault. Although hydrologically linked, massive collapses separate the two.

1. Length 400m   **Depth 21m**
Explored 1888, J. Walker and others; extended 1906/22, YRC; 1969-78, YURT.

WARNING – Lower reaches of streamways liable to severe flooding.

MdL. Hole on S bank of stream 37m downstream of 2 is covered with rocks and branches. Pitch is broken by ledges 3m down and lands in small chamber, with two passages leading off from alcove in N wall. Obvious route steps up, turns left, and ends in choke under stream bed. Right of step up is floor level crawl emerging on fragile chert ledges above small streamway. Downstream is too tight immediately, and tight sandy crawl is too small after two acute bends. Upstream continues to choke under stream bed.

Upper Series

From ledge 3m down entrance pitch is slippery traverse, where rope should be used if necessary, into narrow, winding passage leading to 2.7m deep hole in floor after 30m. Two squeezes at bottom of this emerge in lower series. Beyond hole, passage continues as a crawl and after short drop becomes walking size. Two passages on left lead to Twin Chokes, parts of one large boulder fall. Main route turns right, past 6m long inlet, as crawl under aven and becomes higher, finally descending Rock Steps into North Vein Cavern. Various holes down to stream but way on is near far end of cavern along roof level crawl, then down drop and slide into Far Streamway – crawling for 45m to sump. There are various short side passages in both series.

Tackle – 8m ladder; 3m belay; 10m lifeline. Traverse into Upper Series needs 10m handline.

Lower Series

From chamber at foot of pitch, a crawl over asbestos sheets leads into a larger passage where Traverse Inlet enters on left. Inlet is 30m long to boulder chokes beneath stream bed. Main passage continues beneath squeezes from upper series to The Well, 1.5m climb down, where traverse over top enters 18m crawl which ends in chert bed. Below Well, muddy passage beyond stream sink in tight rift has branch to right, too low after 18m and mud-choked branch to left. Hole up enters 43m crawl which chokes in both directions.

2. Length: Cave 580m, Mine 225m   Depth 19m   Vertical Range 30m
Discovered by lead miners; extended 1906/22, YRC; 1969-77, YURT.

WARNING – Lower passages and pitch flood badly, becoming impassable. The pot is close to a fault and there are numerous loose boulders and much shattered rock.

5YL/MdL. Entrance pitch, covered by boulders, is at N side of stream bed just downstream of old 'marble' sawmill. Large, elliptical shaft is floored with boulders and from S end two series of passages lead off.

Upstream Series

At SW corner of pitch is climb up 2.5m on fragile holds near stream entry. Narrow fissure to 1.2m drop with rift continuing upwards among unstable boulders to choke; in right side partway up rift is bedding plane. Left leads to sand choke after 30m and right reads out into shaft halfway down; passage on opposite side of shaft is boulder-choked after 6m and exposed traverse to it past unstable boulders should not be attempted.

At foot of 1.2m drop is main route, via YRC Crawl, to emerge in roof of fissure. Traverse on at this level ends at calcite choke but dropping down instead leads to muddy squeezes into larger streamway. Inlets here lead into small chambers with water entering through hanging boulders. All water flows into minute, silted downstream sump (water tested to stream in New Series and thence to Far Streamway in No. 1 Pot).

Inviting upstream passage leads past high level oxbows, cascades and dry upper levels with formations (care!). Way divides – stream route to left and lengthy muddy oxbow to right – then rejoins in larger passage and continues to overhanging choke of mine debris. Climb into roof 9m back from this gains further climb and steeply ascending passage emerging in mine levels, choked to right after 75m crawl. Left enters natural chamber, from which mine level runs for 140m to collapse. Upstream passage from chamber ends in massive breakdown after 23m. Stream tested from nearby mine level into upstream passage.

New Series

At SE corner of entrance pitch is route under hanging boulders into descending sandy crawl, which becomes too narrow where hole on right emerges in a parallel passage. To right is climb and crawl into boulder chamber with no way on past massive collapse; this chamber should not be entered as the roof is unsafe in parts and may collapse without warning.

To left is pleasant crawl and drop into larger passage; on left at foot of drop is slot into short, roomy streamway ending at shingle choke upstream with lowering crawl above. Just past foot of drop, the passage opens out 2m above the floor of a large aven. Stream enters from joint and disappears into low, sumped crawl at same level as Far Streamway in No. 1 Pot. Up mud slide in aven is deserted inlet ending in choke which is part of the choke seen in the boulder chamber.

Tackle – 15m Ladder; 3m belay; 20m lifeline.

Permission – High Blayshaw Farm, Lofthouse.

CANAL CAVE NGR SE 100735 Grade III
Alt. 163m   **Length 260m**   **Vertical Range 7.3m**
Extended 1966, HWCPC.

WARNING – Entrance becomes impassable when river Nidd rises in flood.

MdL. Upstream of road bridge at Lofthouse is footbridge over small gorge of river Nidd. Entrance below bridge on W side of gorge where eroded cave passage crosses river bed. Narrow crawl into cold canal and then walking to small chamber. Passage going off above water level is oxbow which can also be entered downstream of climb but way through is choked by gravel and boulders. Canal continues about 1m deep to 3m climb up in 3m high passage. Climb can be done at waterfall or further back and then traverse on very rotten chert ledges. No belay for rope or ladder above climb, where Straw Crawl leads under chert bridges to chamber floored by pool. Stream enters from passage 1m up, which continues as a crawl developing into a tortuous wriggle at end, where walls and calcite flows close in.

About 60m downstream is 3.5m pot in W bank, dug out by CPC, 1985, to bedding which is too low after 4m. Flooded except in dry weather.

CLIFF WOOD SINK NGR SE 087739 Grade III
Alt. 210m   **Length 45m**
Explored 1968, YURT.

WARNING – Floods rapidly and completely.

MdL. Between collapsed blocks beside footpath along How Stean Beck in Cliff Wood, about 30m NW of stile through fence. Probably a flood sink connected with Main Stream Inlet in Eglin's Hole. Crawl through squeeze in pool to flat crawling over shingle, through further pools to tight bedding plane partly blocked by shingle. Impossible to turn round in many places, including final bedding plane.

EGLIN'S HOLE NGR SE 093735 Grade III
Alt. 195m   **Length 1,280m**   **Vertical Range 17m**
Extended 1884, F.C. Armstrong and C.H. Robinson; 1967, YURT; and others unknown.

WARNING – Subject to flooding with numerous lower sections becoming impassable in severe conditions.

MdL. At N side of field across How Stean Gorge from cafe, in small limestone exposure with main entrance beneath; smaller entrance above and to right 10m away. A long and often low cave which was formerly well decorated, but generations of visitors have severely damaged the formations. Main entrance is muddy crawl into wide main passage. Subsidiary entrance is 1.5m deep hole in field followed by slide into main passage. Various short connecting crawls between these entrances. Small stream normally occupies main passage and disappears under boulder choke near entrances to re-emerge at Low Eglin's Hole.

Upstream is passage up to 15m wide and generally 1m high with various crawls out to the extremities of the roof bedding plane on the left. After 150m the way opens into a larger passage with crawl into small, boulder-choked chamber to left. To right is 140m walking along boulder-strewn passage with many damaged formations, succeeded by 60m lower going of back-breaking height which eases where roof lifts and cave bears left. Passage on left at roof level after 15m is oxbow—The Wilderness—with various through routes possible. Main gallery continues as a walk to step up in floor, 30m past which stream emerges from Main Stream Inlet—low bedding plane on right. This is a flat crawl into easier passage 0.7m high which lowers to 15cm high above shingle floor after 110m. Beyond entrance to this inlet, main line continues 1m high for 90m to 15m long tube on left which ends too low.

Bedding plane continues ahead beyond tube entrance as a low crawl to Stalagmite Barrier after 60m followed by muddy inlet on left, 35m long before becoming too low. Another 20m and main bedding plane splits. Right-hand route is followed to reach rock-floored crawl left into wide passage. At far end of this is Northwest Frontier, a network of crawls and squeezes which end in chokes of earth or sand only a short distance from the NE bank of How Stean Beck opposite Waterfall Cave.

Permission—How Stean Cottage, Lofthouse.

GOYDEN POT   NGR SE 099761   Grade II-IV
Alt. 210m   **Length 3.6km**   **Depth 41m**

Extended 1888, G.V. Gaskell; 1912-1934, YRC; 1959, CPC; 1966-1973, ULSA/YURT; 1977-1985, CUCC.

WARNING – Liable to complete flooding, particularly if water is flowing into entrance or reservoirs 4.8km upstream are full.

MdL. Dry river bed plunges into main entrance below tree-lined scar 275m S of Manchester Hole. A complex and impressive major river cave with a variety of routes of differing grades, containing massive caverns and a maze of passages in which a copy of the survey is invaluable. Connects with Manchester Hole and New Goyden Pot to form a system with a combined length of 6.3km and depth of 61m.

Entrance Series and Main River Passage

Walk down entrance passage, over hole with sound of river, to shingle floor and flood debris choke ahead with route to The Window and beyond on left. Right over boulders into Main Chamber, which can also be gained via Back Steps Entrance, a small hole on top of huge block to right of Main Entrance, leading down through boulder chokes and short passage into the

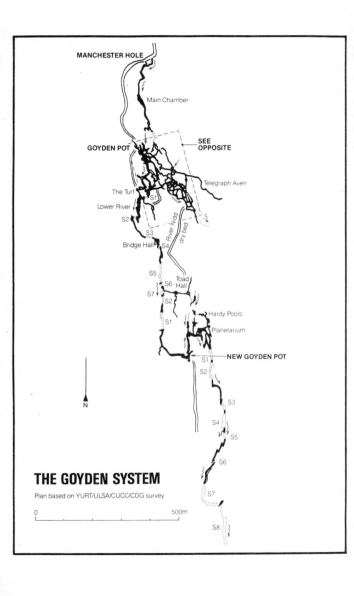

MANCHESTER HOLE

Main Chamber

GOYDEN POT

SEE OPPOSITE

Telegraph Aven

The Turf

Lower River

S1

S2

S3

Bridge Hall

S4

River Nidd dry bed

S5

S6

Toad Hall

S7

S2

S1

Hardy Pools

Planetarium

NEW GOYDEN POT

S1

S2

S3

S4

S5

S6

S7

S8

N

THE GOYDEN SYSTEM

Plan based on YURT/ULSA/CUCC/CDG survey

0   500m

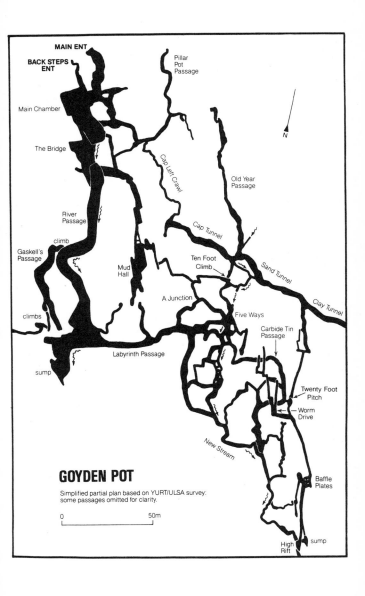

MAIN ENT

BACK STEPS ENT

Pillar Pot Passage

Main Chamber

The Bridge

Cap Left Crawl

Old Year Passage

River Passage

climb

Cap Tunnel

Gaskell's Passage

Sand Tunnel

Mud Hall

Ten Foot Climb

Clay Tunnel

climbs

A Junction

Five Ways

Carbide Tin Passage

N

sump

Labyrinth Passage

Twenty Foot Pitch

Worm Drive

New Stream

Baffle Plates

GOYDEN POT

Simplified partial plan based on YURT/ULSA survey: some passages omitted for clarity.

0   50m

High Rift

sump

chamber. Down boulder slope to river Nidd, entering from narrow rift 20m long which becomes too tight. Downstream The Cascades are descended under The Bridge, a deserted upper level with crawl to avens off it on right. Huge boulder-strewn river canyon continues to left bend with Gaskell's Passage at top of 4.5m sloping climb on right. Beyond, the way lowers to a stoop over cobbles away from the river, past a trickle of water from the 25m long, narrow, boulder-choked Limley Inlet on left, to Labyrinth Passage just past step up in roof. River gallery lowers to Sump 1, which is bypassed via Gaskell's Passage and is 20m long.

Gaskell's Passage

From top of climb out of river, muddy tunnel descends to sump. Before this is fissure on right into The Pinnacle, 6m climb to crawl and further short climbs in twisting canyon – The Spiral – ending in mud crawl. Direct ascent of 6m above first small climb reaches short bedding into The Chapel – chamber with 25m long boulder-choked roof passage. Walking size canyon from Chapel ends in pitch – The Turf.

Lower River Passage and beyond

Below The Turf a short passage over mudbanks meets Lower River Passage, with October Passage directly upstream on outside of corner before lower end of Sump 1. Downstream, river runs into choked bedding plane but to left, route over cobbles emerges in high, boulder-strewn gallery with river in parallel rift to right. Both ways unite at sump pool, with opening into adjoining fissure at end. Sump 2 consists of dives of 1.2m, 2.5m and 3m in deepening water and emerges in high passage 100m long ending at Sump 3. This is 27m long and emerges in Bridge Hall – a large chamber with a natural rock bridge. After 40m of spacious river passage is Sump 4 – 1.5m long to 34m of walking passage and the inevitable Sump 5. About 27m into the sump is a slope of poised boulders leading up into a further 30m of submerged passage and another less stable boulder slope ascending to a lake airbell with choked inlet rift in the roof. Sump 6 is very low and 12m long to an airbell. Sump 7 becomes very low after 15m but alternative route to left in sump reaches low airspace after 5m, then 3m sump to low bedding connecting with Alf's Airbell in New Goyden Pot.

From airbell between Sumps 6 and 7 a roof passage leads off. Phreatic tunnel continues for 80m, through Toad Hall – with side passage which enlarges to walking size and chokes – to reach area of cross rifts and a static sump. Left here is passage to choke and small stream after 50m. Static sump is 30m long in low, silted bedding, into stream passage. Upstream through duck leads to sump, dived for 15m to where way on was lost. Downstream is undived. Stream is presumed to be that from New Stream Sump to Main Inlet Sump of New Goyden.

October Passage

October Passage starts as a climb to tubular crawl 15m long to T-junction where stream flows from choke on right into canal on left. Beyond two ducks are two routes – following stream, or dry crawl descending to rejoin stream in small trench passage after 30m. Downstream, sharp bends and cascade into chamber succeeded by narrow rift and squeeze down to rift canal ending in a sump, dived for 8m in narrow rift.

Labyrinth Passage to Ten Foot Climb

Awkward stooping past 30m boulder-choked crawl on left, round bends and past gour-floored crawl leading to 'A' Junction on left, then floor-level bedding plane on right which is upper end of New Stream Passage, and on beyond aven bearing left past boulder into Five Ways. Gour-floored crawl leads uphill to 'A' Junction where bedding ahead goes to Five Ways and sandy crawl up to left becomes larger at junction with Pyridine Passage over calcite bridge on left. Main way is Pool and Boulder Passage, opening into high chamber with Ten Foot Climb on left.

Five Ways and The Labyrinth

Main route emerges into Five Ways and the heart of the Labyrinth, where a stream flows down-dip from left to right. Crawl from 'A' Junction enters on left and water comes from muddy crawl to Ten Foot Climb. Across the junction an ascending passage enters a choked high-level rift. Downstream is a complex area with numerous oxbows, one of which connects with Carbide Tin Passage, ending where stream sinks and dry crawl emerges in aven with high-level connection to Labyrinth Passage aven. Right from aven joins fissure leading to New Stream Passage while left regains water and crawl to further junction with tube to double aven on left; downstream route emerges in New Stream Passage. There are various confusing oxbows in this area.

Ten Foot Climb, Old Year Passage, Telegraph Aven

Above climb short rift enters chamber with Cap Tunnel to left–45m walking to chamber with aven and crawl down to sump. Cap Left Crawl on right is varied crawling to emergence in Pillar Pot Passage. Right from start of Cap Tunnel, water is followed up through low arches into fine curving rift with massive eroded stalagmite flows. Water emerges from small sump and under calcite shelf is concealed entrance to Old Year Passage, crawl followed by muddy walking to duck, then varied glutinous going to partial choke in pool.

Route along rift with eroded formations is superb highway to junction with way to Twenty Foot Pitch on right. Ahead, muddy going leads to wallow and squeeze – sumped in wet weather – into fissure ending at aven with unsafe scaling ladder in position. Above Telegraph Aven descending passage, also sumped in wet conditions, ends in chamber and inlet to choke. Before wallow is aven on left into high level passage, choked both ways.

Twenty Foot Pitch to High Rift

Descending passage from junction leads via either Silcock's Pool or high-level bypass to straight rift emerging halfway up aven–Twenty Foot Pitch. At the foot a chute on right drops into Carbide Tin Passage, which goes uphill to right to junction. Straight on here ends at pool with choke on right and connection to Five Ways ahead. Left from junction to mud choke, with oxbow to right and crawl to left having branch to double avens near Labyrinth stream, and itself emerging in crawl. This can be followed down to opening in roof of New Stream Passage and up to chute at foot of Twenty Foot Pitch.

Obvious route from foot of pitch passes large opening on right—Worm Drive, a passage which splits and in which both ways drop into parts of Carbide Tin Passage. Next opening on right is aven to high level fissure which becomes tighter and ends as stream outlet partway up Mud Pot aven.

Past this opening, rift meets rock pillars—the Baffle Plates—with Mud Pot aven down to right—and continues to High Rift aven. A 9m climb emerges in roof passage (The Beet Route). Easy going to junction after 30m. Left leads up small aven into low crawl which quickly rejoins the roof passage. Right descends short climbs to a canal and sump after 70m. Sump has been dived for 60m to 6m depth. Upstream from Mud Pot closes; downstream ends in sump with high level crawl to New Stream Passage.

New Stream Passage

Bedding plane from Labyrinth Passage is roof of deserted stream trench which is the upper end of a passage acting as the main watercourse of this part of the cave. After 30m a crawl on left connects via two routes to Labyrinth stream, which actually enters 20m further on. Round the next corner from the stream entry a dry inlet connects to both Carbide Tin Passage and the double aven in Labyrinth. Some distance beyond is a cascade with way to the Twenty Foot Pitch above. New Stream continues as descending rift past inlet ending in clay choke and further downstream past crawl at roof level connecting to Mud Pot. Lower going to short fall into New Stream Sump. Traverse on ledge to right and climb to traverse back over sump to gain fissure emerging close to High Rift.

New Stream Sump starts as a 11m deep flooded pot and after 140m of meandering, submerged passage, reaches the base of an unstable boulder slope. This has been passed into a large flooded shaft leading upwards; the present limit of exploration is beside a precariously balanced flake at 5m depth, with no obvious way on. Water reappears in Main Inlet of New Goyden Pot, presumably by way of the stream passage beyond Toad Hall in Goyden.

Pillar Pot

Both large passages on left 30m in from entrance reunite in walk to junction where passage to right ends at The Window, drop of 5m into Main Chamber. To left, crawl into high rift where crawl on right leads to Mud Hall. Pillar Pot Passage turns left past low entrance to Cap Left Crawl down on right and continues as crawl past Timber Passage on right which ends in 4.5m pot, to Pillar Pot, 3.5m deep to sumped pot and narrow underwater route to large flooded connection with Manchester Hole via 45m sump. Pillar Crawls lead off on right at top of pot and are twin-branched constricted crawls, one sumping and the other becoming too low.

Mud Hall and Nugatory Passages

Crawl over flood debris from start of Pillar Pot Passage over Drum Rift, 12m pitch with excessively low streamway at foot and usually choked with debris at top, to junction. Right to opening high in wall of Main Chamber, left to 1.5m drop into large square tunnel. Right is drop into River Passage but exposed traverse on left (not recommended) gives access to upper

Nugatory Passage. From bottom of 1.5m drop, mud wall to left is ascended into walking passage into Mud Hall, high chamber with steep descent and crawl into aven. Alternative descent to left and short passage to pool with slope and climb across to traverse over sump, then fissure climb down into Pyridine Passage – winding crawl with pools, into Pool and Boulder Passage.

Upper Nugatory Passage is easy going to boulder choke and has branch on right with hole at end into Lower Nugatory Passage. Easiest way into both passages is to climb up joint on left of River Passage 20m upstream of Gaskell's, using bolts at top for 8m ladder. Lower Nugatory is crawl with choked branches to aven and choke close to Limley Inlet.

Lesser Stream Passage

Stream entering on right below Bridge is followed upwards through collapsed bedding cave to passage ending in fissure sumps. From sumps climb of 6m up through shattered area to low bedding plane with inlet through shattered block. On right of Lesser Stream sump, crawl and squeeze into inlet, choked upstream and emerging in larger passage with sump downstream. Upstream in larger passage is boulder choke and roomy inlet on right ending in narrow rift avens. Various unstable boulder chambers can be entered.

Tackle

Pitch	Ladder	Belay	Lifeline
Twenty Foot	6m	1.5m	10m
The Turf	11m	9m	15m

Permission – Limley Farm No. 1 (nearest road). Advisable to check flood risk with Yorkshire Water's superintendent at Scar House Reservoir.

HAZEL CLOSE CAVE   NGR SE 090736   Grade II
Alt. 200m   Length 120m
Extended 1949, CPC.

MdL. From NE end of footbridge on Middlesmoor – Stean path, go downstream following gorge until wall is met. Over this following wall to wall corner in hollow. Entrance is on ledge down face of gorge over wall. Ladder needed to reach ledge and lifeline is advisable. Walking passage can be followed for 37m to small entrance, opening at top of gorge further upstream. Continuing passage encounters gour barriers with pools behind, followed by flat crawl to point where earth floor becomes too close to roof for further progress.

Tackle for pitch to ledge – 3m ladder; 1.5m belay; 6m lifeline.

HOW STEAN TUNNEL   NGR SE 092734   Grade I
[Stean Gill Foot]
Alt. 186m   Length 52m   Depth 4.5m

MdL. Entrance down bank on left where road emerges from between walls into open field a few hundred metres beyond How Stean Cafe entrance.

Interesting and quite impressive through cave. Three entrances at upper end.
Right is fissure, centre is main way and left is high level crawl re-emerging in
roof of main passage below cascade. From main entrance the cascade is
avoided by walk along ledge on left, then drop into streamway and walking
between wide ledges to emerge in deep stream trench flowing into How Stean
Gorge. Quarrying many years ago removed the roof and part of the right wall
of the cave nearest the gorge and the trench is what remains of the passage.
Permission – How Stean Cottage, Lofthouse.

LOFTHOUSE FOSS CAVES   NGR SE 100736   Grade I
Alt. 164m

MdL. On either side of cascade into large pool upstream of footbridge at
Lofthouse. Both caves are submerged when river is in flood, and liable to be
silted up.

1. Length 8m   Explored 1986, YURT
   On E side of pool at water level is excavated crawl to left bend. Lower
continuation ends against silt and flood debris.

2. Length 7m   Explored 1985, YURT.
   On W side of pool is excavated flat-out crawl ending too low over mud and
cobbles.

LOW EGLIN'S HOLE   NGR SE 094734   Grade III
Alt. 189m   **Length 915m**   **Depth 29m**
Explored 1967, YURT.

**WARNING – Passages below Second Climb flood, and entrance becomes
impassable.**

   MdL. Entrance is obvious sink in field, immediately E of Eglin's Hole
field, where stream emerges from narrow passage and falls into cave.
A pleasant linear cave with an interesting variety of passages and formations.
Drop from surface into narrow passage which rapidly enlarges after initial
crawling traverse. Various short inlets in entrance area all end in chokes.
Follow stream down to waterfall and step over into dry passage which
immediately encounters First Climb, 2.7m drop where 5m rope or ladder can
be useful for return. Lower passage continues until opening on right is
encountered. This is Long Inlet, 45m crawling to 2.7m climb up aven and
75m easy passage to extensive boulder chokes.
   Downstream of Long Inlet the stream trench emerges in the side of Jigsaw
Passage which has a wide bedding plane roof. On left is Aurochs Passage
which lowers to a tight bedding plane on left of boulder choke. Low crawl
into higher section followed by crawling to foot of 2.5m climb, at top of
which ascending fissure passage continues until it divides and becomes
excessively tight. Downstream is Jigsaw Passage; Hydra Passage is met on
left after 30m. This is squeeze and crawl followed by squeezes opening into
small aven and ascending rift passage which quickly chokes with boulders. In
main passage walking and crawling downstream past various oxbows on
both sides leads under rotten chert bridges and ledges to where roof lowers
and Second Climb is met. Easy climb of 2.5m down into pool.

Lower Streamway beyond ends after 40m where stream turns sharp right into Downstream Bedding. This is 37m of flat wet crawling to point where passage suddenly lowers to 12cm high. Crawl on left connects with Flood Passage, main way into which is 3m upstream of entrance to Downstream Bedding on left of passage. Muddy crawl into chamber and larger passage leading to The Canal, 45m long ending in crawl over boulders. Floor lowers rapidly to give easy walking followed by Switchback – mudbanks of increasing height across passage. Wriggle over final mudbank leads to wallow through pool and crawl to final pool where roof drops to give decreasing airspace in tight bedding plane with glutinous floor.

LOWER CANAL CAVE   NGR SE 100736   Grade III
Alt. 162m   Length 30m

WARNING – Floods completely and quickly.

MdL. Entrance, now virtually silted up, at opposite side of river bed to Canal Cave. Part of river sinks into entrance, which was body-size and extremely tight even when not silted. Passage led to T-Junction with inlet from sink further down river bed on right and short passage to sump on left.

MANCHESTER HOLE   NGR SE 100764   Grade I
Alt. 222m   Length 503m   Depth 17m

WARNING – Fills to roof in severe floods, when river flows into entrance.

MdL. At base of scar next to river, 110m SE of old railway tunnel. Basically a single large passage forming the upstream end of the Goyden system, and connecting with Goyden Pot and New Goyden Pot to form a cave with a combined length of 6.3km and depth of 61m.

Entrance slope 2m above and 10m back from normally dry river bed leads down into obvious upstream passage ending in block falls under bed of river. Two minor inlets on left also end rapidly, one in block fall and other becomes too low. Downstream from entrance under lower roof and traverse across large blocks to slide down into river passage. Easy walk for 110m past large stalactite curtains to foot of mud slope up into huge Main Chamber, 30m long. Steps in mud lead up to traverse on mud ledges above craters which go down to the river. Short level passage beyond traverse followed by slide down into river, which emerges through blocks. Possible to follow water along lower edge of chamber. Downstream walking until roof dips to 0.6m high, then crawling for short distance to high fissure. Oxbow up slope on right rejoins main passage after a short distance. Main route is along fissure to corner with deeper pool, soon after which the oxbow re-enters down a slope on the right. Opposite on the left wall is a slope up to a crawl which leads downwards to a static sump 45m long connecting to Pillar Pot in Goyden. Ahead in the main passage the river appears to sump but low opening on right in pool leads to further short walk and true sump.
Permission and flood risk check – as Goyden Pot.

NEW GOYDEN POT   NGR SE 102754   Grade III
Alt. 195m   **Length 2.2km**   **Depth 32m**

Explored 1956, CPC; extended 1973/1974, ULSA; 1980-1982, CDG.

WARNING – Liable to sudden and complete flooding.

MdL. Original entrance now completely choked. S entrance is below small cliff on W bank of dry bed of Nidd where track from Lofthouse along E side of valley descends to river, 110m S of Dry Wath. Approach along public footpath beside river, not directly across field from road. A major river cave with a superb railway-tunnel sized main streamway. Connects with Manchester Hole and Goyden Pot to form a cave with a combined length of 6.3km and depth of 61m. Crawl, becoming higher, leads to 1st pitch under boulder choke. Belay to rocks embedded in mud bank 6m back from pitch should not be wholly trusted. Behind foot of ladder, ascending fissure, Vulcan Rifts, chokes just below surface. 2nd pitch belayed to insecure boulder descends into large river passage.

Upstream Passages

Upstream to corner where narrow rift at top of boulder slope emerges in South Avens, where Postmaster General's Passage goes back over entry point as muddy climbs into narrow rift emerging 4.5m down 1st pitch and having connection with aven in Vulcan Rifts. Up-river passage lowers beyond duck and after 120m, past short low inlet on left, Top Sump is met. This is 76m long and is followed by 37m of low, wide going to a further sump. After 33m it is possible to surface in Alf's Airbell. The main upstream sump is choked after 6m, very close to the choke in Goyden Sump 7, but a low bedding to the right links through to Goyden Pot via a sump.

Downstream Passages

Downstream from foot of 2nd pitch, river passage turns right and Main Inlet continues straight ahead at this corner to a sump; this has been dived for 25m, reaching 3m depth, at the foot of a rift beneath poised flakes, where an excessively tight passage led off. Dry Wath Inlet is a narrow fissure entering left wall 20m downstream from Main Inlet and can be followed as traverse and crawls to foot of 12m aven, former pitch from original Dry Wath entrance with short high level passages above. Middle Sump is soon encountered by continuing down river but large mud slope on left before sump and route up through boulders on right lead into The Planetarium, large chamber with inlet stream from Astronomers' Passage, steeply rising and becoming too low.

At lowest point of Planetarium (SE corner) is climb down boulders into a tunnel which increases in size past an opening in the left wall and ends at the Downstream Sump. Upstream of the sump leads to the lower end of Middle Sump, 12m long and not free-diveable as it is fairly deep and contains a squeeze.

Downstream Sumps

Downstream, Sump 1 is 37m long in a roomy passage to a large airbell. Sump 2 is also roomy but route finding is awkward, and right wall is followed from airbell. After 64m, sump ends and 110m of large river passage ensues, ending at Sump 3, 24m to a large airbell. Sump 4 follows immediately, 55m long to a short section of passage with a dry side passage 30m long, ending in a choke one way and a sump – possibly connected with Sump 4 – in the other direction. Sump 5 is 24m long to more river passage, ending after about 90m at Sump 6, only 9m to 70m of passage with a parallel passage on the left. The passage lowers to Sump 7, 110m long to an airbell and flooded pot. The way on is part way down this, and Sump 8 doubles back beneath the airbell, entering a large underwater passage after about 40m. The present limit of exploration is where a slope of shingle rises up to the roof, about 1200m from the upstream limit in Nidd Head NW rising.

Hardy Pools Passage

From NE corner of Planetarium a short passage drops into Hardy Pools Passage. Right leads down climb and eventually enters tunnel leading from Planetarium to Downstream Sump. Left along Hardy Pools Passage leads past two steeply rising rifts which both end in blind avens, through the Hardy Pools to a 4.3m pitch with a 9m sump at the foot. At the other side a climb is followed by a short passage ascending to two choked muddy chambers. Down rift before chambers a squeeze leads to a low bedding plane with sumps in both directions. Upstream sump is too tight after 3m; downstream sump has been dived for 6m to a large hole in the floor, choked with shingle at the foot.

Tackle

Pitch	Ladder	Belay	Lifeline
1st	15m	12m	20m
2nd	12m	3m	15m

Permission and flood risk check – as Goyden Pot.

NIDD HEAD NW RISING   NGR SE 104731   Grade III
Alt. 160m   Length 700m
Extended, 1961/62, CDG; 1973, ULSA; 1980/82, CDG.

WARNING – Liable to severe flooding.

MdL. Entrance immediately below road 400m SE of Lofthouse. Major resurgence of the Nidd, forming part of the Goyden drainage system. Obvious large entrance is joined a few metres in by crawl from smaller entrance to left, then wading in 1.5m deep water to junction. Turn right and leaving first passage on left, which is oxbow, take second left into wide chamber with Main Rising at far side. This has been dived but found impenetrable. Continuing past second left, passage leads to hole up into roomy chamber which connects across to chamber at Main Rising by way of a bouldery crawl. Against right wall of dry chamber two holes drop back to water. One is dead end but other, nearest entry point, is long duck into further dry chamber with branch to left connecting with bouldery crawl near Main Rising by way of wet crawl. To right of 2nd dry chamber is 1st Sump, 12m, followed by 20m passage to Sump 2, dived for 550m. There is an airbell off to the left after about 100m, and after another 75m the Dog's Front Door, at 3m depth, drops into a large passage, frequently at 15m depth, which has been followed for 375m and continues. The end is about 1200m from the downstream limit in New Goyden.

From junction in entrance passage, straight on then left, crawling below and to left of large poised blocks leads through several sizeable dry chambers and short wet crawls to Tributary Rising, where water emerges from tight flooded bedding plane.

NIDD HEAD SE RISING   NGR SE 105730   Grade I
Alt. 159m   **Length 250m**
Extended 1960, 1985, CDG.
WARNING – Liable to severe flooding.

MdL. Entrance 120m SE of NW Rising. Another major resurgence for the Goyden system, but with only a few metres of passage accessible to non-divers. T-junction is met immediately inside entrance. Left is Sump 1, 33m to 10m of passage and a Sump 2, 10m long to dangerously poised boulders. There is an airbell through a sump off to the left between Sumps 1 and 2, and an airbell to the left in Sump 2.

Right from the T-junction is Outer Chamber, with 6m sump to Backwater Chamber. A further sump has been followed from the far side of the chamber. It divides after about 80m, right choking after 30m and left heading W, past a sandbank after 10m to end at crossjoints 30m further on. Right over the sandbank is continuing sump with good water flow, followed for 30m, at which point a squeeze up boulders for 2m enters a low bedding plane. The sump has not been followed past this point.

OXBOW CAVE   NGR SE 090736   Grade I
Alt. 200m   **Length 25m**

Entrance on 12m wide ledge on N side of How Stean Gorge, 75m downstream from Hazel Close Cave. Passage to right re-emerges into gorge. Crawl to left under large block opens into passage which ends in small earth-filled tubes.

STEAN BRIDGE CAVE   NGR SE 088736   Grade II
Alt. 205m   **Length 14m**
Extended 1970, YURT.

On SW side of How Stean Gorge immediately adjoining upstream side of footbridge, on path from Middlesmoor to Stean. Behind block 2.5m down face of gorge is lower entrance from which tortuous dry crawl continues to very low bedding plane where daylight is visible just ahead. On surface nearby is short roomy through cave.

TOM TAYLOR'S CAVE   NGR SE 093735   Grade I
[Cat Hole]
Alt. 190m
Length 180m   **Depth 15m**
Entrances in shakehole 30m E of Eglin's Hole. Lower entrance on N side of How Stean Gorge behind path between two foot-bridges. Roomy through

cave associated with Eglin's/Low Eglin's system. From lower entrance, roomy passage to fence where climb of 2m up on left followed by similar climb into Roof Bedding, crawl 20m long which emerges through hole beneath railway sleepers in field. From fence wooden steps down over stream outlet give access to high fissure with the lower passage accessible from near water level in gorge. Canyon passage continues to chamber, The Steeple, where route divides. Both ways lead to surface in a few metres. Left-hand passage can be followed as unroofed trench on surface to small entrance with short crawl leading to two small blockfall chambers, flood overflows for Eglin's Hole. Right-hand passage emerges and short upper passage on right chokes beneath small cave over wall.

Permission – How Stean Cottage, Lofthouse.

TUFA RIFT   NGR SE 092734   Grade II
Alt. 180m   **Length 25m**
Explored 1970, YURT.

On easily accessible ledge halfway down side of How Stean Gorge, 45m downstream of How Stean Tunnel. Narrow fissure passage, mostly crawling, terminates at choke of earth and boulders.

Permission – How Stean Cottage, Lofthouse.

WATERFALL CAVE   NGR SE 088739   Grade II
Alt. 210m   **Length 67m**

Entrance beneath small waterfall among fallen limestone blocks, 30m downstream of Cliff Wood Sink, on W side of How Stean Beck. Narrow crawl into wider passage. Inlet on left too tight after 8m. Main water comes from right where wallow through damp tube is followed by crawling past 3m aven on to perforated chert floor. Passage abruptly lowers and widens and route onwards is blocked by thick chert.

WHIT BECK CAVE   NGR SE 096733   Grade I
Alt. 170m   **Length 17m**

Entrance 2.5m up in S side of gorge halfway between How Stean Cottage and road bridge. Stream falls into gorge from narrow passage, becoming lower. Crawl opens into small chamber with waterfall. Immediately upstream passage ends at low bedding blocked with chert.

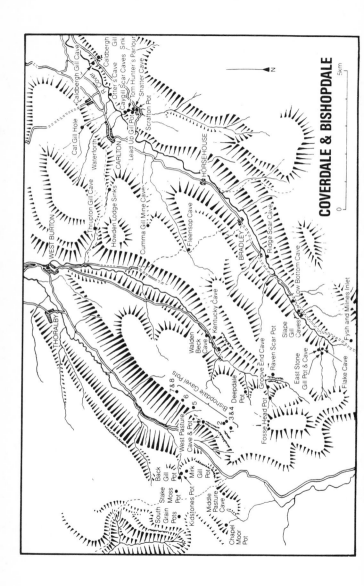

COVERDALE & BISHOPDALE

N

0   5km

Caldbergh Gill Cave
Caldbergh Gill
Otter's Cave
Cat Gill Hole
Cavgill Scar Caves Sink
Lead Up Gill Pot
Tom Hunter's Parlour
Waterforth
Shatter Cave
WEST BURTON
CARLTON
Scrafton Pot
Trupton Gill Cave
Howden Lodge Sinks
Cumma Gill Mine Cave
HORSEHOUSE
Fleensop Cave
THORALBY
BRADLEY
Ridge Scar Cave
Walden Beck Cave
Low Bottom Cave
Kentucky Cave
Fysh and Mines Inlet
Slape Gill Caves
Groove End Cave
Raven Scar Pot
Deepdale Pot
East Stone Gill Pot & Cave
Fosse Head Pot
Flake Cave
Bishopdale Gavel Pots
7 & 8
6
5
West Pasture Cave & Pot
2
3 & 4
1
Back Gill Pot
Mirk Gill Pot
South Stake Moss Pots
Slake Moss Pot
Kidstones Pot
Middle Pasture Cave
Chapel Moor Pot

COVERDALE AND BISHOPDALE

BACK GILL POT NGR SD 943822 **Grade II**
Alt. 500m Depth 6m

UnL. Narrow fissure close to stream is choked by rocks but water can be heard below.

Tackle – 6m ladder; stake and sling belay; 9m lifeline.

BISHOPDALE GAVEL POTS **Grade II**
1 and 2 explored 1930, NCFC; 3, 4 and 6 explored 1934, YRC.

ML. The pots lie on a long, rather featureless bench on the SE side of Bishopdale. They are well spaced out and difficult to locate.

1. NGR SD 961803 Alt. 535m Depth 23m
Cross-shaped shaft with hawthorn tree. Small stream sinks at S end and scramble down N end leads to pitch. Behind ladder at bottom is 9m deep rift choked at the foot.

Tackle – 8m ladder; sling belay; 15m lifeline.

2. NGR SD 962805 Alt. 535m Depth 23m
Square shaft in large, dry depression is first pitch. At bottom is 6m scramble down fissure to two separate rift pitches which are choked.

Tackle

Pitch	Ladder	Belay	Lifeline
1st	8m	9m	15m
Rifts	8m	Sling	11m

3. NGR SD 963805 Alt. 535m Depth 27m
In small depression where stream sinks is 3m climb down to 4.5m crawl in stream. A 2m descent into pool is followed immediately by a very fine pitch at the foot of which the water sinks in a narrow rift among boulders.

Tackle – 23m ladder; 6m belay; 30m lifeline.

4. NGR SD 963805 Alt. 535m Depth 27m
In same depression as 3 is 3m climb down to head of pitch which is choked at foot.

Tackle – 30m ladder; stake and sling belay; 30m lifeline.

5. NGR SD 968816 Alt. 517m Depth 11m
Choked double pitch beyond watercourse through gap in bench.

Tackle – 12m ladder; stake and sling belay; 15m lifeline.

6. NGR SD 970820 Alt. 510m Depth 30m
An 18m deep shakehole with scramble down at W end. Three shafts on SW side:

Right hand. Climb down 2.5m to narrow fissure opening into rounded chamber where water runs into tight rift.

Centre. Belay to pillar on left for shaft into fissure 1m wide and 15m high. Fissure ends in a high, fluted chamber with sump on left and inlet from right hand shaft on right.

Tackle – 8m ladder; sling belay; 15m lifeline.

Left hand. Shaft filled with chockstones connects with centre shaft at foot of pitch.

7. NGR SD 971822   **Alt 500m**   **Depth 12m**
   Single choked pitch in rocky depression with stream sink.

Tackle – 15m ladder; 6m belay; 25m lifeline.

8. NGR SD 971822   **Alt. 500m**   **Depth 9m**
   Two shafts in same depression as 7, the first being a scramble down boulders to a high, fluted chamber, choked at the bottom. To left of this hole a short passage leads to a pitch into a fine chamber with choked fissures leading off.

Tackle – 8m ladder; 6m belay; 15m lifeline.

CALDBERGH GILL CAVE   NGR SE 091853   Grade I
Alt. 185m   **Length 73m**
Extended 1975 and 1977, CDG and UWFRA.

MdL. Resurgence cave on W side of gill where gorge opens out several hundred metres below road bridge. Dry entrance into upstream crawl past two fallen blocks to sharp bend and Sump 1, with unuseable airspace. A 0.6m dive in a low, silty slot emerges in a low airspace canal ending after 30m at Sump 2. This is 9m long with an airbell half way, but should not be free-dived as it is low and heavily silted with a double bend. At the far side a short stretch of decorated joint passage degenerates into a further canal crawl, and after 9m Sump 3 is reached. This has been dived to a chert obstruction after 3m.

CALDBERGH GILL SINK   NGR SE 092852   Grade I
Alt. 195m   **Length 9m**

MdL. Large open joint in E bank of gill, below waterfall just upstream of road bridge, ends at partial blockage beyond which the way on can be seen to continue as a tight rift.

   Just downstream is a smaller joint enterable for a short distance, with an impassable connection with the main sink.

CAT GILL HOLE   NGR SE 067856   Grade I
Alt. 320m   **Depth 5m**

ML. Entrance 232m upstream from moor wall. Where small stream from E sinks in Cat Gill is tight squeeze between boulders into climbable, irregular fissure.

CAYGILL SCAR CAVES   NGR SE 074840   Grade I
Alt. 220m

MdL. In gorge of Lead Up Gill 0.8km downstream of West Scrafton are several obvious entrances to short dry caves with two through trips, the longest being 9m. Large entrance at head of gorge is Tom Hunter's Parlour (described elsewhere).

CHAPEL MOOR POT   NGR SD 927805   Grade II
Alt. 520m   **Depth 8m**
Explored 1976, YURT.

UnL. About 1.2km SW of Stake Moss track, and about 30m NE of scar below sink. Tight entrance to choked shaft with water running across floor and sinking in boulders. Probable resurgence close by.

Tackle – 9m ladder; stake and sling belay; 12m lifeline.

CUMMA GILL MINE CAVE   NGR SE 031832   Grade I
Alt. 370m   **Length 12m**

ML. At head of Turn Beck, below small scar on SW side of Cumma Gill, is mine level about 20m long to dead end. Hole in floor below rise near entrance enters sandy crawl in phreatic tube, choked below mine level and ending at sumped joints in the other direction. Partly widened by miners. Permission – Fleensop House.

DEEPDALE POT   NGR SD 973798   Grade II
Alt. 500m   **Depth 9m**

ML. Sink on N side of Deepdale. Roomy shaft is choked at foot.

Tackle – 11m ladder; 1.5m belay; 15m lifeline.

EAST STONE GILL CAVE   NGR SE 988772   Grade I
Alt. 475m   **Length 29m**
Explored 1968, YURT.

ML. Resurgence near head of gorge. Water emerges from several fissures leading to interconnecting cross rifts. Upstream is collapse chamber and downstream a short, dry crawl enters two blockfall chambers with an exit to the gorge at the top of an earth slope.

EAST STONE GILL POT   NGR SE 987771   Grade II
Alt. 490m   **Length 30m**   **Depth 6.7m**
Explored 1969, UWFRA.

ML. Stream bed above gorge is normally dry. Just downstream of sink is 3m climbable pot on S bank. At foot is slide into passage which enters cross rift. Stream enters from excessively tight passage ahead and flows through squeeze to right. Crawl downstream on chert floor leads to 1.5m waterfall into constricted rift sump. Water emerges at East Stone Gill Cave.

FLAKE CAVE   NGR SE 988772   Grade I
Alt. 475m   **Length 9m**

ML. At top of boulder pile downstream and on opposite side of gorge to East Stone Gill Cave is slope down into crawl which becomes too low.

FLEENSOP CAVE   NGR SE 023818   Grade I
Alt. 410m   **Length 4.5m**
Explored 1968, YURT.

ML. Where bridle track crosses Fleemis Gill is sink in pool below waterfall. Small hole on SE bank drops into roomy passage blocked by mud. Permission – Fleensop House.

FOSSE HEAD POT   NGR SD 972789   Grade II
Alt. 520m   **Length 40m**   **Depth 18m**

ML. Entrance above stream in small gorge at head of waterfall in Fosse Gill, on N bank of beck. Crawl to boulder and hole into cross rift. This is choked ahead but to the right the passage floor suddenly ends at the head of a fine, free-hanging pitch. At the bottom a fissure leads off and degenerates to a low airspace over liquid mud.

Tackle – 20m ladder; bar and sling belay; 25m lifeline.

FYSH AND MILNES INLET   NGR SD 992759   Grade II
Alt. 495m   **Length 13m**
Explored 1987, CPC.

ML. Entrance is stream sink in 2m deep rectangular shaft. Dry bedding to N is too low after 3m and crawl downstream is blocked after 5m. Inlet at S end has been followed for 6m and continues.

GROOVE END CAVE   NGR SD 974790   Grade I
Alt. 440m   **Length 168m**
Extended 1970, YURT.

UnL. Two entrances on S side of Fosse Gill 400m above junction with Walden Beck. Stream falls out of Backhouse Passage which is short and roomy to exit squeeze over boulders. Main entrance 11m W of exit leads down boulders into attractive upstream passage eventually ending at a very small sump. Crawl on right 25m from entrance ends at very low bedding plane where daylight is visible.

HOWDEN LODGE SINKS   NGR SE 045847   Grade I
Alt. 390m

ML. A number of small holes in twin dry valleys near the head of Howden Gill, W of Carlton.

1. Length 8m
Hole near rubbish tip in grassy dry gill drops into crawl to a mass of rusty iron and broken glass which extends to the right and chokes any possible continuation.

2. Length 4.5m

Short cave on S bank of southern gill, above a small gorge. Crawl into small chamber with no way on.

3. Length 8m

In southern gill is narrow fissure in middle of last waterfall (normally dry). Tight downward slope to narrow cross rift; rope useful for return.

4. Depth 7m   **Grade II**

In S bank of southern gill is tight entrance, probably walled (please replace). Narrow, fluted pitch widens and chokes at bottom.

Tackle – 8m ladder; 4.5m belay; 12m lifeline.

KENTUCKY CAVE   NGR SD 992809   Grade II
Alt. 340m   **Length 45m**

Extended, Buxton Speleological Group.

MdL. Cave entrance beneath prominent fir tree on S side of road 0.4km before Kentucky House. Roomy boulder-strewn rift lowers to crawl which rounds several bends and becomes extremely narrow.

KIDSTONES POT   NGR SD 944821   Grade II
Alt. 495m   **Length 12m**   **Depth 8m**

UnL. Stream sink in narrow valley S of Back Gill. Pitch into large chamber with outlet passage blocked by large boulders.

Tackle – 8m ladder; stake and sling belay; 12m lifeline.

LEAD UP GILL POT   NGR SE 073838   Grade II
Alt. 240m   **Length 35m**   **Depth 15m**
WARNING – Floods severely.

MdL. On W bank of Gill about halfway between Scrafton Pot and Caygill Scar, 1.5m above stream, is 3.5m climb down through loose boulders to squeeze into large steeply descending rift passage ending in blank wall; on left is short bedding crawl into aven with good formations.

LOW BOTTOM CAVE   NGR SE 007782   Grade II
Alt. 340m   **Length 15m**

Explored 1970, YURT.

MdL. Next rising NE of Slape Gill Caves, some way further along scar, below bird cherry tree. Crawl steps up, turns right and becomes too low.

MIDDLE PASTURE CAVE   NGR SD 938806   Grade I
Alt. 480m   **Length 6m**

UnL. Conspicuous undercut in small scar to SW of Stake Moss track.

MIRK GILL POT   NGR SD 945819   Grade II
Alt. 500m   **Depth 6m**

UnL. Entrance in base of large double shakehole 100m N of stream sink. Slide down through boulders on to pitch with water disappearing into blind tube.

Tackle – 6m ladder; stake and sling belay; 9m lifeline.

OTTER'S CAVE   NGR SE 080846   Grade I
Alt. 185m   **Length 470m**
Extended 1974, 1985, CDG.

WARNING – The boulder chokes are unstable in places.

MdL. Resurgence on S bank of river just upstream of Thorow Gill. Easy walking for about 75m to Sump 1 in large chamber. Sump 1 is 4.5m dive to airbell; in far right hand corner of this is Sump 2, 125m long and about 4.5m deep in a passage 3.6m wide and 1.2m high. Large upstream passage with many formations including long straws ends at Sump 3, which is 4.5m long. More streamway is interrupted by the 6m long Sump 4 and ends at a boulder choke. Complicated route on left through choke leads to two further chambers with good formations, and further unstable choke .

RAVEN SCAR POT   NGR SD 980788   Grade II
Alt. 490m   **Depth 6m**

ML. Choked shaft near sink above scar at head of Waldendale.

Tackle – 8m ladder; stake and sling belay; 10m lifeline.

RIDGE SCAR CAVE   NGR SE 022791   Grade II
Alt. 285m   **Length 80m**
Explored 1962, BPC; extended 1968/76, YURT.

MdL. Three entrances in tree-covered scar opposite Woodale. Stream cascades from upstream passage which is a walk lowering to rift and squeeze to right into bedding. Slit up to higher bedding which drops back into streamway, ending too low but hole in left wall regains part of flow in fissures ending at choked sumps. Traverse left from entrance reaches short passage connecting other entrances.

SCRAFTON POT   NGR SE 073836   Grade III
Alt. 240m   **Length 900m**   **Depth 44m**
Explored 1964/68, CPC; extended 1986, Swaledale Fell Rescue Team.

WARNING – Floods as stream flows down entrance in wet weather.

MdL. Interesting and complex pot which drains to Otter's Cave; park down road to NE, not in village. Just downstream of road bridge is fissure in W side of small gorge, dropping to rift to left and 1st Pitch, belayed to bar. Fine free-hanging climb lands on massive boulder at junction. Alternative route is step (while lifelined) up to left at head of pitch through boulders into rift passage; step across 18m pitch into rift to 5m Alternative Pitch and then 2m climb down into Big Bedding Plane.

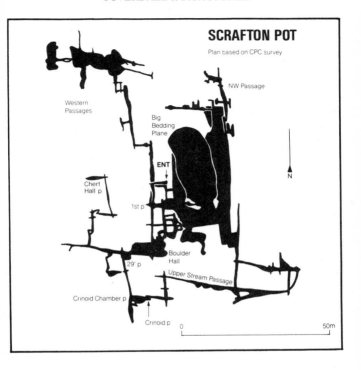

Opposite foot of 1st pitch ladder is high rift down into Boulder Hall and Main Stream Passage. leading down to Stream Corner, where narrow high level inlets enter, and continuing to 6m climb down into Chert Hall, a choked, sumped rift.

Right (NE) of foot of 1st Pitch a fissure leads past maze of passages connecting with Boulder Hall on right, to emerge in widening chamber, near start of which is 6m climb up on left to Western Passages. Beyond the climb main way rises into Five Ways Chamber; on right here is drop into blind chamber and on left is steep slope up into Big Bedding Plane, low chamber 12m wide and over 25m long, becoming too low.

At far end of Five Ways Chamber is passage to left leading through collapse blocks into North West Passage and pitch choked at foot; on left at head of pitch is series of interconnecting rifts with loose boulders. From blockfall other lower chambers can be reached, leading down through Cellar

Chamber to choked passage at same level as Chert Hall, the lowest points in the pot. Right from end of Five Ways Chamber passes Block Chamber and several routes emerge in the spacious Upper Stream Passage. To right of inlet aven the way contracts to Crinoid Pitch, followed by pitch into Crinoid Chamber, a blind rift. Traverse right above Crinoid Chamber Pitch gains small fissure and 29ft Pitch (8.8m) landing in Main Stream Passage upstream of Stream Corner. Traverse over pitch enters choked crawls.

Above climb into Western Passages the way leads past connection to a large chamber and high level link to 1st Pitch on left, then into high rift chamber. Several short passages lead off and water from aven inlets sinks in tight fissure.

Tackle

Pitch	Ladder	Belay	Lifeline
1st	20m	Bar and sling	25m
Alternative	5m	Sling	20m (for traverse and lifeline)
Crinoid	8m	Bar and sling	10m
Crinoid Chamber	8m	Bar and sling	10m
NW Passage	9m	Bar and sling	12m
29ft	9m	Bar and sling	12m

Permission – Secretary, West Scrafton Village Committee, Coverdale.

SHATTER CAVE   NGR SE 073836   Grade III
Alt. 240m   **Length 30m**   **Depth 7m**
Explored 1977, UWFRA.

WARNING – Beware of the many loose boulders.

MdL. A short distance downstream from Scrafton Pot is obvious climb up fissure in right bank of gill. Low crawl off to right quickly leads to head of short pitch into rift passage. Dangerous crawl off to left among loose blocks quickly chokes, while crawl straight ahead enters 6m wide chamber with water sinking through boulder floor. A 3m climb to a shelf gains access to a short choked crawl.

Tackle – 6m ladder; bar and spreader; 8m lifeline.

SLAPE GILL CAVES

MdL. Sinks downstream of road bridge, including cave 3, feed two caves in scar beside river Cover.

1. East Cave   **NGR SE 001778**   **Grade III**
Alt. 345m   **Length 320m**
Explored 1968, YURT.

Small resurgence 100m down valley from mouth of Slape Gill. Flat crawling in water to left turn into straight fissure which is followed by wallowing to a calcite-floored passage rising up on left. Sharp progress up this to The Lagoon, a static canal oxbow returning to the stream on far side of low section. More crawling and stooping to junction, where water enters from right out of tube ending in tight duck.

Left at junction along decorated crawl past long curtains and sharp bends to columns (care!) beyond which is squeeze and wriggle into cross rift entering Omega Chamber, 4.5m diameter and 1.5m high with inlet ending too low.

2. West Cave   **NGR SE 000777**   **Grade I**
Alt. 349m   **Length 105m**
Explored 1968, YURT.

Resurgence 30m up valley from mouth of Slape Gill. Single, joint-determined streamway of crawling size ends at partial choke of sandstone cobbles in low passage.

3.   **NGR SE 001777**   **Grade I**
Alt. 357m   **Length 16m**
Explored 1980, WRPC.

Small excavated entrance in W bank of Slape Gill, some 10m below the road bridge, leads to climb down boulder pile into rift passage. Small stream sinks into the boulders and cannot be followed. Upstream the passage gradually narrows to where further progress is impossible.

SOUTH GRAIN POTS   NGR SD 928820   Grade II
Alt. 577m

ML. Two pots in adjacent shakeholes which are wet weather stream sinks, 300m NE of South Grain Tarn.

1. Depth 14m
In side of easternmost shakehole, which is shallow and grassy, is pitch broken by boulder ledge and landing on shingle floor with no way out.

Tackle – 15m ladder; stake and sling belay; 20m lifeline.

2. Depth 4.5m
In deeper adjacent shakehole to W is scramble down boulders in choked fissure.

STAKE MOSS POT   NGR SD 938822   Grade II
Alt. 555m   **Depth 27m**
Explored 1970, CPC.

ML. In small, steep-sided shakehole 250m E of track. Pitch with unstable rocks in upper section opens into fine shaft with boulder floor.

Tackle – 30m ladder; stake and sling belay; 40m lifeline.

THRUPTON GILL CAVE   NGR SE 030851   Grade II
Alt. 410m   **Length 8m**
Explored 1979, MSG.

ML. At foot of small waterfall. Small entrance opens into 5m wide blockfall chamber with choked exits. All very loose.

TOM HUNTER'S PARLOUR   NGR SE 074840   Grade I
Alt. 220m   **Length 73m**
Extended CPC.

MdL. Large entrance in head of gorge 0.8km downstream of West Scrafton. Climb up into 8m long narrow crawl which opens into a roomy rift passage, ending in a choked inlet. On the left of the main rift are two small parallel rifts with connecting fissures.

WALDEN BECK CAVE   NGR SD 993812   Grade II
Alt. 305m   **Length 70m**
Explored 1969, YURT; extended 1974, Buxton Speleological Group.

SiL. Resurgence in NW bank of Walden Beck 300m NNE of Kentucky Cave. Crawl in water to sump, but passage on left leads through duck into hands and knees crawl to final collapse chamber. Sump is 3m long and a short crawl beyond leads to a second sump which becomes too low after 3m.

WATERFORTH   NGR SE 061850   Grade II
Alt. 335m   **Length 18m**
Explored 1966, MSG.

ML. Small entrance in boulders above obvious rising behind Carlton. Crawl into small chamber and scramble up through boulders into further small choked chambers.

WEST PASTURE CAVE   NGR SD 963813   Grade II
Alt. 490m   **Length 370m**
Explored 1972, CPC.

ML. Resurgence at foot of West Pasture Scar. Wet rift passage into higher section followed by passage of varying height with many chert ledges. Beyond collapse blocks is duck to wet crawls and sideways walking to aven and choke.

WEST PASTURE POT   NGR SD 963813   Grade II
Alt. 490m   **Depth 27m**
Explored 1972, CPC.

WARNING – Whole pot contains a mass of dangerously loose boulders, especially on 2nd pitch.

UnL. Water from West Pasture Cave sinks into a small rift, close to which a capped shaft drops down two pitches to end in joints, with the water entering on the right and sinking into the floor to reappear at the foot of Dale Head Scar directly below.

Tackle (both pitches together) – 40m ladder; stake and sling belay; 45m lifeline.

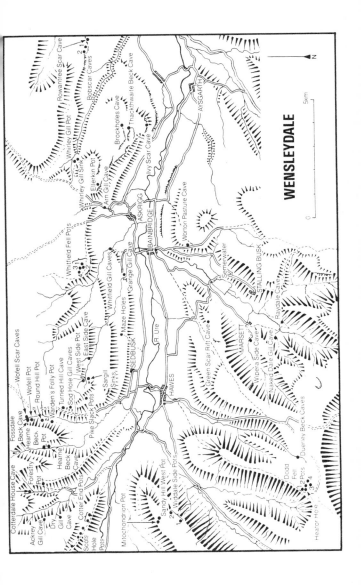

WENSLEYDALE

ACKREY GILL CAVE   NGR SD 820951   **Grade III**
Alt. 472m   **Length 240m**   **Depth 21m**
Explored 1961, NPC.

ML. Entrance shaft near sink of Ackrey Gill. Narrow pitch into linear stream passage, then mostly crawling to where daylight is seen at rising, but too tight to emerge.

Tackle – 20m ladder; stake and sling belay; 25m lifeline.

ARN GILL CAVE   NGR SD 952922   **Grade I**
Alt. 335m   **Length 6m**

MdL. Small resurgence cave in short gorge on W side of Askrigg-Healaugh road ends too low after damp going.

BOBSCAR CAVES   NGR SD 021929   **Grade II**
Extended 1970, CPC.

UnL. Two dissimilar caves in Bob Scar, NW of Castle Bolton.

1. Alt. 415m   **Length 75m**   **Depth 4.5m**
Entrance at head of bank close to fence which crosses scar, marked by remains of crashed aircraft. Square tunnel to blockfall and cross passage, choked both ways. Low crawl ahead leads past calcite slope, with choked upper and lower passages, to muddy choke with strong draught from nearby surface hole.

2. Alt. 415m   **Length 25m**   **Depth 5.5m**
Obvious entrance in scar 100m NW of 1. Muddy walk to climb down and further short walk to end in earth slope with small solution tubes.

BROCKHOLES CAVE   NGR SD 988914   **Grade II**
Alt. 410m   **Length 11m**
Explored 1977, M. Ridealgh & MSG.

ML. Follow valley above Thackthwaite Cave up to scar, in which is small cave entrance. Slide down to junction; ahead is pool and dead end, to left is bedding plane and impassable tube.

CAT SCAR CAVE   NGR SE 035940   Grade I
Alt. 360m   **Length 5m**

ML. On N side of Apedale Beck near Harker's Level is rift entrance in scar above sinks which take part of beck. Passage opens into small chamber with only an excessively tight fissure leading off.

(For location see Northern England map on front endpaper).

COTTERDALE HOUSE CAVE   NGR SD 831957 Grade I
Alt. 410m   **Length 70m**

ML. In gorge of East Gill, Cotterdale, on E bank and 8m above beck, may be walled up. Bouldery entrance chamber lowers to small upstream passage, passing two dry branches on left which end low and silted, before splitting into two inlets, ending too tight.

COTTER END POTS   NGR SD 821931   Grade I
Alt. 500m
Explored 1972, YURT.

ML. A series of small pots close to the bridle path along Cotter End on either side of slight depression.

1. Depth 4.5m
In small shakehole where path begins to descend into depression, almost due N of old railway tunnel on S side of dale. Wriggle under and over boulders into climbable mud-floored shaft.

2. Length 9m   **Depth 3m**
About 50m W of 1 in E side of larger rocky shakehole. Climb down into small fissure, too tight to S and mud choked to N.

3. Depth 3m
Beyond shallow valley, 150m W of 2. Straight fluted climb becoming narrow and choked.

DODD FELL POTS   Grade II
Explored 1975, NCC.

ML. A series of small pots high on SW slopes of Dodd Fell.

1. Alt. 585m   **NGR SD 831838**   **Length 6m**   **Depth 6m**
Sink about 100m N of Heator Hole. Tight rift becomes impossibly tight. No tackle needed.

2. Alt. 590m   **NGR SD 832837**   **Depth 6m**
In boggy area 50m E of Heator Hole. Straight shaft into boulder-strewn chamber. Small stream sinks through choked floor.

3. Alt. 587m   **NGR SD 832836**   **Depth 8m**
Close to two prominent sinks about 150m SE of Heator Hole. Tight shaft becomes excessively narrow.

4. Alt. 605m   **NGR SD 834837**   **Depth 4.5m**
Over wall from 3, about 90m NE. Small hole into a shattered chamber 4.5m square, with no passable outlet. No tackle needed.

Tackle for 2 and 3 – 8m ladder; stake and sling belay; 12m lifeline.

DRY GILL CAVE   NGR SD 822944   Grade III
Alt. 450m   **Length 90m**
Explored 1961/66, NPC.

ML. Entrance at rising of a tributary of Dry Gill. Low airspace crawl leading to higher but tight passages.

DUERLEY BECK CAVES   NGR SD 846843   Grade I
Alt. 560m

ML. In gorge near head of Duerley Beck.

Resurgence Cave   **Length 6m**
On S bank at foot of gorge. Crawl to where daylight enters from collapse chamber in shakehole.

Flood Sink Cave   **Length 9m**
On N side of usually dry stream bed a few metres upstream from the resurgence. Drop of 2.5m into stream passage which ends too tight.

EAST SIDE CAVE   NGR SD 888932   Grade II
[Jerry's Cave]
Alt. 520m   **Length 27m**
Explored 1967, ULSA.

ML. Entrance behind boulders in V-section valley E of West Side Pot. Low, wet crawl to a short step in the floor and a waterlogged passage. Water emerges only a short distance away.

ELLERKIN POT   NGR SD 965924   Grade III
Alt. 515m   **Length 6m**   **Depth 23m**
Explored 1984, YURT.

ML. In small shakehole at lowest point of large depression behind Ellerkin Scar. Short crawl leads to first drop of 3m onto ledge, followed by climb down to top of second drop of 2m. From foot of drop is choice of routes; 14m pitch choked at the bottom or exposed climb down separate fissure, rejoining main shaft 5m above the floor, which can be reached by a climb.

Second drop needs ladder due to lack of holds; easiest and safest to ladder the whole pot.

Tackle – 30m ladder; stake and sling belay; 40m lifeline.

FORESTRY POT   NGR SD 835951   Grade I
Alt. 460m   **Length 3.5m**   **Depth 4.5m**
Explored 1971, YURT.

ML. Stream sink in tributary of East Gill above forestry track 1.2km NNE of Cotterdale. Climbable descent into small unstable boulder chamber with excessively tight outlet.

FOSSDALE BECK CAVE   NGR SD 863955   Grade II
Alt. 460m   **Length 410m**
Explored 1972/75, MSG.

ML. Three entrances on W side of beck. Main Entrance, 4.5m above beck behind dry wall opposite Wofell Scar Caves 1 and 2, and Matins Entrance, 11m further S at same level, enter Upper Series, Tube Entrance near stream level by mouth of gorge enters Lower Series.

Upper Series
Main Entrance drops into walking-size passage. After 6m Pitch Passage is to left and to right is step across Blind Pitch – 5.5m deep and climbable – into Shuffle Inlet, tight rift to chamber with avens and impassable rift to daylight. Main streamway continues past avens and 20m inlet on right, entered by tight crawl and becoming too low, to Stalagmite Corner (care!). Passage lowers to crawl and becomes too low where stream runs through to Lower Streamway a short distance away.

Pitch Passage is easy crawl to head of pitch. Traverse across top to Matins Entrance and larger passage to Matins Chamber, ending choked. Pitch needs tackle and passage at foot ends in choked fissure beneath Matins Chamber; very low branch on left connects with Lower Series.

Tackle – 6m ladder; 1.5m belay; 10m lifeline.

Lower Series
Tube Entrance is crawl to complex area with short side passages. Main way to left enlarges, then muddy crawl past two avens ends at T-junction. Right is Lower Streamway, too low after 20m; left is climb up into Great Aven. Left from aven is passage ending too low after another aven. Rift passes Eyehole Aven to 2m drop. Traverse ahead gains crawl to West Aven, with inlet and dangerous boulder slope. Below drop is crawl to junction; left ends too low and right is squeeze over boulder into South Aven with awkward floor level squeeze into West Aven.

GRANGE GILL CAVE   NGR SD 924913   Grade II
Alt. 267m   **Length 40m**
Extended 1972, MSG.

HScL. Resurgence cave in N bank of Grange Gill, 300m downstream of Skell Gill hamlet. Immediately inside, entrance divides into two passages; right inlet a tight crawl ending in a loose chamber. Left inlet roomy to 1m waterfall, then closes to impenetrable bedding. On right below waterfall is squeeze at roof level into small bedding chamber.

GREEN SCAR RIFT CAVE   NGR SD 904878   Grade I
Alt. 495m   **Length 25m**   **Depth 8m**
Explored 1968, MSG.

UnL. Near NE end of plateau about 50m S of wall. Descending rift cave ending in a boulder ruckle. Other small caves nearby.

HEARNE BECK CAVE   NGR SD 850948   Grade III
Alt. 470m   Length 120m
Explored 1969/1976, MSG.

ML. Resurgence cave on E bank of Hearne Beck. Crawl into roomy chamber, then series of wet crawls and small chambers until stream emerges from impassable bedding. On left here is The Squirm – squeeze under boulder – into easy dry crawl to sandy chamber. Straight ahead is small passage to aven chamber, with impassable inlet and outlet rifts. To left in sandy chamber is low crawl to The Gurgle – an awkward duck – into easier passage and Shrimp Chamber with silted inlet sump.

HEARNE BECK POT   NGR SD 851950   Grade II
Alt. 490m   Length 45m   Depth 11m
Explored 1976, MSG.

ML. Follow stream from Hearne Beck Cave; pot is in large rocky shakehole next to small gorge. Drop (rope useful) into chamber, and low crawl to where daylight visible from gorge. Main route descends steep, narrow chute to short series of passages, with small stream entering and sinking into impassable fissure.

HEATOR HOLE   NGR SD 832838   Grade III
Alt. 587m   Length 90m   Depth 15m
Explored 1972, LUCC.

ML. At S end of line of shakeholes on W side of Dodd Fell. Entrance pitch has now collapsed at top. Tight section at bottom is followed immediately by 2m drop into streamway. About 90m of boring, muddy, formationless passage with some constrictions becomes too low soon after crawl over large block. Beside track 400m N is 3.5m choked pot.

Tackle – 8m ladder; stake and sling belay; 12m lifeline.

IVY SCAR CAVE   NGR SD 986904   Grade I
Alt. 330m   Length 14m

UnL. Obvious entrance in scar N of mine level lowers to crawl and then divides and becomes tight. Tube to left before crawl also emerges in face of scar. Other holes nearby are all mine workings.

KELDHEADS CAVE   NGR SE 075916   Grade IV
Alt. 270m   Length 610m
Extended 1970/73, MSG.

WARNING – Floods badly and easily sumps in places. Loose boulders are a hazard.

ML. Stream rises below small cliff E of road opposite ruined barns. Crawl for 12m to inlet splitting into three – left choked, right is an oxbow and ahead enters Inlet Chamber, loose and choked. Main crawl continues to collapse chambers linked by squeeze beside poised blocks, then down into bedding

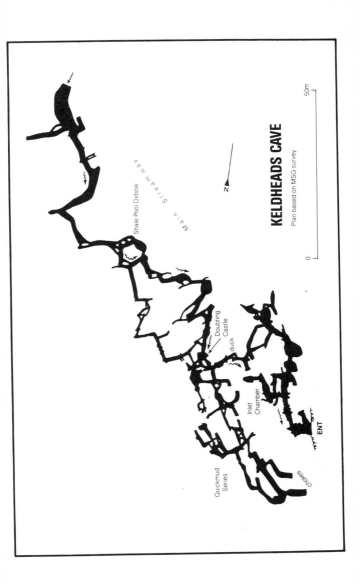

KELDHEADS CAVE

Plan based on MSG survey

N

0   50m

Main Streamway

Shale Pool Oxbow

Doubting Castle

duck

Inlet Chamber

Quickmud Series

ENT

CHOKES

with short branches; first two on left join at small aven where way on is wet
crawl to loose choke with tube on right to duck followed by small collapse
chamber and narrow arch—The Postern—into Doubting Castle—a roomier
chamber.

Main Streamway

Right from Doubting Castle wet, bouldery crawls lead upstream past
Shale Pool Oxbow. From stream route here series of crawls and wallows lead
back to rejoin just downstream of Doubting Castle. Main stream continues
as crawling to 2m step up into bedding and side passage, both too low.

Quickmud Series

By going left from either Doubting Castle through collapse chambers or
small chamber before The Postern, Quickmud Series is reached, an
unpleasant collection of low, wet crawls and collapse chambers. Further
reaches beyond constricted liquid mud duck are slightly larger and end in
chokes with tree roots, close to surface S of entrance.

Permission—Estate Office, Wensley.

(For location see Northern England map on front endpaper).

LADY ALGETHA'S CAVE   NGR SE 090911
Alt. 240m   Length 6m

ML. In scar 1.6km W of Leyburn. Small cave, was minor archaeological
site, has been destroyed by collapse of scar.

(For location see Northern England map on front endpaper).

MAZE HOLES   NGR SD 899915   Grade I
[Mease Hole]
Alt. 360m   Length 45m   Depth 9m

MdL. Follow old road E above Litherskew and after barn on right is open
field with sink to left. Entrance in shakehole next to sink drops into first
chamber, from end of which route spirals down left through two more
chambers into fourth chamber. Small window links first and fourth
chambers. In wet weather stream enters roof of fourth chamber and sinks in
gravel floor.

Permission—Mr E. Chapman, Litherskew.

MITOCHONDRION POT   NGR SD 821903   Grade II
Alt. 528m   Depth 9m
Excavated 1974, CPC.

ML. Fluted shaft 50m NW of Sandy Hill West Pot has choked bedding at
the foot.

Tackle—8m ladder; 0.6m belay; 12m lifeline.

NAKED DALE GILL CAVE

HwL. Single cave passage which is obstructed by cobbles, preventing a
through trip.

Upper Cave   NGR SD 896849   Grade II
Alt. 300m   **Length 64m**   **Depth 6m**
Explored 1978, YURT.

Entrance on N side of beck just below moor wall, near Startling Fall. Drop of 3.5m into small aven, followed by further aven, then hands and knees crawl, lowering to flat-out crawl over cobbles which becomes too low just short of the end of the lower cave.

Lower Cave   NGR SD 896850   Grade I
Alt. 290m   **Length 12m**
Explored 1976, YURT.

On N side of gill W of Raydale Grange is rising in small scar. Crawl to left bend and narrower crawl to collapse from surface. Passage beyond is too low, being part-filled with cobbles which have accumulated behind the collapse. Permission – Raydale Grange.

PIKE SLACK POTS   NGR SD 872930   Grade II
Alt. 525m   **Depth 9m**

ML. In Pike Slack, to S of stream sink. Two small narrow pots, choked at the bottom. Both require tackle.

Tackle – 9m ladder; stake and sling belay; 15m lifeline.

RAYDALE CAVE   NGR SD 904847   Grade I
Alt. 290m   **Length 6m**
Explored 1978, YURT.

HwL. Rising below track, 400m NE of Raydale House. Entrance over wall 1.5m up rock face. Low wet crawl which becomes tight after second bend.

ROUND HILL POT   NGR SD 862951   Grade II
Alt. 490m   **Length 20m**   **Depth 9m**
Explored 1968, MSG.

ML. In small shakehole on N side of obvious stream gully, in line of shakeholes about 800m S of Wofell Scar. Climb down 6m to tight squeeze into small chambers and rifts. Lifeline useful.

ROWANTREE SCAR CAVE   NGR SE 023928   Grade I
Alt. 390m   **Length 12m**

UnL. Small cave towards W end of scar has two entrances which link into a single fissure. Crawl leads to narrow section beyond which there appears to be a drop although it is very small.

SANDY HILL WEST POT   NGR SD 821903   Grade II
Alt. 528m   **Depth 12m**
Explored 1974, GC.

ML. Open shaft in a large irregular depression with tree, midway between Sandy Hill and Rooting Gill. Pitch enters a boulder-floored rift with secondary inlet fissures. A further 3m climb down at W end leads to choke and E end of rift narrows to tight squeeze to rift chamber with daylight entering.

Tackle – 9m ladder; 4.5m belay; 15m lifeline.

SARGILL SINKS   NGR SD 880931   Grade II
[**Sargill Head Sinks**]
Alt. 520m

1. Explored 1967, ULSA.   **Depth 8m**
   ML. In right bank of most northerly stream at Sargill Head. Very tight 4.5m shaft needing foot stirrup for return is succeeded by wriggle into narrow, shingle-choked parallel fissure.

2.   **Depth 6m**
   ML. Small fissure in side of large rocky shakehole S of the choked main sink at head of Sargill. Steep boulder slope ends at narrow drop, choked at foot.

Tackle – 8m ladder; stake and sling belay; 9m lifeline.

SCOTS HOLE POTS   Grade II
Nos. 1, 2, 4, 5 explored 1929, YRC; No. 3 explored 1972, YURT.

   ML. A series of small pots in a long line of shakeholes close to the old highway along Thwaite Bridge Common.

1. Alt. 491m   NGR SD 818932   Length 14m   Depth 8m
   Smal sink S of Cotter End Tarn. Passage from foot of pitch connects with fissure which becomes too tight in both directions.

2. Alt. 491m   NGR SD 817932   Length 18m   Depth 6m
   Double pot a few shakeholes W of 1. Larger shaft has awkward connection with smaller pot. Fissure leading off main pot enters parallel rift which closes in in both directions.

3. Alt. 488m   NGR SD 814935   Depth 6m
   On slight mound above the main line of shakeholes is a collapse through shale into a choked pitch.

4. Alt. 485m   NGR SD 811936   Depth 9m
   Open pot about 200m NW of large sink. Fluted pitch onto boulder floor which descends steeply to a choke.

5. Alt. 484m   NGR SD 809937   Depth 4.5m
   Small choked pitch on SE side of wall running down fell.

6. Alt. 473m   NGR SD 807939   Depth 8.2m
   Pitch concealed under rocks in small shakehole SE of stream sink. Narrow rift choked with boulders at foot.

Tackle (all pots) – 10m ladder; stake and sling belay; 15m lifeline.

SOD HOLE GILL CAVES   Grade II
   ML. Caves appear to be remnants of old phreatic network and are reached by following gully E of Buttertubs road up past 4.5m long boulder-choked resurgence to line of shakeholes containing caves.

1. Alt. 528m   NGR SD 868937   Length 80m   Depth 11m
Explored 1958, NPC.

Fissure in shakehole 400m S of gully narrows to descending rift, then over mud bank into larger chamber with choked galleries on both sides. Over boulders is traverse to clay choke and left of boulders is entry to clay-choked rift.

2. Alt. 525m   NGR SD 868938   Length 90m   Depth 10m
Explored 1958, NPC.

In large, deep shakehole 150m N of 1 is hole under small cliff dropping into small chamber. Descend boulders into chamber with 3m deep choked pot. Muddy passage to S leads past choked branches to boulder choke. Crawling over boulders to N reaches large collapse with small muddy inlet to left ending at a fall.

3. Alt. 525m   NGR SD 868939   Length 207m   Depth 14.5m
Explored 1958, NPC.

Two entrances, needing tackle, 27m apart in shakeholes 250m N of 1. Entrances are connected by straight bouldery passages with choked passages to E and four links to W into main rift, choked to N and with three ways choked to S. On W side of main rift is short loop and small stream runs into impassable rift. Main rift is up to 6m high, with narrow trench below 2.5m diameter phreatic tube.

Tackle – 6m ladder; 1.5m belay; 8m lifeline.

4. Alt. 520m   NGR SD 868940   Length 33m   Depth 10m
Explored 1967, ULSA.

Sink 30m S of gully. Boulder slope down into square tunnel with branch to right, both ending at collapses. Now blocked by collapse 12m from entrance.

5. Alt. 520m   NGR SD 868938   Length 15m   Depth 3.5m
Explored 1972, YURT.

Entrance in hollow just beyond lower end of long, rocky hollow S of 2. Slide into roomy passage with stalagmites in alcoves (care !). Roof lowers to boulder choke.

6. Alt. 525m   NGR SD 868936   Length 14m   Depth 4.5m
In line of small shakeholes 210m S of 5 is walk-down rift to choke.

7. Alt. 525m   NGR SD 868936   Length 8m   Depth 4.2m
Descent among blocks in small shakehole 30m S of 6 enters passage running E to boulder choke.

THACKTHWAITE BECK CAVE
NGR SD 987911   Grade III
Alt. 380m   Length 800m
Explored 1960, NPC.

UnL. Entrances on either side of fence above resurgence below Blue Scar are blocked at present. Fine linear stream cave with large chambers. Original entrance was via sharp, wet crawl on left, soon entering main passage. Right hand entrance was at foot of scree funnel and entered main passage directly.

Dry going for a short way to stream, flowing left into passage ending at fissures. Upstream walk becomes canal to blockfall chamber with wet bedding plane beyond leading to extensive collapse. When route-finding becomes difficult, best to keep right over slabs into stream and crawl forward into Stalactite Chamber, with good formations (care !).

Just upstream is start of massive collapse, avoided by rifts and 'duck' to right. Up into boulder chamber then descend to stream in crawl which enlarges to small blockfall. Up and over to right is canal to junction; right with stream or left over mound of boulders both enter first large boulder cavern, about 30m long, 15m wide and up to 8m high. Way on is through more gloomy halls until passage form is completely obscured by collapse. Complex routes at different levels become confusing and choke at about the same point; some are very muddy.

Permission – Estate Office, Wensley.

TURNED HILL CAVE   NGR SD 868942   Grade I
Alt. 505m   Length 8m   Depth 4.5m
Explored 1977, R.S.W. Gibson.

ML. In shakehole NW of obvious impenetrable rising by road. Squeeze down into little chamber with 5m aven and some formations.

WARDEN'S FOLLY POT   NGR SD 863947   Grade I
Alt. 435m   Depth 6m
Explored 1971, MSG.

UnL. Small stream sink on W side of valley about 30m above beck level opposite old mine tip. Climbable descent into choked rift chamber.

WEST SIDE POT   NGR SD 887933   Grade II
Alt. 520m   Length 55m   Depth 15m
Explored 1967, ULSA.

WARNING – Very loose boulders at entrance, now collapsed.

ML. In large, blind valley where three streams unite and sink. Climb down through grit boulders into clean limestone passage dropping quickly to a low crawl and high rift to a friable 3m climb. Comfortable flat-roofed passage lowers to a crawl into a 6m wide chamber floored by the terminal sump. Outlet too tight for diving 4.5m forward.

WHIRLEY GILL POT   NGR SD 972935   Grade III
Alt. 463m   Length 625m   Depth 29m
Explored 1959, NPC; extended 1966 and 1969, ULSA.

WARNING – Lower parts flood in wet weather.

ML. A fine example of a streamway controlled by impervious beds at the base of the Main Limestone. Entrance in large shakehole near Beldon Beck 350m NW of prominent sink. Pitch with boulder belay is succeeded by three short climbs down a rift into stream passage.

Upstream, two easy ducks gain roomy fissure and short, muddy inlet on

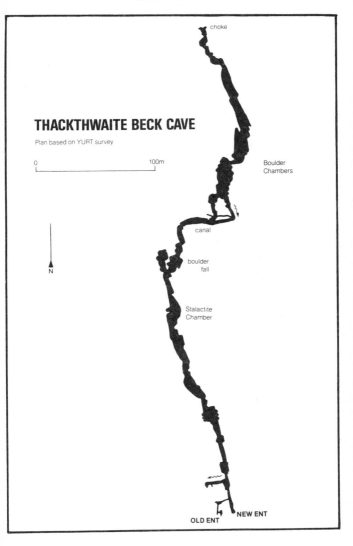

THACKTHWAITE BECK CAVE

Plan based on YURT survey

0   100m

N

choke

Boulder
Chambers

canal

boulder
fall

Stalactite
Chamber

OLD ENT   NEW ENT

left. Main way is canal with high level oxbows which unite into walking-size streamway before slowly contracting to a wet hands and knees crawl. At junction, right branch soon ends in calcite choke, while streamway becomes tortuous and silted up only 45m short of sink.

Main Cave
   Downstream, the cave changes abruptly to a wide bedding plane crawl giving awkward hands and knees progress from pool to pool. Just beyond a low oxbow on the right the bedding lowers and swings left at the top of an inclined series unique in Yorkshire. The water cascades down a wide bedding dipping at 15° and abandoned oxbow routes within the same bedding plane occur over a width of 18m. Similar oxbows bypass two shingle chokes in the stream and the series terminates in a third such choke. Water has been tested to Crackpot Cave.

Tackle – 8m ladder; 2m belay; 9m lifeline.

WHIRLEY GILL SINK   NGR SD 974933   Grade I
Alt. 465m   **Length 8m**
   ML. Prominent sink above Beldon Beck. Water sinks at base of 4.5m waterfall but entrance is on opposite side of rocky shakehole. Crawl over boulders into mud-choked bedding plane.

WHITFIELD FELL POTS   Grade II
Alt. 515m
Explored 1972, MSG.
   ML. A group of small pots about 3km NW of Askrigg.

1. NGR SD 926931   **Depth 9m**
   Small entrance in corner of shakehole near the back of the limestone bench. Tight shaft, 4.5m down which is step off ladder and squeeze into small blind chamber beneath the shakehole. Shaft is too tight below this level.

2. NGR SD 926931   **Depth 4.5m**
   In shallow shakehole SW of 1. Obvious open shaft dropping to a choked rift.

3. NGR SD 926934   **Depth 8m**
   Smaller of two stream sinks at rear of bench. After 2m drop is 5m shaft, tight at the top and narrowing down to an impenetrable choked fissure.

4. NGR SD 925934   **Depth 8m**
   The larger sink, a short way W of 3. Two holes in shakehole floor and one in the side all drop into a 9m long, roomy rift. Stream enters from boulder ruckle and sinks where rift suddenly becomes impassably narrow. Rift can be climbed via entrance in corner of shakehole floor, but a ladder is helpful.

Tackle (all pots) – 9m ladder; 6m belay; 15m lifeline.

WHITFIELD GILL CAVES   NGR SD 935921   Grade II
Alt. 290m

SiL. On opposite banks of Whitfield Gill 150m upstream of a small footbridge.

1. Length 24m. Explored 1968, Yoredale Limestone Group

On N bank of stream. Three entrances all link to low chamber with impassable inlets.

2. Length 8m

On S bank of stream. Tubular crawl to choke.

WIDDALE SIDE POTS   Grade II
1. Alt. 555m   **NGR SD 819891**   **Depth 8m**

ML. Obvious sink close to scar on edge of Widdale Fell. Climbable descent with stream to where water flows away between large collapsed blocks.

2. Alt. 565m   **NGR SD 822895**   **Depth 6m**

ML. Entrance in shallow shakehole, with limestone blocks, near edge of Western End Crag, SE of large depression with sink. Tight opening to pitch into choked rift.

Tackle – 6m ladder; 3m belay; 9m lifeline.

WIPERA SIDE CAVE   NGR SD 895861   Grade I
Alt. 295m   **Length 12m**

HwL. Three entrances in small cliff where Bardale widens out, 800m W of Marsett. Middle entrance is stream outlet from chamber with ways out to left via tubular crawl and to right through squeeze over boulders.

WOFELL POT   NGR SD 863955   Grade II
Alt. 480m   **Length 36m**   **Depth 9m**

Explored 1972, MSG.

ML. On W side of Fossdale, just S of Wofell Scar, in rocky gully. Entrance where stream sinks is awkward 6m climb (rope useful) with many loose rocks. Entrance pitch drops into chamber and stream sink becomes too tight, but large inlet passage with oxbow on left ends in silt choke.

WOFELL SCAR CAVES   NGR SD 863955   Grade I
Alt. 460m

ML. In gorge of Fossdale Beck, on E bank of stream.

Explored 1972, MSG.

1. Length 14m

Small entrance at foot of cliff. Narrow crawl to junction; right passage too tight; left passage narrow crawl to choke.

2. Length 6m

Just N of 1, and 2.5m higher up rock face. Obvious entrance, low crawling becoming too low after left bend.

3. Length 9m

About 50m further N; obvious resurgence cave. Hands and knees crawl turning left and becoming too tight, with narrow aven on right. The cave stream is fed by sinks in the side of the beck a few metres away.

WORTON PASTURE CAVE   NGR SD 935886   Grade II
Alt. 360m   **Length 55m**
Explored 1976, South West Essex Technical College CC.

MdL. Entrance near E side of Bainbridge to Carpley Green road is obvious alcove in low scar. At foot of alcove is tight squeeze into low bedding passage, closing down after a pool. Several short side passages, all crawling.

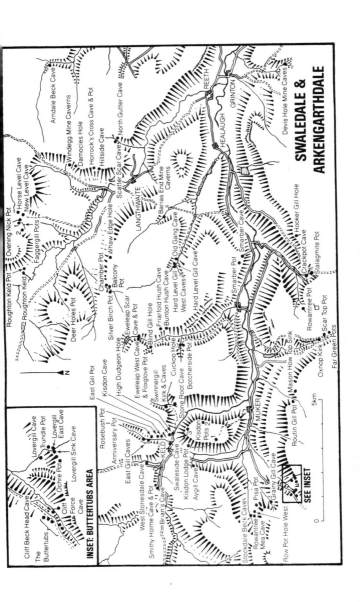

SWALEDALE & ARKENGARTHDALE

INSET: BUTTERTUBS AREA

N

0   5km

SEE INSET

Arndale Beck Cave
Windegg Mine Caverns
Damocles Hole
Horrock's Cross Cave & Pot
Hillside Cave
Scatter Scar Cave
North Gutter Cave

REETH
HEALAUGH
GRINTON

Devis Hole Mine Caves

Horse Level Cave
Ovening Nick Pot
New Level Cave
Roughton Keld Pot
Roughton Keld
Faggergill Pots

Deer Holes Pot
Chamber Pot
Whaw Edge Hole
Silver Birch Cave
Balcony Pot
Eweleap Scar Cave & Pot
Blind Hole

LANGTHWAITE
Barras End Mine Caverns

Smarber Cave
Crackpot Cave
Hooker Gill Hole
Stalagmite Pot

East Gill Pot
Kisdon Cave
High Dudgeon Hole
Eweleap West Cave
& Foxglove Pot
Swinnergill
Kirk & Caves
Cuckoo Hole
Stone Root Cave
Botcherside Pot

Friarfold Hush Cave
Bunton Hush Cave
Hard Level Gill
West Caves
Hard Level Gill Cave
Old Gang Cave

Smarber Pot
Rowantree Pot
Scar Top Pot
Far Green Pots

Rosebush Pot
Anniversary Pot
East Gill Caves
Smithy Holme Cave & Pot
West Stonesdale Cave
Brian's Cave
Swaleside Cave
Kisdon Lodge Pot
Aygill Cave

KELD

Kisdon
Pots

MUKER

Oxnop Kirk
Routin Gill Pot
Mason How Top Sink

Stockdale Beck Caves
Rowantree
Mea Cave
Pisa Pot
Row Pot Hole West
Granny Gill Cave

INSET: BUTTERTUBS AREA

Cliff Beck Head Cave
The Buttertubs
Cliff Force Cave
Ochre Cave
Lovergill Sink Cave
Lovergill Cave
Trundle Pot
Lovergill East Cave

SWALEDALE & ARKENGARTHDALE

ANNIVERSARY POT NGR NY 898016 Grade II
Alt. 405m Length 12m Depth 12m
Explored 1987, MSG/Haymarket Caving Club.

ML. In shakehole 40m N of gate in second wall from barn. Squeeze and series of climbable descents to blind rift with tiny eyehole into deeper shaft.

ARNDALE BECK CAVE NGR NZ 053059 Grade I
Alt. 350m Length 6m
ML. At foot of cliff on S side of beck. Crawl becoming too tight.

AYGILL CAVE NGR NY 886002 Grade II
Alt. 370m Length 67m
ML. Follow Aygill up from road to entrance on S side of stream. First 9m of cave has been removed by quarrying. Bedding crawl to junction. Right is narrow crawl to 3.5m climb up to exit in gorge. Left is main upstream passage, crawl in muddy canal to small chamber, then lowering crawl ending in two inlets, both too low.

BALCONY POT NGR NY 961037 Grade I
Alt. 465m Length 4.5m Depth 9m
Explored 1969, MSG.

ML. On E side of gorge, opposite and a few metres downstream of Silver Birch Pot. Obvious cave entrance in cliff 3.5m above silted flood sink. Crawl 4.5m to squeeze onto head of 9m climbable pitch which ends in choked fissures.

BARRAS END MINE CAVERNS NGR NY 988012
Alt. 420m Length 1km
ML. A series of caverns intersected by Barras End High Level (also known as Reform Level) about 1.2km from the adit entrance. Collapse of mine workings has thwarted attempts to regain access.

BLIND GILL HOLE
NGR NY 934019   **Grade II**
Alt. 470m   **Length 28m**   **Depth 11m**
Explored 1968, MSG.

ML. Right at first fork up Blind Gill is entrance on E bank below small waterfall, dropping into chamber. Left becomes too tight, right is climbable 4.5m blind pitch. Straight ahead over boulder is tight, descending rift to rift chamber with daylight entering in roof from smaller entrance, which would require a ladder.

BOTCHERSIDE POT
NGR NY 935005   **Grade I**
Alt. 450m   **Depth 6.5m**
Explored 1970, MSG.

ML. Narrow, fluted shaft in small shakehole adjacent to S side of track. Climbable blind pitch.

BRIAN'S CAVE
NGR NY 876016   **Grade I**
Alt. 350m   **Length 9m**

ML. Small fissure above and to left of impenetrable rising enters higher rift leading through boulders into aven with joint inlet.

BUNTON HUSH CAVE
NGR NY 942012   **Grade I**
Alt. 480m   **Length 9m**

ML. In S wall of hush on E side of Gunnerside Gill, behind ruined building and Bunting (or Bunton) Level. Small, dry cave ending in unstable draughting choke.

THE BUTTERTUBS
NGR SD 875961   **Grade II**
Alt. 480m   **Depths to 25m**

ML. Several pots on either side of road, with no horizontal passages. Main pot, next to road, takes small stream and has short 2nd pitch (climbable) to choke where running water can be heard. Same tackle for each hole.

Tackle – 20m ladder; 6m belay; 30m lifeline.

CHAMBER POT
NGR NY 961037   **Grade II**
[Stones Pot]
Alt. 465m   **Length 25m**   **Depth 11m**
Explored 1969, MSG.

ML. At foot of gorge of Little Punchard Gill, up E bank of stream behind ruined mine building. Large shakehole with small cave entering roomy chamber, On right a large rift drops to a choke; on left, window onto blind wet pitch needing tackle.

Tackle – 9m ladder; 3m belay; 12m lifeline.

CLIFF BECK HEAD CAVE   NGR SD 874960   Grade II
Alt. 450m   **Length 135m**
Extended 1967, MSG.

ML. Resurgence cave for The Buttertubs, in valley bottom below pots. Two passages inside entrance arch. Left is roomy, with inlet on right from sump, then lowers to very wet crawl with duck and ends in a higher section with roof inlets. Right passage in small stream has some tight sections. Dry oxbow on left by-passes impassable section of streamway, then squeeze over boulder and wet crawl lead to 3m high aven, at foot of which stream issues from low bedding becoming too tight.

CLIFF FORCE CAVE   NGR SD 875960   Grade III
Alt. 445m   **Length 2km**
Entrance series explored 1962, NPC; main exploration 1976/77, MSG; extended 1980, CPC.

WARNING – Entrance shaft is now unstable. Crawl into Fault Hall rapidly becomes impassable in flood and most of the cave downstream of Fault Hall appears to be affected by floodwater ponded up in severe conditions. Some areas are unstable, notably Shower Chamber series and the vicinity of The Room of Dangling Doom.

ML. Entrance shaft at foot of cliff above rising opposite The Buttertubs.

Entrance Series
Easy, narrow climb down shaft into bouldery chamber. Left passage is muddy crawl to choked aven; ahead is crawl which becomes too low and main route is walking passage to right. Beyond jammed boulder a crawl lowers to an impassably tight sump; left above boulder is Overflow Passage, mostly muddy crawling for 30m before opening into small chamber with boulder floor. Straight ahead is crawl to climb up through ruckle into Shower Chamber and high level passages and avens.

Main way is 2m climb down to left, then skirting base of boulder fall a larger passage is reached. This ends at a drop into the Ducking Pond – duck under or scramble over rock bridge to regain higher passage above mud wall. Two routes lead into bedding chamber and at junctions ahead keep right through complex area until streamway is reached.

Main Streamway
Roomy, muddy passage with boulder obstacles and occasional oxbows lowers to crawl after ending at boulders. Just before these is hole in roof on left into short crawl emerging at the bottom of the impressive Fault Hall, about 9m high with stream cascading down boulders. Attractive canal passage upstream to duck after 180m, by-passed 30m back via passage on left. More canal passage to wide, low collapse chamber, The Room of Dangling Doom. At far side are two low level streamways, both becoming too tight. Hole at roof level between slabs enters dry crawl over blocks rejoining stream after 60m. Small streamway to 26m sump with squeeze between blocks in middle. Small, shattered passage beyond has been explored for 245m, partly in the stream, and continues to second sump, dived but too low. Water comes from Sargill Head area.

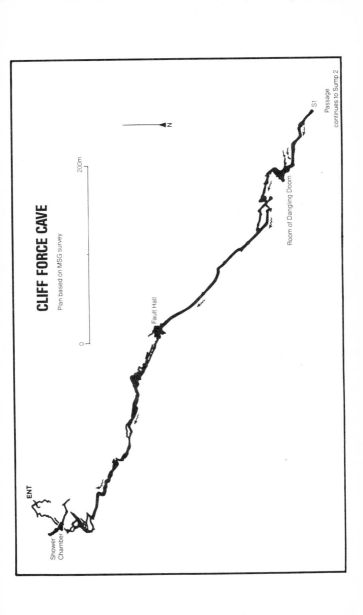

CLIFF FORCE CAVE

Plan based on MSG survey

N

0   200m

ENT

Shower
Chamber

Fault Hall

Room of Dangling Doom

S1

Passage
continues to Sump 2

Spar Shop Series

About 80m upstream of entry into Main Streamway on right of passage is 7m climb up right into dry high level series. Rifts in downstream direction end too tight close to aven above entry to streamway: in upstream direction is varied going with some tight sections. Follow high level beyond the Spar Shop (a small chamber) to lower crawl ending in 6m pitch, requiring tackle, into Fault Hall.

CRACKPOT CAVE   NGR SD 964954   Grade II
[**Summer Lodge Cave**] [**Fairy Hole**]
Alt. 386m   **Length 550m**
Extended 1958, Richmond Grammar School Caving Club.
WARNING – Final choke has collapsed recently and is very dangerous.

ML. Large rising on W bank of beck 400m S of farm is fed by sinks in Wensleydale and Swaledale, including Whirley Gill Pot and Hooker Gill Hole. Main Entrance is obvious, large unstable opening at top of boulder pile; Kneewrecker Entrance is 12m S at foot of cliff.

Hole down through blocks at Main Entrance emerges in roomy passage. At left bend are series of crawls on right, becoming too tight. Main way degenerates to hole down into crawls through boulders, heading left then right to emerge in open passage. Right chokes and walk to left enters main streamway.

Kneewrecker Entrance enters streamway on opposite side after a series of easy crawls which enlarge into spacious passage. Upstream is walk in attractive decorated streamway through three boulder chambers linked by oxbows on left. From Column Chamber with excellent, recently-cleaned stalagmite column (do not touch!) are two ways. In stream, canal leads to boulder choke. Behind column is muddy passage into chamber with despoiled formations. From highest point way down passes choked crawl on left to reach stream. Downstream are narrow joints, upstream is collapse. Short passage on left to dig beneath recent slump on surface, 15m above. Hole between packwalls on left of main passage should not be entered as it emerges in very unstable final choke.

In gill near cave entrance is 5.5m long descending cave under waterfall, becoming too low.
Permission – Summer Lodge.

CUCKOO HOLE   NGR NY 935005   Grade I
Alt. 430m   **Length 8m**   **Vertical Range 4.5m**
Extended 1975, YURT.

ML. In S side of gorge of Botcher Gill, below track. Slit into fissure passing squeeze to choke. Climb up above squeeze to exit at top of cliff.

CRACKPOT CAVE

Plan based on YURT survey

0   50m

MAIN ENT

KNEEWRECKER ENT

Intestines

Block
Chamber

Column
Chamber

The Dig

N

DAMOCLES HOLE
NGR NZ 010048   **Grade I**

Alt. 500m   Length 36m   Depth 11m

Explored 1969, MSG.

WARNING – This cave contains dangerous loose boulders.

ML. Small entrance in S end of shakehole, on bench above Little Windegg Scar. Loose slope drops into short section of phreatic passage, blocked by major collapse and very unsafe chamber with two unsafe choked crawls leading off.

DEER HOLES POT
NGR NY 954054   **Grade II**

Alt. 465m   Depth 18m

ML. A few metres E of Roe Beck, on slight plateau, just below a steepening of the hillside is group of large shakeholes. Open pot is free-hanging pitch into rift 6m long, narrowing down at both ends. Belay ladder to large boulders in adjacent shakehole.

Tackle – 15m ladder; 30m belay; 20m lifeline.

DEVIS HOLE MINE CAVES
NGR SE 051960   **Grade III**

Alt. 355m   Length of cave passages 2.1km

Discovered by lead miners; extended 1973/75, EMRG & MSG.

WARNING – In flood conditions the surface stream can flow into the mine level and fill the first section to the roof. Parts of the mine workings are dangerously unstable.

ML. Follow Cogden Gill above old lead smelting mill, to where valley forks above mine tips. Entrance a few metres up W branch is timbered shaft dropping into level. After 12m of crawling through heavily-silted level is roof fall, passed by squeezing through metal drum 0.33m in diameter. After 120m is Pearson's Level going off on the left for 250m to a forehead.

Ahead from the junction after 45m the level intersects the Central Maze. This has several entrances and is a remarkable phreatic maze with about 1.7km of natural passages, sometimes fairly roomy, crammed into an area little more than 120m by 45m.

Continuing beyond the Central Maze, a further 120m of level leads to a junction. To the left is East Level and to the right West Level, both following the line of a natural passage, considerable evidence of which remains. Straight ahead the entrance cross-cut continues for 93m to a forehead. Just before the end is a rift in the floor dropping into a short series of natural rifts.

East Level leads into a series of mined passages with occasional natural fragments, and the long South East Level with several shafts in its floor.

West Level shows more evidence of natural passages, and is in places almost entirely natural. Passing the short, but mostly natural, South West Level on the left, a series of roof falls is encountered – great care is essential here and the area should be avoided.

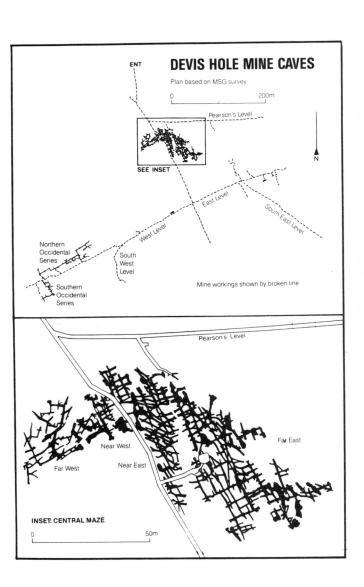

DEVIS HOLE MINE CAVES

Plan based on MSG survey

0   200m

ENT

Pearson's Level

SEE INSET

N

East Level

South East Level

West Level

Northern
Occidental
Series

South
West
Level

Southern
Occidental
Series

Mine workings shown by broken line

Pearson's Level

Far East

Near West

Far West   Near East

INSET: CENTRAL MAZE

0   50m

Where more solid passage is regained after the roof falls, a crawl over miners' deads in a short branch level on the right leads into Northern Occidental Series, 300m of natural passages, mostly crawling, with some good formations. A short distance further along West Level, on the left, is the entrance to Southern Occidental Series, 155m of natural passages, generally narrow with some squeezes. West Level, itself an enlarged natural rift, continues to a fork, each branch soon ending in a forehead.

EAST GILL CAVES   NGR NY 897020   Grade II
Alt. 380m

ML. A group of caves about 800m up East Gill, NNE of Keld.

1. Length 150m
Explored 1933, YRC; extended 1969-87, MSG.

WARNING – A few centimetres rise in stream level will cause the gill to flow into the entrance and flood the cave.

On W bank of gill at foot of cliff just above stream level is small entrance divided into two by horizontal flake of rock. Descending crawl forks and enters streamway. Downstream are two high avens then crawl under left wall to small chamber, branch on left to three more avens, one with high level crawl rejoining entrance passage through squeeze. Downstream, tight crawl ends too low. Upstream easy walking to very tight Aidan's Exit on right; left is low crawl and squeeze into boulder-choked avens with impassable rift connection to tiny cave in stream bank.

2. Length 150m
On W side of gill 180m N of 1, in large rift in cliff. Entrance, which may be walled up, closes to narrow passage. Cross rift system, with climbs over mud banks and crawls. Far reaches take a stream in wet conditions. Ends too tight.

3. Length 9m
In cliff between 1 and 2. Short passage with good formations.

4. Length 9m
On E bank, opposite to and a little further downstream than 1, is small entrance from which a stream falls 4.5m into the gill. Winding, jagged crawl, ending too low.

5. Length 4.5m
Explored 1970, MSG.

On E bank further downstream than 4, in scar above choked risings. Very tight, jagged rift, becoming too tight.

6. NGR NY 897019   Length 9m
Explored 1978, MSG.

To the S of choked risings on E bank. Tight squeeze into wet bedding which opens to 1.2m high scalloped passage running to loose choke.

EAST GILL POT
NGR NY 898015
Grade II
Alt. 396m
Depth 29m

Explored 1962, BCC; re-opened 1978, MSG.

ML. In shakehole 50m S of gate in second wall from barn. Grassy shakehole with entrance beneath metal sheets and old rails. Broken pitch with ledges and inlets, to pebble floor.

Tackle – 30m ladder or rope; stake and sling belay; 35m lifeline.

EWELEAP SCAR CAVE
NGR NY 939024
Grade I
Alt. 465m   **Length 4.5m**

ML. In gorge of Gunnerside Gill, 800m above ruined Blakethwaite smelt mill. Entrance on E side of stream at foot of cliff opens into high aven. Squeeze on right into small chamber with impenetrable connection to Eweleap Scar Pot.

EWELEAP SCAR POT
NGR NY 939024
Grade II
Alt. 480m   **Length 30m**
Depth 20m

ML. At top of cliff on E side of gorge, up gully near entrance of Eweleap Scar Cave. Care required on loose scree above entrance. 1st pitch in roomy shaft with 2nd pitch in narrow, choked shaft directly below. At top of 2nd pitch is rift leading to 3rd pitch into chamber. Small stream passage with oxbow leads to squeeze down into old mine level with dangerously deep, clinging mud. Tackle for 1st and 2nd pitches can be pulled through rift and used for 3rd pitch, with an additional lifeline man at 3rd pitch.

Tackle listed below is adequate for all pitches.

Tackle – 20m ladder; 3m belay; 25m lifeline.

EWELEAP WEST CAVE
NGR NY 939024
Grade II
Alt. 480m   **Length 35m**
Depth 12m

Explored 1971, MSG.

ML. On W side of gorge, opposite and to S of Eweleap Scar Cave. Scramble up gully to small entrance 12m above stream. Junction is reached after 4.5m; to left is too low and to right is an excessively tight pitch. Straight ahead a tight, sandy crawl bears right into a descending rift and an aven chamber, followed by a pitch with a tight take-off, choked at the bottom.

Tackle – 9m ladder; stake and sling belay; 15m lifeline.

FAGGERGILL POTS
Grade II
1. NGR NY 987073   **Alt. 438m**
Depth 18m

ML. Open shaft in small shakehole W of sharp bend in gill, 100m upstream of Ovening Nick Pot. About 3m down, a large boulder is wedged across and two mine levels lead off but both rapidly choke. At foot of ladder is rift chamber floored with bones.

Tackle – 25m ladder; stake and sling belay; 30m lifeline.

2. NGR NY 985071   **Alt. 432m**   **Length 15m**   **Depth 6m**

ML. A few hundred metres W of 1 in shallow, boggy shakehole. Pitch intersects small cave passage which chokes in both directions.

Tackle – 8m ladder; stake and sling belay; 9m lifeline.

FAR GREEN POTS   NGR SD 940945   Grade II
Alt. 500m

ML. Group of pots at head of Oxnop Gill, surrounded by peat bogs. 1-3 are in northernmost of short row of shakeholes, 5 and 6 in the southernmost, and 4 in between.

1. Depth 12m
The obvious stream sink. Climb down 3m into open pot, then narrow, descending rift to head of 5.5m pitch into blind rift.

2. Depth 11m
Obvious entrance in centre of shakehole; roomy, dry 9m shaft, closing to an impenetrable descending fissure.

3. Depth 5m
At the end of shakehole. Narrow shaft, choked floor.

4. Depth 6m
Two shakeholes further S is obvious hole with fence round. Roomy shaft, choked at bottom.

5. Depth 14m. Explored 1972, MSG
Against W side of shakehole. Narrow rift, initially very tight and jagged, then widening and opening into aven with choked floor.

6. Depth 8m
Just S of 5. Obvious circular, smooth-walled pitch to choked floor, above the aven at the bottom of 5.

Tackle (all pots) – 15m ladder; stake and sling belay; 20m lifeline.

FOXGLOVE POT   NGR NY 939024   Grade II
Alt. 475m   Length 17m   Depth 11m
Explored 1970, MSG.

ML. In same gully as Eweleap West Cave, West Cave, but 3.5m higher up, is small entrance. Narrow 3.5m climb to platform, then roomy shaft, climbable but a ladder is helpful. On far side of shaft, half way down, is chamber leading to ascending rift passage and sand choke.

Tackle – 9m ladder; 0.6m belay; 12m lifeline.

FRIARFOLD HUSH CAVE   NGR NY 942013   Grade I
Alt. 480m   Length 23m
Explored 1969, MSG.

ML. In northernmost of two prominent hushes on E side of Gunnerside Gill. In S wall of hush is dry passage with two small avens and 3m deep hole in the floor, ending suddenly at a blank wall.

GRAINY GILL CAVE   NGR SD 871971   Grade II
Alt. 470m   **Length 70m**
Explored 1978, MSG.

ML. Obvious rising on E bank of Grainy Gill. Stream entrance is tight wet crawl to climb through loose boulders into walking-sized passage, also reached via a squeeze from dry entrance at cliff foot above rising. Upstream passage easy going but ends abruptly in impassable rift.

GREAT SLEDDALE POTS   NGR SD 827988   Grade II
Alt. 510m   **Length 15m**   **Depth 25m**

ML. Main pot is where stream sinks above Long Scar. Large open shaft, easily scrambled down, to short passage ending in aven. Climb down behind boulders against left wall of shaft leads to head of underground pitch, followed by descending stream passage becoming too low.

Other shallower pots nearby, with no passages, up to 9m deep, some requiring ladders. Same tackle for each pot, including main pot.

(For location see Northern England map on front endpaper).

Tackle – 9m ladder; 3m belay; 12m lifeline.

HARD LEVEL GILL CAVE   NGR NY 969007   Grade III
Alt. 420m   **Length 220m**   **Depth 12m**
Explored 1955, NPC; extended 1967/1970, MSG.

UnL. On E side of small gorge directly below Hard Level Gill Force, waterfall 800m above ruined Old Gang smelt mill. Entrance 1.2m above stream level. After 3.5m is tight 3m chimney down and crawl into small chamber. Water enters but sinks in tight passage. Right is chamber and slide down into larger passage. To right ends in choke, to left divides into a high level passage through boulder ruckle and a low level crawl, which re-unite at Crypt Junction. On left here is low crawl to where the stream can be heard, ending too tight after another 20m.

High and low levels continue from Crypt Junction and re-unite in small chamber. Straight ahead is choked, but flat crawl under right wall leads to parallel low crawl through pools, to tight squeeze under low arch into February Series. Right is choked by silt, left is main downstream passage, easy crawling to T-junction. To left climb up into small chamber, to right squeeze past boulder and turn left again, in descending streamway ending in tight crawl to fallen block which completely obstructs the passage.

HARD LEVEL GILL WEST CAVES
NGR NY 969007   Grade II
Alt. 420m
Explored 1970, MSG.

1. Length 12m
UnL. Directly opposite Hard Level Gill Cave on other side of gorge. The larger of two small entrances, nearer the waterfall. Narrow drop into roomier rift, closing to narrow inlet passage. In wider section of rift, on left, is short,

narrow passage dropping into small chamber with stalactite curtain and impassable connection with 2.

2. Length 6m
   UnL. Small entrance a few metres S of 1. Tight squeeze into short rift with impassable branch on right connecting with 1.

HIGH DUDGEON HOLE   NGR NY 899010   Grade I
Alt. 300m   **Length 6m**
Explored 1982, EPC.

   ML. Resurgence at base of cliff. Wet crawl over sandstone floor ends too low.

HILLSIDE CAVE   NGR NZ 009039   Grade II
Alt. 470m   **Length 9m**
Explored 1971/79, MSG.

   ML. Project line of E-W wall up slope to scar to find small cave entrance. Short scalloped crawl into ruckle-roofed chamber; cautious ascent into upper chamber above ruckle, with tall choked rift.

HOLGATE MOOR CAVE   NGR NZ 068058   Grade I
Alt. 375m   **Length 8m**   **Depth 3m**
Explored 1972, YURT.

   ML. Entrance under boulder in small stream sink 50m W of Marske–Newsham road. Slide down into small passage choked at both ends, with narrow choked rift to one side.
   (For location see Northern England map on front endpaper).

HOOKER GILL HOLE   NGR SD 980957   Grade II
Alt. 475m   **Length 15m**   **Depth 18m**
   ML. Entrance blocked by earth and rocks, above stream at sink 100m S of shooting box. First pitch extremely tight, second in wider rift, and short climbs lead to final choke. Pitches climbable but 30m rope helpful. Water emerges at Crackpot Cave.

HORROCK'S CROSS CAVE   NGR NZ 009041   Grade I
Alt. 500m   **Length 15m**   **Depth 15m**
Explored 1969, MSG.

   ML. Entrance on the brink of Windegg Scar into descending rift cave. Easy passage to 6m climb down, then crawl to second 6m climb into choked rift. Traverse along rift above first climb leads to small chamber with loose boulders.

HORROCK'S CROSS POT   NGR NZ 009041   Grade II
Alt. 485m   **Length 46m**   **Depth 8m**
Explored 1970, MSG.

   ML. Pothole entrance between foot of scar and scree slope, below obvious joint in cliff, directly below Horrock's Cross Cave. Climbable descent and squeeze into series of old mine workings and partly natural rifts, with some loose boulders. Original entrance into mine workings now blocked.

HORSE LEVEL CAVE   NGR NY 990071   Grade II
Alt. 417m   Length 54m
Explored 1970/76, MSG and BACC.

ML. Mine level entrance in valley bottom alongside old tips; level runs SE and 73m from entrance is 3m climb on left, where water enters. Squeeze through boulders into upstream cave, a low crawl to a choke; downstream passage is also choked. Continuing along mine level for 6m, natural passage cuts level, on left is choke, on right low, muddy crawl to squeeze through pool, and further low crawls and pools to choke.

About 310m from the level entrance, the mine has cut a natural rift 8m high, but immediately choked in both directions and containing much loose rock.

KISDON CAVE   NGR NY 899010   Grade II
Alt. 355m   Length 238m
Extended 1962, BCC and EPC.

ML. Follow Crackpot Hall track from Keld for 800m E of bridge over East Gill, to old mine tip above track, just before gate. Small entrance in grass bank above tip leads into mine level with knee-deep water. After 67m natural cave runs off on each side. Level continues for another 120m passing small natural passage on left leading to an aven after 3m, to end in a collapse. Main cave on left of level is crawl down slope into chamber, with two avens, and low, muddy crawl at floor level which ends after 15m in a choke. To right of the level drops into a small chamber, and then sandy passages lead to slope up into Fault Chamber. In left wall at roof level is entrance to Mud Slide (reached by slippery 4.5m climb), tight tubular crawl for 33m to a choke. Main passage continues, roomy at first, but lowers to a muddy crawl, with oxbows, ending at low choked bedding on left and narrow rift with loose choke on right.

KISDON LODGE POT   NGR SD 894999   Grade III
Alt. 400m   Length 27m   Depth 32m
Explored 1975, Michelin Caving Club.
WARNING – Unstable boulders in climbs following entrance pitch.

ML. Lidded entrance shaft 10m from Keld-Muker track, beyond the top gate. Pitch into chamber with dig in boulders to one side and 2m climb into aven at other side. Loose 9m climb down to cross rift and 3.5m climb down on right. Slope down to final 7.5m climb down into rift chamber with narrow fissures in floor.

Tackle – 9m ladder; 0.6m belay; 12m lifeline.

KISDON POTS

1. Alt. 470m   **NGR SD 896993**   **Grade I**
                        Length 4.5m   **Depth 4.5m**

ML. In centre of field N of walled lane and old mine tip. Entrance at N end of rocky rift-like shakehole; climb down into chamber.

2. Alt. 440m   **NGR SD 904998**   **Grade II**
                          Length 6m   **Depth 6.5m**

ML. In shakehole just N of S wall of field N of open moor running down to edge of scars. Entrance in NW corner of shakehole; pitch into chamber with loose boulders. Rift runs back under shakehole to boulder, and narrow 2m hole in floor.

Tackle – 4.5m ladder; 3m belay; 9m lifeline.

3. Alt. 415m   **NGR NY 901004**   **Depth 4.5m**   **Grade II**

ML. In largest of line of shakeholes, on hillside above shooting box. Entrance under large boulders on S side of shakehole; pitch in fluted shaft to boulder floor. A rift too narrow to enter drops at least 6m further. Boulder floor is apparently choke in deeper shaft, and could perhaps be dug.

Tackle – 4.5m ladder; 3m belay; 9m lifeline.

LONG SCAR CAVES   Grade II

1 explored 1969, MSG; 2 and 3 explored 1975, MSG.

1. (Long Scar East Cave)   NGR SD 829990
Alt. 495m   **Length 20m**

ML. Obvious pair of tubular entrances at E end of Long Scar, on S side of Great Sleddale Beck. Dry crawl ending too tight.

2. NGR SD 828989   **Alt. 495m**   **Length 6m**

ML. Resurgence at foot of dry valley running down from Great Sleddale Pot. Tight squeeze over or grovel beside large fallen slab to choke and impassable wet bedding.

3. NGR SD 827989   **Alt. 495m**   **Length 12m**

ML. A short distance W of 2, just before old copper mine. Small entrance beside stream opens into wet crawl, suddenly closing down.

(For location see Northern England map on front endpaper).

LOVERGILL CAVE   **NGR SD 881961**   **Grade III**
Alt. 480m   **Length 120m**

Explored 1958, NPC; extended 1971, MSG.

WARNING – The Duck will sump with a slight rise in water level.

ML. Resurgence from cliff on W side of Lovergill. Stream enters from left 4.5m in. Ahead through chamber is dry crawl through narrow section to squeeze over boulder before rejoining streamway which continues as easy crawl to two chambers, then lower wet crawl, passing low oxbow on left, to awkward duck 45m from entrance. This may silt up and become very tight. Duck is 2.5m long with 5cm airspace. Further crawls and small chambers continue until passage turns left to sump.

LOVERGILL EAST CAVE   NGR SD 882961   Grade II
Alt. 505m   **Length 52m**   **Depth 7.5m**
Explored 1958, NPC.

ML. Opposite Lovergill Sink Cave, on E side of stream. Entrance opens into large passage and boulder ruckle; climb down through boulders into cross rift series of passages, all ending in chokes. Loose boulders in parts.

LOVERGILL SINK CAVE   NGR SD 882961   Grade II
Alt. 505m   **Length 245m**   **Depth 17m**
Explored 1958, NPC; extended 1971/78, MSG.

ML. Follow gill above Lovergill Cave to entrance on W side of gorge at stream level. Drop of 2m to junction. Left is choked inlet, right leads to choke and hole into parallel rift leading back into Main Rift. Straight ahead at junction is Main Rift, steeply descending. A handline is a help on initial 3m drop. At second junction, short choked passage to right, to left high chamber, lowering to choked crawl. Main Rift continues ahead to end in easy climb down of a further 3m. Tight fissure running back under climb leads to winding crawl, with one tight section, ending in a drop into large boulder ruckle. Left at bottom of drop at end of Main Rift leads to another high chamber, then crawl through pool to another junction. To right opens into Straw Rift – right here rejoins main passage behind fallen boulders, left leads to high and low level passages both rapidly becoming too tight. Turning left at junction leads into South East Rift with avens and small chambers, ending in choked fissures after 20m. Scaling reached short upper levels in places.

MASON HOW TOP SINK   NGR SD 917960   Grade I
Alt. 505m   **Length 8m**   **Depth 3m**
Explored 1968, YURT.

ML. Stream sink in shakehole at E end of series of open quarry-like pots and shakeholes. Fissure beneath large gritstone slab is a slide down into chamber with bouldery alcove. All ways out are too tight.

NEW LEVEL CAVE   NGR NY 991073   Grade II
Alt. 430m   **Length 135m**
Extended 1970, BACC and MSG.

ML. Mine level at valley head has collapsed for some distance. Present entrance in the last of a line of collapsed depressions may be walled up. Flat crawl through unstable, silted-up level gradually gains height. After 150m the level cuts a natural passage 1.5m above the level floor. Right is too tight after 9m; to left 27m of passage, including a fine aven with stalagmites, ends choked. Another 3m along level is hole in floor, which is a tight 3.5m drop into a natural stream passage. Upstream, a narrow crawl, becoming larger, ends in a boulder ruckle after 20m. Downstream through a duck leads to a crawl with some formations, descending to a canal which ends in a sump. The sump goes under left wall for 3m to cross joint with minimal airspace and after a further 4.5m dive the way is low and silted.

NORTH GUTTER CAVE
NGR NZ 021031
Grade I
Alt. 340m Length 26m

ML. On E bank of Slei Gill, directly opposite to and on same joint as Scatter Scar Cave. Rift cave modified by mining ends in choke.

OCHRE POT
NGR SD 880960
Grade I
Alt. 510m Length 6m Depth 6m
Explored 1972, YURT.

ML. In shakehole W of sink 100m W of Lovergill. Short drop followed by crawl under block into small chamber from which climbable pitch descends and becomes too tight.

OLD GANG CAVE
NGR NY 971006
Grade I
Alt. 410m Length 9m
Explored 1968, MSG.

UnL. At foot of small scar N of track, just W of small stone building. Small entrance drops into a muddy crawl ending in a choke.

OVENING NICK POT
NGR NY 988072
Grade II
Alt. 435m Depth 15m

ML. Stream from N side of Faggergill sinks and dry miniature gorge meanders on through grass. Hole in narrowest part of 'gorge' 200m NNW of hut at end of mine tips, opens into side of roomy shaft choked at foot and with a sumped alcove opposite the ladder. The walls of this pot are shattered and loose.

Tackle – 20m ladder; 6m belay; 25m lifeline.

OXNOP KIRK
NGR SD 937949
Grade I
Alt. 480m Length 4.5m Vertical Range 9m

ML. Large rift in scar on E side of Oxnop Gill, prominent from N. Dead end but hole in roof emerges at top of scar, and would need ladder for descent.

PISA POT
NGR SD 869977
Grade II
Alt. 550m Depth 8m
Explored 1978, NSG.

ML. In shakehole with leaning tower of fluted limestone, 400m E of Rowantree Mea Cave. At foot of tower is crawl to climb down rift and choke.

ROSEBUSH POT
NGR NY 897019
Grade II
Alt. 400m Depth 12m

ML. On E side of East Gill in line of shakes 50m downstream from East Gill Cave 1. Rift climbable with rope ends choked. Pot is now blocked.

ROUGHTON KELD
NGR NY 965071   **Grade I**

Alt. 380m   **Length 20m**

Explored 1965/66, ULSA.

ML. Above S branch of Roughton Keld rising. To the right is a dangerous choke of boulders and black mud, while straight ahead a narrow fissure with a small stream becomes too tight.

ROUGHTON KELD POT
NGR NY 967071   **Grade II**

Alt. 395m   **Depth 11m**

Explored 1964, ULSA.

ML. Sinkhole 200m away from and 15m higher than the rising at Roughton Keld. Large shaft covered by boards ends abruptly in choke of mud and boulders.

Tackle – 9m ladder; 0.6m belay; 15m lifeline.

ROUTIN GILL POT
NGR SD 911961   **Grade IV**

Alt. 530m   **Length 60m**   **Depth 15m**

Explored 1981, MSG.

WARNING – The Whirlpool is extremely wet and narrow.

ML. Entrance under large boulder on W side of depression. A short length of stooping-height passage to Waterfall Pitch 8m. Tall canyon passage becomes too tight but climb leads to squeeze which rejoins stream at Whirlpool. Very narrow 4m squeeze down to water chute and short section of canal continuing to junction. Straight on is a chamber; to right stream flows along a very narrow tube, ending too tight.

Tackle – 8m ladder, stake and sling belay, 10m lifeline.

ROWANTREE MEA CAVE
NGR SD 866978   **Grade II**

Alt. 490m   **Length 57m**   **Depth 6m**

Explored 1978, MSG.

ML. In small grassy shakehole to E of Row Pot Hole West. Hole under a slab into an interesting little complex of rift passages.

ROWANTREE POT
NGR SD 951955   **Grade II**

[Broken Rift Pot]

Alt. 472m   **Length 12m**   **Depth 9m**

WARNING – Unstable boulder floor near foot of pitch.

ML. Sink 1.2km W of Summer Lodge has pitch on SE bank of depression. Pitch opens into two adjacent rift chambers with some straw stalactites.

Tackle – 12m ladder; stake and sling belay; 15m lifeline.

ROW POT HOLE WEST
NGR SD 865978   **Grade II**

Alt. 490m   **Depth 8m**

Explored 1978, MSG.

ML. High on W side of large rocky shakehole with boulder-choked rift is small hole with clayey wriggle down to tight chimney descent (rope useful). Other small holes nearby.

SCAR TOP POT   NGR SD 938946   Grade II
Alt. 495m   Depth 11m
Explored 1972, Cotham Cave Group.

ML. In SE corner of bench adjacent to road, above Oxnop Scar. In shallow shakehole without any rock exposure is small hole which may be covered by stones. Tight shaft, choked floor.

Tackle – 12m ladder, stake and sling belay; 14m lifeline.

SCATTER SCAR CAVE   NGR NZ 020031   Grade I
Alt. 350m   Length 33m

ML. In Scatter Scar, on W side of Slei Gill. Dry rift cave with two entrances and roomy passage ending in small chamber.

SILVER BIRCH POT   NGR NY 959035   Grade II
Alt. 465m   Length 27m   Depth 14m
Explored 1969, MSG.

ML. Near head of gorge in Little Punchard Gill. Entrance on W side of gorge near the top directly beneath shale scar. Three short pitches, all climbable but tackle helpful, ending in short rift passage to choke.

Tackle – 15m ladder; 6m belay; 20m lifeline.

SMARBER CAVE   NGR NY 971980   Grade II
Alt. 370m   Length 20m
Explored 1970, MSG.

MdL. Rising from scar, just below track. Small entrance drops into streamway. Water sinks into impenetrable fissures, but upstream is tight crawl through squeezes, with no room to turn round. Ends too tight.

SMARBER POT   NGR NY 969981   Grade II
Alt. 390m   Depth 9m

MdL. In shakehole at rear of bench, W of sink, is blind shaft.

Tackle – 9m ladder; 6m belay; 12m lifeline.

SMITHY HOLME CAVE   NGR NY 876016   Grade II
Alt. 354m   Length 14m
Explored 1962, BCC.

ML. Rising 3.5m up from base of scar 20m E of Brian's Cave. Crawl past boulder becomes too low after bends.

SMITHY HOLME POT   NGR NY 876016   Grade II
Alt. 365m   Depth 10m
Explored 1972, YURT.

ML. On N side of track to farm in gully E of wall behind Smithy Holme Cave. Hole covered by boards drops onto boulders and further rift pitch descends to choked floor with choked aven to one side.

Tackle – 11m ladder; stake and sling belay; 12m lifeline.

STALAGMITE POT   NGR SD 965951   Grade II
Alt. 380m   Length 3m   Depth 9m

ML. In small cliff up E fork of gill above Crackpot Cave. Small shaft to pool and short, low crawl ending in boulder choke. On the opposite side of the beck a short way upstream is an obvious sink with a narrow fissure about 4.5m long above.

Tackle – 9m ladder; 2.5m belay; 12m lifeline.

Permission – Summer Lodge.

STOCKDALE BECK CAVE   NGR SD 865980   Grade I
Alt. 440m   Length 6m
Explored 1978, MSG.

UnL. Obvious entrance on S bank of Beck closes to silty tube which could be pushed further.

STONE ROOT CAVE   NGR NY 911010   Grade II
Alt. 360m   Length 33m
Explored 1973, MSG.

ML. On E side of Swinnergill, at stream level, just below a narrowing and sharp double bend in the gorge. Entrance may now be blocked by rockfall. Low crawl to tight squeeze and small chamber, with choked tubes leading off and one rift ending too tight where daylight visible.

SWALESIDE CAVE   NGR NY 895011   Grade II
Alt. 305m   Length 46m
Explored 1978, MSG.

WARNING – Floods completely when river is high.

ML. Several entrances in cliff on N bank of Swale, on either side of Pennine Way footbridge. Crawly passage, tight in places; often choked by flood debris.

SWINNERGILL CAVES   NGR NY 911013   Grade II

ML. Nos. 1, 2 and 3 are in the upper gorge, N of junction with East Grain, No. 4 is in lower gorge, downstream of junction.

1. Alt. 415m   **Length 148m**   **Depth 12m**

Entrance on W bank a few metres below waterfall. Crawl to climbable descent to streamway. Upstream above 1.2m waterfall is tight ascending side passage on right to junction; right too tight, left descends to rejoin upstream passage. Upstream passage ends where water enters through roof, directly below sink in surface stream bed. Downstream, walking-size passage with inlet on right at floor level which ends too low. Main passage ends at 6m high chamber and choked bedding.

2. Length 12m

In E bank of gill a few metres downstream from 1. Two entrances, one on ledge 3m above stream, join in tubular tight crawl to a choke.

3. Length 12m

In bank of gill further downstream, near sink, Steeply descending crawl to junction. To left, ascending passage to choke with stream entering and 3m high aven with crawl at top becoming too tight. To right, stream sinks in impenetrable slot.

Further downstream again, also in E side of gorge, are several short caves up to 6m long.

4. NGR NY 911010   **Alt. 370m**   **Length 12m**

Explored 1969, GC.

On W side of lower gorge is fissure crawl into 4.5m high rift passage. Water enters from above but rift pinches out in both directions.

SWINNERGILL KIRK   **NGR NY 911012**   **Grade I**
Alt. 415m   **Length 65m**   **Depth 11m**

ML. Large entrance on W side of waterfall at head of upper gorge takes part of stream. Roomy, straight passage suddenly closes to descending tight crawl which turns left to constricted sump, dived for 4m. Water resurges at East Gill, about 1.5km away.

THREE NEUKS POT   **NGR NZ 132036**   **Grade I**
Alt. 302m   **Depth 4.5m**

Explored 1968, YURT.

ML. On E side of Marske-Ravensworth road, 1.2km N of Marske-Richmond road. Entrance in shallow, grassy shakehole is 3m deep collapse through drift. Short crawl in limestone on blocks over top of pitch estimated at 9m deep, but undescended due to sudden collapse of large boulders.

(For location see Northern England map on front endpaper).

TRUNDLE POT   **NGR SD 882961**   **Grade II**
Alt. 510m   **Depth 8m**

Explored 1972, YURT.

ML. Entrance around corner E of Lovergill East Cave under large blocks at top of gully. Climbable pitch choked with earth and boulders.

WEST STONESDALE CAVE   NGR NY 888021   Grade I
Alt. 340m   **Depth 8m**
Explored 1970, MSG.

ML. On W side of gorge just S of impenetrable rising. Small entrance in gully, 3m above stream level. Low crawl into small chamber where floor steps up to within 7.5cm of roof.

WHAW EDGE HOLE   NGR NY 971034   Grade I
Alt. 500m   **Length 12m**   **Depth 6m**
Explored 1979, MSG.

WARNING – Dangerous loose rock.

ML. Walk up fellside W of Danby Level, keeping old sheds at end of track in line with Whaw Bridge. Climbable 3m square shaft; to E is blind chamber, to W unsafe chamber with unstable rift in floor, probably dropping into old mine workings.

WHITCLIFFE SCAR CAVES   NGR NZ 131020   Grade II
Alt. 275m

ML. The caves are 400m S of the Marske road, about 4km from Richmond.

1. Gel's Pot   **Length 110m**   **Depth 17m**
Entrance at head of gully, on E side of prominent break in the scars. A dry rift cave, apparently formed largely by slip action. Large passage to junction. To left impassable fissure connecting with 2, straight on is descending rift to choke, with easy traverse into higher level above choke, which ends in a stalagmite slope. To right at junction, cross tight hole in floor and turn left, then tight descent into large rift passage. Traverse over hole in floor, then passage ends in a boulder ruckle.

2.   **Length 40m**   **Depth 12m**
Entrance a few metres N of 1, with smaller entrance just above. Rift passage descends to 4.5m pitch, smaller entrance joins at roof level. Pitch climbable, although rope helpful; no way on at bottom. Impassable fissure on right connects with 1. Traversing over head of pitch leads to a further rift passage which ends too tight.

3.   **Length 100m**   **Depth 12m**
Extended 1973, MSG.

On W side of break in scars, behind bushes in gully reached by following ledge round. Large upper entrance into short, roomy passage; hole to right is climb down into rift passage. To left ends too tight, to right is junction; passage on left to lower entrance, on right ending in boulder-choked rift, and straight ahead a squeeze into narrow rift with unsafe boulder bridges, eventually ending choked.

4.   **Length 12m**   **Depth 12m**
Explored 1974, MSG.

In grassy bank above cliff a few metres SW of 3. Rift, very tight at first, descends in a series of steps, ends choked.

There are several other small caves of similar type along Whitcliffe Scar to the E and W of the above group. About 800m E is a large cave entrance on a ledge just above base of scar, leading via an ascending series of partly-mined small chambers and passage to a second entrance half way up the scars.

(For location see Northern England map on front endpaper).

WINDEGG MINE CAVERNS NGR NZ 012052 Grade III
Alt. 460m   Length 1.2km

Entered by lead miners; re-discovered 1968, EMRG; extended 1970/76, MSG.

WARNING–The mine level, especially Clay Vein Level, is prone to accumulations of carbon dioxide. The natural caverns contain many very unstable boulder ruckles, especially in the Creaking Boulder Cavern area, which is extremely dangerous. Take great care throughout.

ML. Alcocks Level is entered by dug shaft now provided with plastic pipe, a few metres from the original collapsed entrance, above large mine tip visible from road. Follow level to junction – on left is Clay Vein Level, ending in clay choke. Straight ahead at junction is right turn below old ore chute. Level continues to Third Rise and then to a collapse.

Climb of 6m up Third Rise enters mined passage 120m long, partly natural and with several sections of natural passage leading off. Two 4.5m rises are connected by 45m of narrow natural rifts.

Main Caverns

Climb up alongside old ore chute, on unsafe timbers, into mined passage. Rise above is a slippery 8m climb into Carlisle Cavern. Easiest route into caverns is to follow mined passage, turning left at junction (right ends in choked natural rift) and passing base of Climbing Rise (unsafe and should not be used) to muddy 4.5m climb up into Durham Rift.

From Durham Rift, first right turn enters small chamber with large slab, and then right again to Nineways Junction. Right again here to squeeze up over boulder into the low, wide Carlisle Cavern, the largest chamber in the system. Right through the Cavern leads to head of Climbing Rise; beyond is head of slippery climb above ore chute. Left at head of Climbing Rise a series of rifts leads to traverse over 6m deep miners' sump and then partly-mined passages, past mine wagon, to a sump down into Clay Vein Level – this is unsafe and should not be descended. Left at Nineways Junction, along the largest passage, leads to 2.5m climb up and right along another large passage leads to foot of high boulder slope ascending to Creaking Boulder Cavern, which should be avoided. Other passages extend in all directions; some areas are very complex.

Tackle – 3m ladder and long belay for entrance pipe.

Permission – Mr Greenhalge, Shaw House Farm.

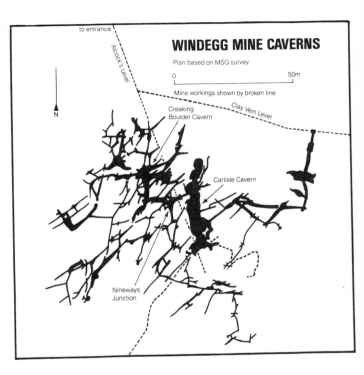

WINDEGG MINE CAVERNS

Plan based on MSG survey

0   50m

Mine workings shown by broken line

to entrance

Alcock's Level

Clay Vein Level

N

Creaking
Boulder Cavern

Carlisle Cavern

Nineways
Junction

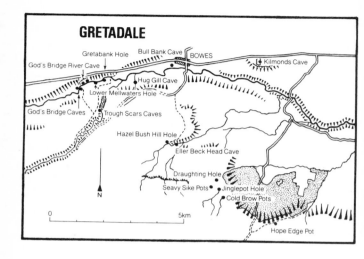

GRETADALE

BARNINGHAM MOOR CAVE
NGR NZ 077098
Grade I
Alt. 260m   **Length 8m**
Explored 1969, MSG.

3YL. In stream bed below track from W end of Barningham village to monument on Brown Hill, where stream sinks. Small entrance drops into stream passage, too tight both ways.

(For location see Northern England map on front endpaper).

BULL BANK CAVE   NGR NY 990133   **Grade I**
Alt. 270m   **Length 9m**

ML. In cliff on N side of river Greta, directly S of Bowes Castle. Small entrance and tubular crawl ending in small aven.

COLD BROW POTS   NGR NZ 011083   **Grade II**
Alt. 495m

ML. Two pots about 400m SSE of Jinglepot Hole, in plantation.

Main Sink   **Depth 15m**
   Large shakehole with trees growing near rear of limestone bench. Small entrance in corner is pitch into rift becoming too tight.

Tackle – 15m ladder; 3m belay; 20m lifeline.

Cold Brow 2   **Length 90m**   **Depth 15m**
   NW of Main Sink, hole in last of prominent line of shakes, covered with iron sheets and other debris. Awkward rope climb into rift which continues for 90m beneath surface shakeholes, with climbs over unstable boulders. At foot of entrance pitch in opposite direction to main rift passage is a further pitch too tight to descend.

DRAUGHTING HOLE   NGR NZ 007090   Grade II
Alt. 450m   **Length 18m**   Depth 11m
Explored 1968, MSG.

   ML. On wide bench NW of Jinglepot Hole and N of Seavy Sike Pots, in corner of large shakehole, is tight squeeze under loose rocks to head of 6m drop, an awkward climb into narrow rift (rope helpful). Side passage on right becomes too tight. Main rift descends to muddy pool and then ascends to wedged block; rift beyond closes down. Draughts very strongly at times.

ELLER BECK HEAD CAVE
NGR NY 992102   Grade IV
Alt. 380m   **Length 200m**
Explored 1968/1970, MSG.

WARNING – This cave is tight, wet and very arduous. Several low airspace sections will sump readily with a slight rise in water level.

   GL. At foot of gorge where Eller Beck resurges from cliff. Easy walking in waist-deep water for 12m to T-junction. Right is narrow rift with deep water to small chamber.
   Main route is left up into dry tube and past narrow branch on left to drop back into deep water. Right round second double bend and past low airspace passage on left leading to 0.6m sump. Right into sideways crawl over mudbank then sharp left into wider passage; ahead at bend is very tight squeeze into 20m of tight, wet rift. Paranoid Passage is easy crawl to boulder and unpleasant duck, just beyond which is tight passage on left to other end of 0.6m sump.
   Main passage enters chamber with fallen boulder. Right is oxbow, and ways ahead and at roof level on left enter a large chamber, Disillusion Way, with Worm Sewer on right at start – 20m of crawl in deep, liquid mud with no room to turn. Disillusion Way becomes lower and water deepens until airspace is unusable.

GOD'S BRIDGE CAVES   NGR NY 956125   Grade III
Alt. 305m

1. Length 45m
   ML. Obvious entrance on S side of river bed a few metres W of the natural

bridge, usually dry but acts as a resurgence in wet conditions. Varied crawling ends too low.

2. Upper Cave   **Length 12m**

ML. About 150m further S and 50m E of river, at foot of hillside. Tight fissure drops into small stream; upstream ends too low after 9m, downstream is a boulder choke.

3. NGR NY 955124   **Length 30m**

Explored 1977, MSG.

ML. Hole in field 200m N of bend in river bed 200m above natural bridge; narrow upstream passage with boulder clay roof.

4. Flood Sink Cave   **NGR NY 955124**   **Length 11m**

ML. On N side of bend in river bed. Crawl to sump.

Permission – Pasture End Farm, near Bowes.

GOD'S BRIDGE RIVER CAVE
NGR NY 958126   Grade III

Alt. 305m   **Length 855m**

Explored DCC; extended 1967/1971, MSG; 1976, CDG.

WARNING – In wet conditions large sections fill completely.

ML. From natural bridge follow N bank of river Greta downstream. After 40m is tight hole in small scar – The Exit – and after another 100m, small disused quarry is set back from the river bank. Main entrance is in NW corner of quarry. Drop down into bedding crawl through deep, liquid mud for 60m to junction with River Passage. Branch on left half way through crawl is oxbow with small chamber, joining the river further upstream. Downstream from junction after 25m is short crawl (this sumps readily in wet weather) to walking-size passage, with low wet crawl on left to a sump, taking part of the stream, and on right, short oxbow. Right at large aven avoids ducks on River Passage, and dry route rejoins stream after second aven, with side passage on right which becomes too tight after a difficult bend. Downstream leads to an awkward duck after 15m, sumped except in drought, entering a series of rifts with deep water (swimming is necessary in places) and another aven, ending in a sump.

Upstream from junction, River Passage continues stooping and walking height to oxbow on left. From this oxbow a low, muddy crawl, then a squeeze up into a collapse chamber lead back to The Exit. Rejoining River Passage, a mud bank on the left leads to Stalagmite Aven, with a 25m crawl leading off. Continuing upstream through a low bedding leads to a larger passage which suddenly ends. Turning left leads into a narrow rift with deep water and small airspace. A series of awkward ducks leads for 20m to the Upstream Sump. Sump is 27m dive (best done as 46m dive from commencement of ducks) to large chamber and 60m of roomy passage, lowering to a crawl for 15m and then second sump, which has been dived for 15m to where underwater passage became too tight.

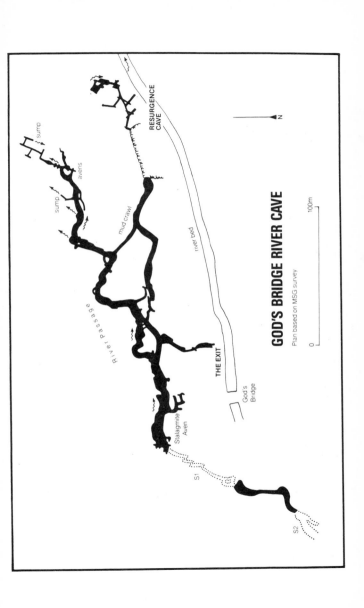

GOD'S BRIDGE RIVER CAVE

Plan based on MSG survey

RESURGENCE CAVE

THE EXIT

God's Bridge

river bed

River Passage

mud crawl

avens

sump

sump

Stalagmite Aven

S1

S2

N

0   100m

Resurgence Cave
Entrance in NE corner of old quarry with further entrances on the river bank near the resurgence of the river Greta (from a boulder ruckle). Series of easy crawls leads to a point where daylight is visible; turning left leads to the river, upstream a wet crawl leads to a sump.
Permission – Pasture End Farm, near Bowes.

GRETABANK HOLE   NGR NY 965127   Grade II
Alt. 300m   Length 37m
Explored 1986, MSG & GC.

ML. Obvious small entrance in low cliff on S side of normally dry bed of Greta. Tight grovel through pool into sharp bedding crawl, through squeeze to boulder blockage where faint daylight can be seen through a side passage.

HAZEL BUSH HILL HOLE   NGR NY 990102   Grade II
Alt. 400m   Length 82m   Depth 12m
Explored 1968, MSG.

WARNING – This cave floods to the roof in wet conditions.
GL. In gorge (usually dry) above Eller Beck Head is a hole behind some large boulders on N side of stream bed, just below a pool where the beck normally sinks. Climb down to chamber with stream entering through roof. Downstream passage is mostly crawling, passing oxbow on left, to climbable descents of 3m and 2.7m below which the stream sinks and the passage beyond closes to a choked fissure.

HOPE EDGE POT   NGR NZ 030075   Grade II
Alt. 480m   Depth 8m
Explored 1969, MSG.

ML. Small hole in top of plantation near edge of escarpment, covered by barbed wire. Single pitch, choked at bottom, with stalagmite flow on one wall.

Tackle – 8m ladder; stake and sling belay; 9m lifeline.

HUG GILL CAVE   NGR NY 977125   Grade I
Alt. 310m   Length 8m
Explored 1974, MSG.

ML. In gorge below Huggill Force, on E side of stream below floodgate. Short through trip.

JINGLEPOT HOLE   NGR NZ 009086   Grade I
Alt. 465m   Length 12m
Explored 1968, MSG.

ML. In large depression where sizeable stream sinks at edge of plantation. Rift becoming too narrow, may be choked at entrance by flood debris.

KILMONDS CAVE   NGR NZ 023135   Grade I
Alt. 295m   **Length 18m**
Explored 1977, YURT.

ML. In E side of disused quarry S of A66 road SW of Boldron is obvious opening 2.5m above quarry floor. Climb into entrance then traverse ahead to jammed boulders, beyond which is sharp left bend. Cave ends at a blank wall.

LOWER MELLWATERS HOLE
NGR NY 963127   **Grade II**
Alt. 297m   **Length 12m**   **Depth 3.5m**
Explored 1969, MSG.

ML. Tight shaft in grass bank a few metres S of river Greta, near where river sinks in dry weather, drops into small stream; downstream a boulder choke, upstream easy crawl becomes too low.

SEAVY SIKE POTS   NGR NZ 006087   Grade II
Alt. 465m   **Depth 9m**

ML. Two small potholes, on wide plateau W of Jinglepot Hole, are both blind shafts. Same tackle for each hole.

Tackle – 9m ladder; 3m belay; 12m lifeline.

TROUGH SCARS CAVES   Grade II
ML. The caves are in the wooded gorge of Sleightholme Beck.

1. Main Cave   **NGR NY 964119**   **Alt. 310m**   **Length 60m**
Extended 1969, MSG.

Easiest approach from E side of stream where easy descent into gorge can be made near ruined limekiln. Obvious small entrance 4.5m above beck. Crawl and climb over boulder into wide bedding chamber. To left, passage with good formations runs back to side of gorge. On right of main bedding tight crawl to low chamber. Main bedding with some good formations ends in stalactite barrier. Passage on right at end becomes too low.

2. NGR NY 964118   **Alt. 310m**   **Length 23m**
Explored 1967, MSG.

About 100m S of Main Cave. Lower Entrance in cliff 2m above stream. Squeeze over block and muddy bedding crawl to small chamber with boulders. Passage beyond becomes too tight. In roof of chamber easy 4.5m climb into narrow rift leading to Upper Entrance.

3. NGR NY 964116   **Alt. 320m**   **Length 18m**
Explored 1972, MSG.

About 200m S of 2 at stream level above 3m waterfall. Small hole behind fallen block leads into 3.5m high chamber and stream passage. Upstream passage ends too tight, downstream passage is a crawl through a pool to a pebble choke.

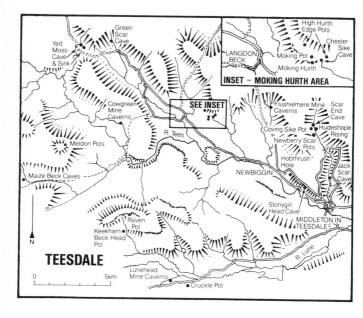

TEESDALE

CHESTER SIKE CAVE   NGR NY 870311   Grade II
Alt. 488m   **Length 25m**
Explored 1969, BACC.

    GL. In scarp 270m E of Moking Hurth, beside a wall, where Chester Sike rises. Wet crawl ending too tight after small chamber.

COVING SIKE POT   NGR NY 937304   Grade II
At. 410m   **Length 17m**   **Depth 8m**
Extended 1976, MSG.

    GL. In S bank of Coving Sike at top of limestone outcrop, where stream may be sinking. Climbable descent into roomy chamber, closing to impenetrable slot. By scaling 4.2m on right of chamber a tubular crawl is reached, becoming very tight where a stream is audible ahead.

COWGREEN MINE CAVERNS   NGR NY 809309
Alt. 500m

MSL. A series of caverns found in this mine are now lost. The mine site, at the edge of Cowgreen Reservoir, has been bulldozed and the caves are presumably flooded.

CRUCKLE POT   NGR NY 856202   Grade II
Alt. 437m   Length 12m   Depth 18m
Explored 1968, MSG.

GL. In large rocky shakehole at rear of limestone bench. Climb down through ruckle of large loose boulders to pitch into choked rift. Take care when selecting belay as most boulders are unsafe.

Tackle – 6m ladder; 6m belay; 12m lifeline.

FLUSHIEMERE MINE CAVERNS   NGR NY 909316
Alt. 460m

Level on E bank of beck has now collapsed but formerly intersected a large chamber containing good formations. Attempts to reach the cave by the mine shafts have been thwarted by massive collapses.

GREEN SCAR CAVE   NGR NY 804360   Grade I
Alt. 600m   Length 8m
Explored 1967, MSG.

GL. In Ashgill, 800m above road, on W side of stream in small gorge. Tubular crawl becoming too tight and having a vocal connection with a small pot above cliff (too tight 4.5m down).

HIGH HURTH EDGE POTS   Grade I
Alt. 500m

1. NGR NY 866316   Length 6m   Depth 6m

GL. In grassy shakehole near W end of line of shakeholes at rear of bench is 2m drop into low chamber. Crawl to 3.5m drop, climbable, to a pebble floor.

2. Ramshorn Pot   NGR NY 871313   Length 9m   Depth 8m
Explored 1972, MSG.

At rear of bench; second shakehole to E of the track. Two entrances, the lower opening onto an easy climb down into a rift chamber, ending too tight.

In line of shakeholes between these two pots, and also out on the bench, are several small holes, up to 6m in depth, all climbable.

HOBTHRUSH HOLE   NGR NY 922275   Grade I
Alt. 330m   **Length 9m**

GL. Below Low Ravelin farm, at head of wooded gorge used as rubbish tip. Obvious entrance 3m above foot of cliff. Tubular crawl becoming too tight.

HUDESHOPE RISING   NGR NY 938304   Grade I
Alt. 395m   **Length 5.5m**

GL. Rising at base of scar on E bank of Hudeshope Beck. Low, wet crawl to impassably-small tubes. Cave entrance higher in scar a few metres to S is an earthy crawl 4.5m long to choke.

JACK SCAR CAVE   NGR NY 948276   Grade II
Alt. 290m   **Length 140m**
Extended 1971, MSG.

GL. Follow track alongside Hudeshope Beck from Middleton-in-Teesdale. On E side of beck near start of Jack Scar gorge is cave entrance with small rising immediately below. Sandy hands-and-knees crawl to where main passage turns left. Ahead is a small aven, and a 3m drop reaches the stream, which cannot be followed. Along the main passage traversing past two small avens is followed by walking in stream to a small chamber. Through low arch and climb up 2m to rejoin stream. At second chamber there is a 5.5m climb into a high level passage, choked by a fallen slab. Stream passage continues as a tight crawl, left into a roomier section with some formations, then right again, to become too tight. At final corner is tight squeeze into higher level which is too tight.

KEEKHAM BECK HEAD POT   NGR NY 814236 Grade I
Alt. 620m   **Depth 4.5m**

In dry streambed. Fluted shaft to boulder floor and narrow fissure. Rising 100m away.

LUNEHEAD MINE CAVERNS NGR NY 845205 Grade II
Alt. 430m   **Length of cave passage 755m**
Explored by miners; small extensions 1975/76, MSG.

GL. Various short sections of cave have been intersected and often modified by old mine workings. Water in level is about 1.2m deep, dammed up by shale fall at entrance, which may now be blocked.

Wading past short branch levels, ending in collapses, on Read, Nacky and White Veins. Natural passage on White Vein, 460m in, is reached from branch level with deep mud, or from main level just beyond. Right of level is 20m of small passage; left is 30m of passage to chamber and massive collapse. Main level continues a further 157m to fork. Left is Cavern Vein East, right is Cavern Vein West.

Cavern Vein West

Level intersects two natural chambers with Scallop Passage – 60m natural

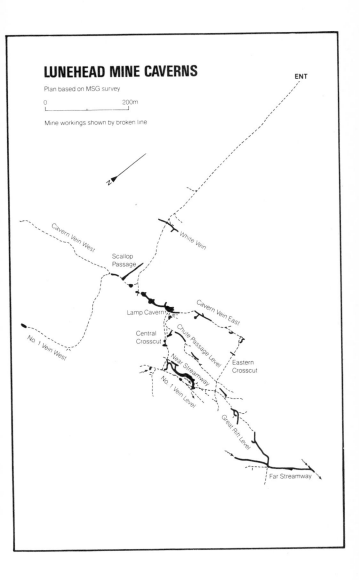

LUNEHEAD MINE CAVERNS

Plan based on MSG survey

0   200m

Mine workings shown by broken line

ENT

N

Cavern Vein West

White Vein

Scallop Passage

Cavern Vein East

Lamp Cavern

Central Crosscut

Chute Passage Level

No 1 Vein West

Eastern Crosscut

Near Streamway

No 1 Vein Level

Great Rift Level

Far Streamway

rift to choke – up slope on right in second. Level continues to fork; ahead ends in fall and left is No. 1 Vein West, ending after 370m at natural chamber and forehead.

Cavern Vein East

Level passes through two natural caverns, flat-roofed and stacked with deads, into a third, even larger: Lamp Cavern. At far end is high level chamber with unsafe, mined sub-level. Also at far end is continuation of Cavern Vein East over boulders to left. Mined and natural passages, lead past mud slope up into chamber and 25m of passage on right, to forehead. On right before this is 6m climb down into Eastern Crosscut.

Central Crosscut

Main level from Lamp Cavern goes to fork. Left is Chute Passage Level, right is Central Crosscut, descending to junction just before which is 3m climb up into 27m of sandy crawls to choke. At junction, way back to right is collapsed under Lamp Cavern. Ahead continues, past way on left into chamber with squeeze down on right into Near Streamway, to T-junction with No. 1 Vein.

Chute Passage Level

Easy walking in modified natural passage with short branches. After 113m is crawl on left up into 27m crawl ending too tight. Level continues to junction with Eastern Crosscut. Left past stream from tight inlet leads to climb to Cavern Vein East. Ahead leads to forehead; right, to a junction. Left at junction is Great Rift Level, right is No. 1 Vein Level.

No. 1 Vein and Near Streamway

Level passes short mined branches on left, then branch on right drops into natural Stream Chamber. Downstream is low crawl to 0.6m waterfall into bedding ending too low. Upstream is low, wide crawl; where stream route becomes too low, tube against right wall leads to further crawls, becoming too low after dry chamber on right with link to chamber off Central Crosscut. Main level passes dead end branch on left to unsafe arching with deads above. Passage beyond should be entered from Central Crosscut. From Central Crosscut, No. 1 Vein Level is enlarged streamway. Mined branch on left ends in fall, ahead is natural aven with floor level inlet crawl sumped after 6m. Level ends in forehead.

Left on No. 1 Vein Level from Central Crosscut, then left again, is natural downstream crawl for 27m, becoming too low close to upstream end of Near Streamway.

Great Rift Level

This follows line of natural passage. Mined branch on left has 20m natural crawl on its left. Main way becomes natural rift 1.2m wide and up to 17m high. At start of this section is climb above arching to short cave with very loose 4.5m climb, ending too low.

Great Rift ends where arching restarts – ahead is fork, main way backfilled, right is forehead. At start of arching is Far Streamway on either side of level. Upstream passage under right wall is 67m of miserable wet crawl to minimal airspace. Downstream is reached by careful climb up on left into chamber with climb down on left into rift streamway with battered formations. Walk for 60m then crawl to sump. Inlet on left before sump is too tight.

MAIZE BECK CAVES   NGR NY 749269   Grade II
Alt. 580m

TBL. On W side of gorge immediately downstream from bridge where Pennine Way crosses Maize Beck.

1. Rising on W side of gorge; entrance 0.6m wide and 0.5m high. Tight, wet crawl, may be accessible in drought, fed by sink 11m to W.

2. Length 5m
In side of gorge 12m SW of the sink feeding 1. Dry crawl ending in a choke.

3. Length 32m
Where stream rises 12m W of sink for 1. Low, wet crawl, including duck, for 20m to where daylight visible through a cross joint, and then easier passage to exit at sink.

4. Length 22m
21m E of entrance of 3. Easy crawl through two pools to exit in shakehole.

5. Length 5m
In opposite side of shakehole to exit to 4. Short crawl with pool.

MELDON POTS   NGR NY 774291   Grade II
Alt. 745m   **Depth 8m**
Explored DCC.

GL. Several small pots close to summit of Meldon Hill. Cairns mark the entrances of these choked shafts. Same tackle for each.

Tackle – 9m ladder; stake and sling belay; 12m lifeline.

MOKING HURTH   NGR NY 868310   Grade II
[Backhouse Cave]
Alt. 485m   **Length 300m**
Extended 1970, MSG.

GL. In prominent cliff above ruined limekiln are four entrances to main cave; there are other short caves nearby. The main cave is a series of phreatic cross rifts, some tight. From E entrance turn right into streamway; water sinks to reappear below entrances. Upstream is high, narrow rift with some climbs and traversing. Immediately after crossing first slightly awkward section of traversing (about 4.5m above the stream), on left is entrance to Mud Tube series, narrow crawls. Main passage becomes easy walking and ends where daylight is visible from impassable fissure high on left – this connects with large shakehole beside Moking Pot entrance. Straight ahead, stream issues from a very tight, wet crawl, which is the connection with Moking Pot, passable by thin cavers only.
Permission – Underhurth, Forest in Teesdale.

MOKING POT

NGR NY 868312

Grade II

Alt. 495m

Length 245m

Depth 11m

Extended 1970, MSG.

GL. On plateau above Moking Hurth, in small shakehole adjoining a large rocky depression which contains impenetrable fissure connecting with Moking Hurth. Narrow entrance shaft, belay to beam. At foot of ladder is junction, to right is impassable rift with daylight entering from rocky depression. Turning left, and immediately right again, leads to a narrow crawl through pool to 2.7m drop into the stream. Downstream climb into passage on right above stream sink, and drop down again to stream – this is the upstream end of connection with Moking Hurth, a very tight, wet crawl.

Upstream is a roomy passage to T-junction. Right is a dry side passage ending too tight; left is main upstream passage, with formations. Where the streamway turns right, straight ahead is an inlet passage, with a crawl over or under stal cascades, to an aven. Main upstream passage lowers to hands-and-knees crawl, after crawl through boulders, and continues to very tight section. Beyond this is small chamber, and another narrow jagged crawl – Fossil Crawl – to a large fallen block. Passage beyond is half choked with shingle and too tight to enter.

Tackle – 9m ladder; 1.5m belay; 12m lifeline.

Permission – Underhurth, Forest in Teesdale.

NEWBERRY SCAR POTS

Grade II

1. NGR NY 938300   Alt. 405m   **Length 11m**   **Depth 8m**

GL. Above scar a few metres S of obvious hush. Entrance in shakehole drops into chamber, which closes down to impassable fissures.

Tackle – 4.5m ladder; stake and sling belay; 8m lifeline.

2. NGR NY 938301   **Length 23m**   **Depth 13m**

Explored 1974, MSG.

GL. In grassy gully above scar, where small stream sinks. Narrow slot enlarges into an impressive rift. Downstream easy walk to wet squeeze then climb over boulders before passage becomes too narrow.

Tackle – 14m ladder; stake and sling belay; 18m lifeline.

3. NGR NY 937303

GL. In small shakehole at foot of gully a short distance N of 2. Very tight rift dropping onto pitch, not descended.

RAVEN POT

NGR NY 817247

Grade II

Alt. 720m

Depth 6m

Below crags on Mickle Fell escarpment is 1.5m wide hole in shale into chamber with debris floor. Probable rising is 80m away.

Tackle – 6m ladder; stake and sling belay; 12m lifeline.

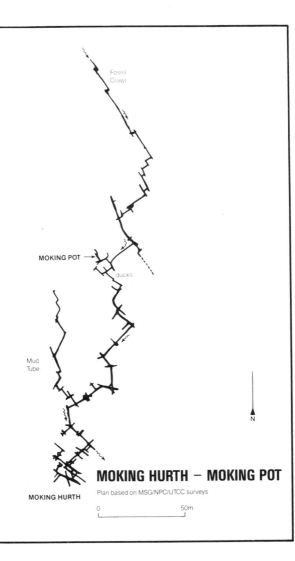

Fossil
Crawl

MOKING POT →

ducks

Mud
Tube

N

MOKING HURTH – MOKING POT

Plan based on MSG/NPC/UTCC surveys

MOKING HURTH

0   50m

SCAR END CAVE   NGR NY 937305   Grade II
Alt. 400m   **Length 21m**
Explored 1975, MSG.

GL. A few metres from end of scar, on W bank of beck, N of Coving Sike. Low entrance, may be walled, into crawl through low section into small rift chamber with some formations.

STONYGILL HEAD CAVE   NGR NY 932267   Grade II
Alt. 320m   **Length 23m**
Explored 1970, MSG.

GL. Entrance 100m W of rising, beside farmhouse. Low passage to junction with streamway, downstream choked with boulders, upstream a narrow crawl through an oxbow to choke.
This cave is used as a water supply and should not be entered.

YAD MOSS CAVE   NGR NY 783358   Grade II
Alt. 600m   **Length 190m**
Explored 1974, YURT; extended 1975, MSG.

ScL. Entrance on SE side of Crook Burn in small gorge. Wet crawl quickly opens into roomy passage with old choked outlet to right. Upstream walking passage with formations lowers to squeeze through vein. Crawling leads to two further squeezes and final stalagmite blockage.

YAD MOSS SINK   NGR NY 784356   Grade II
Alt. 610m   **Length 9m**
Explored 1974, YURT; extended 1975, MSG.

ScL. Entrance at obvious sink 200m SE of Yad Moss Cave. Slot with loose blocks drops into chamber with excessively tight inlet. Drop into downstream passage which becomes very low.

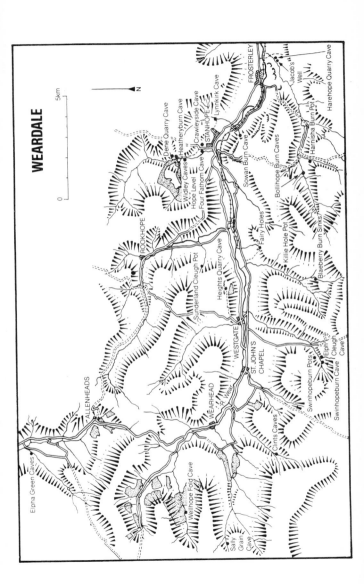

WEARDALE

5km

N

Elpha Green Caves

ALLENHEADS

Sally Grant Cave

Wellhope Fold Cave

WEARHEAD

Wear

Clints Caves

ST. JOHN'S CHAPEL

Swinhopeburn Pots

Elpha Cleugh Cave

Swinhopeburn Cave

WESTGATE

Sunderland Cleugh Pot

Heights Quarry Cave

Fairy Holes

Killie Hole Pot

ROOKHOPE

Dene Quarry Cave

Heatheryburn Cave

Widley Caves

Hope Level

Four Fathom Cave

Crawleyside Cave

STANHOPE

Lynnkirk Cave

Sowan Burn Cave

Bollihope Burn Caves

Blaeberry Burn Sinks

FROSTERLEY

Jacob's Well

Harnisha Burn Pot

Harehope Quarry Cave

WEARDALE

BLAEBERRY BURN SINKS
NGR NY 928344 **Grade I**
Alt. 420m **Depth 8m**

GL. Two small holes in Blaeberry Burn are sinks for Fairy Holes.

1. Shaft 3m deep just above stream on W bank becomes too tight.

2. On W side of stream a short distance upstream is 8m deep climbable rift, which may be covered over, dropping to an impenetrably narrow fissure into which the stream sinks.

BOLLIHOPE BURN CAVES
Grade I

1. Alt. 305m **NGR NY 978349** **Length 3m**
Explored 1973, DUSA.

GL. On N side of burn, beside a small tributary. Squeeze into aven chamber.

2. Alt. 305m **NGR NY 979349** **Length 17m**

GL. On S side of burn in prominent scar; a straight rift passage.

3. Resurgence Cave **NGR NY 982350** **Alt. 300m** **Length 4.5m**
Explored 1973/74, DUSA.

GL. Upstream one of two resurgences on S bank. Excavated way into boulder fall gains wet bedding which becomes too tight. Entrance blocked by fallen boulder.

CLINTS CAVES
NGR NY 843366 **Grade II**
Alt. 440m

1. Length 90m

GL. Below waterfall on Grooves Cleugh just above confluence with Ireshopeburn. On W side of stream is steadily lowering crawl with several inlets, becoming too low after rift aven.

2. Length 60m

GL. On opposite bank of Grooves Cleugh to 1. Small stream passage ending in sump and short, tight branch passage on right.

3. Length 15m

GL. In E bank of Grooves Cleugh a short distance above the waterfall. Rift drops to junction with streamway. Upstream is too tight; downstream closes down after fallen blocks.

4. Length 9m
Explored 1986, MSG.

GL. Dry entrance in S bank of Cutthroat Sike 150m upstream of confluence with Grooves Cleugh. Scalloped rift to 5m climb down into rift chamber with all exits too tight.

CRAWLEYSIDE CAVE   NGR NY 992398   Grade I
Alt. 240m   **Length 30m**
Explored 1975, MSG.

GL. In NW end of disused quarry. Scramble up into hands-and-knees crawl ending in sandy bedding.

DENE QUARRY CAVE   NGR NY 988411   Grade I
Alt. 260m   **Length 37m**
Explored 1977/79, MSG.

GL. In old quarry in Stanhope Dene. Tubular crawl, largely excavated, to choke. Perhaps a remnant of Heatheryburn Cave.
Permission – Stanhopeburn Mine.

ELPHA GREEN CAVES   NGR NY 846485   Grade II
Alt. 335m

GL. In disused quarry on N bank of Swinhopeburn, beside track from road to Elpha Green farm, Allendale.

Rift Cave   **Length 9m**
Obvious entrance in W end of quarry wall. Crawl to squeeze up into small chamber with stalagmite floor.

Main Cave   **Length 250m**
Extended 1973, MSG.

Main entrance, on N bank of stream just over wall from E end of quarry opens into chamber. Left is passage leading to tight entrance in quarry wall. Right leads to third entrance, but immediately left leads through crawl to small aven, then long tubular crawl to junction with stream passage. To right, downstream passage through low crawls and small boulder chambers to Ruckle Entrance, tight squeeze through boulders out onto stream bank 100m downstream of main entrance. Left is upstream passage to duck which can be by-passed by crawl up into chamber on right, and tube on left at end of chamber dropping back to stream. About 9m after rejoining the stream a climb up on left leads into the well-decorated 4.5m high Penguin Chamber. Continuing upstream through wet crawls to final chamber, with eroding stalagmites. Low, wet bedding continues (Feather End), and connects with low hole in quarry wall 15m away, but is obnoxious due to farm debris.
Permission – Elpha Green Farm (may be refused).

ELPH CLEUGH CAVE   NGR NY 889342   Grade II
Alt. 460m   Length 245m
Extended 1971/73, MSG.

GL. Entrance on E bank of Elph Cleugh, a few metres above confluence with Swinhope Burn. Hands-and-knees crawl to a small chamber, then continues upstream to junction, 20m from entrance. Right is Cake Inlet, tight and low at first but opening out to easier crawling and ending in choke beneath bed of Elph Cleugh 25m upstream of entrance. Main streamway continues as easy crawling and walking to a second junction, just after low bedding containing pool avoidable on right. At second junction, ahead is the Main Inlet, at first easy crawling but then becoming low and wet, to end in wet crawl, too low after a shingle bank. Passage on the right at the junction, at first low, is Green Elf Passage. Branch on right, 9m from junction becomes too tight after an aven. Green Elf Passage ends in boulder choke after walking-sized section and climbs up three small cascades. Final choke is only 12m horizontally from Elph Cleugh Pot, sink in 4.5m deep choked shaft, now covered over.

FAIRY HOLES   NGR NY 943369   Grade III
Alt. 370m   Length 3.2km
Explored 1844; main exploration 1953, DCC.

GL. Original entrance above resurgence has been left in a little hillock by vast quarrying operations which have destroyed about 600m of passage. Present quarry face is just upstream of site of Boulder Chamber and cave is blocked at this point.

From here the cave continues past The Duck — easily missed — into comfortable rifts, passing a muddy fissure on right which is too tight after 30m. From this junction up to The Choir there is often a deserted upper level to the streamway. Main way becomes more bouldery and reaches a climb up through boulders into Vein Chamber, 8m diameter and 1.5m high, 1km in.

From Vein Chamber the high level Coral Gallery is followed for a short way to a loose climb down to stream at first hole in floor. Coral Gallery contains formations and protruding fossil corals — care! Continuing upstream walk with boulder obstructions for about 600m to 5.5m climb up into the low, sandy Grave Chamber. Over slab to right is tight crawl out into a boulder chamber and the stream again. After more rift passage, boulders herald the 2.5m climb up into The Choir, a low chamber about 30m long and 6m wide, with stalagmites on the left.

Streamway is blocked with boulders at The Choir but a bedding plane crawl emerges on a balcony overlooking The Vestry. Stream is regained but quickly sumps. Way on is climb and traverse into rift chamber with Via Dolorosa down on the right. This low crawl, which floods in extreme conditions, continues past a spiky oxbow on the left to a letterbox and higher going. A pit in the floor gives access to the stream but it is easier to continue at high level and scramble down into an antechamber where Myers' Passage, 275m long to a choke, is seen up on right. The Antechamber opens into The

Sarcophagus, a larger cavern with a way over blocks to the stream again. Good going up the main streamway for 520m to an abrupt sump with no by-pass.

Permission to visit the cave is not given because it is in an active quarry.

HAREHOPE QUARRY CAVE   NGR NZ 036362   Grade I
Alt. 180m   **Length 110m**
Explored DCC.

GL. In S wall of Frosterley Quarry; dry cave with formations. Now quarried away.

HARNISHA BURN POT   NGR NY 986346   Grade I
Alt. 310m   **Depth 8m**
WARNING – Entrance frequented by adders in summer.

GL. On W side of Harnisha Burn just above small waterfall in wooded gorge is shaft into which part of burn falls. Climbable descent ends too tight. Below waterfall are two impenetrable sinks.

HEATHERYBURN CAVE   NGR NY 987412
Alt. 260m

GL. A large hoard of Bronze Age material was found in this cave in 1861. Cave was subsequently quarried away and the quarry, beside Stanhope Burn, is now partly filled with mine waste.

HEIGHTS QUARRY CAVE   NGR NY 923390   Grade I
Alt. 400m   **Length 6m**

GL. On W side of narrow section of Heights Quarry, near NW corner where quarry cuts through veins. Muddy, descending passage to choke. Other open holes nearby are old mine workings.

HOPE LEVEL FOUR FATHOM CAVE
NGR NY 990397   Grade III
Alt. 215m   **Length of cave passage 760m**
Explored NPC; extended DCC.

4FL. Hope Level entrance is on E bank of Stanhope Burn beside cottages. After 646m, level has cut a natural stream passage. On right (downstream) is 120m of dry passage, at first easy going, then climbs over and through boulder ruckles, ending in a complex and muddy ruckle. Upstream passage is over 600m long, at first easy walking in a high rift, then climbs over boulder ruckles. For one climb, from stream up into a fairly large chamber, a rope or an 8m ladder belayed by the first man up is useful. Beyond a small chamber, where passage cuts mineral veins, the cave is wider and lower to a low chamber, with a hole in the floor dropping into a low, wet crawl. Short, wet crawls alternating with higher sections lead to small chamber with a large fallen slab. Straight ahead, at end of chamber, a small hole leads into an aven, The Glory Hole, with very fine formations. On right of chamber, behind fallen block, a very wet and muddy crawl leads to the final sump – too tight to pass. On left here a short, tight crawl appears to be by-passing the sump, but ends after a tight squeeze in a pool and boulder ruckle.

Mine gated and not working at present due to dangerous concentrations of radon (radioactive gas) which prohibit any visit to the cave.

JACOB'S WELL   NGR NZ 035361   Grade II
Alt. 185m   Length 300m
Explored DCC; extended BACC and MSG.

GL. In SW corner of Frosterley Quarry, damaged by quarrying. Obvious arched entrance just below quarry bench, on S side of Bollihope Burn where it enters the quarry. Choked hole in floor at junction immediately inside entrance led into Lower Series, now blocked. Left at junction is roomy tunnel to boulder ruckle and exit onto quarry bench; passages and chambers of Flood Rising Series beyond are now inaccessible. Right at junction is easy route past original entrance on right, now choked by quarry debris, to concrete wall across passage. Tight squeeze through hole in wall to large passage beyond, with stream entering through inlets on right and sinking in floor. Straight ahead is massive ruckle; to right is wet crawl in streamway ending in choke.

KILLIE HOLE POT   NGR NY 934358   Grade I
Alt. 415m   Length 10m   Depth 7m
GL. In large shakehole on drift-covered bench. Climb down through dangerous boulders into descending rift which becomes tight.

LYNNKIRK CAVE   NGR NZ 006392   Grade I
Alt. 250m   Length 110m
Extended 1962, Weardale Speleological and Rambling Society.

GL. On Shittlehope Burn, best reached from footbridge on path from Jolly Body farm. Follow stream down to Upper Entrance on W bank, opening into small chamber. Left is easy crawl through bedding to large passage where stream enters on left. Downstream passage and roomy, dry passage with gours rejoin just inside large Lower Entrance opening into gorge. Ahead at small chamber near Upper Entrance leads to junction with low streamway. Left rejoins main route at bedding crawl; right (upstream) forks, both branches being too tight.

SALLY GRAIN CAVE   NGR NY 801291   Grade II
Alt. 570m   Length 98m   Depth 8.5m
Explored 1968, YURT.

GL. Entrance in small solitary outcrop on S side of Sally Grain Burn, 2.5m above stream. Slide down into straight fissure passage, narrow walking and short crawl for 52m to mud choke. Claw Crawl on right is short, sharp wriggle into further rift which steps across into parallel fissure, becoming low and tight. Water may flow to Priorsdale Cave.

SOWAN BURN CAVE NGR NY 998380 Grade II
Alt. 270m **Length 260m**

GL. In N wall of disused quarry. W entrance is hole behind tree half way up quarry wall, a few metres E of rising. Entrance drops into chamber. To right climb down into a series of dry rift passages, with some climbs and traverses, leading to E entrance. To left in chamber drop down into roomy, bouldery passage where stream is met, sinking in floor fissure – stream is local water supply and should not be entered. Upstream is canal passage to sump, which has been dived to two airbells and then chokes with silt.
Permission – Parson Byers Farm, Stanhope.

SUNDERLAND CLEUGH POT NGR NY 934400 Grade II
Alt. 365m **Length 15m** **Depth 9m**

GL. Collapse close to N bank of Cleugh. Climb down through earth and boulders into solid rock rift and chamber; two windows link to second chamber.

SWINHOPEBURN CAVE NGR NY 888342 Grade I
Alt. 460m **Length 20m**

GL. In small scar on S bank of Swinhope Burn, 200m upstream from Elph Cleugh. Small, winding passage leads into roomier chamber, ending in a silt choke.

SWINHOPEBURN POTS Grade II
1. NGR NY 888343 **Alt. 480m** **Length 20m** **Depth 9m**
Explored 1975, MSG.

GL. On N side of Swinhope Burn in large bouldery shakehole about 300m N of Swinhopeburn Cave. Most obvious entrance is 3.5m climb down into chamber. Narrow rift descends to showerbath beneath Sink Entrance, stream sinks into impassable rift.

2. NGR NY 888343 **Alt. 480m** **Depth 9m**
Explored 1975, MSG.

GL. About 100m SW of 1. Hole covered by fence posts, very earthy at the top, drops to choke.

Tackle – 9m ladder; stake and sling belay; 12m lifeline.

3. NGR NY 890347 **Alt. 490m** **Length 8m** **Depth 3.5m**
GL. Follow line of shakeholes N from 1 and 2. Small stream sink, narrow descending crawl to a boulder choke.

WELLHOPE FOLD CAVE NGR NY 815410 Grade I
Alt. 490m **Length 11m**
Explored 1969, MSG.

4FL. Entrance at stream level on S side of Wellhope Burn. Hands-and-knees crawl, ending too low where the passage turns right and runs back towards the stream bank.

WIDLEY CAVES   NGR NY 987402   Grade I
Alt. 240m

4FL. Three small caves on W side of Stanhope Burn, by waterfall 100m S of footbridge.

1. Length 4.5m
Narrow fissure N of waterfall becomes tight and choked.

2. Length 4.5m
Under waterfall is low entrance into higher passage with flowstone covered walls and floor, ending at blank wall.

3. Length 5m
Rectangular entrance S of waterfall closes down to tiny hole with water emerging.

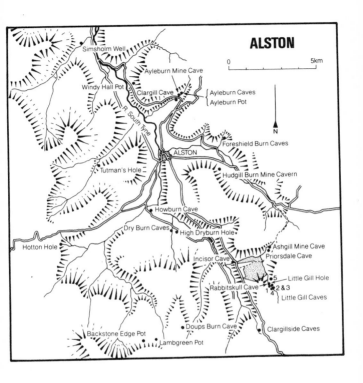

ALSTON

ASHGILL MINE CAVE   NGR NY 778413   Grade I
Alt. 500m   **Length 9m**

GL. On S bank of Ashgill 200m upstream from Priorsdale Cave. Entrance above small rising leads into low, mined passage with crawl on left into natural bedding with stream entering and sinking. Mined passage ends in collapse after 4.5m high natural aven on right.

AYLEBURN CAVES NGR NY 730500 Grade II
Alt. 345m

GL. On N bank of Ayle Burn 200m upstream of Ayleburn Mine entrance.

1. Length 43m

Obvious 1.2m high entrance opens into a chamber with aven, and on right a crawl into a second chamber, with continuing passage beyond ending too narrow. About 9m from end of this a tube on right blocked with stalactites communicates with 2.

2. Length 48m

Small entrance on N bank of Ayle Burn 20m upstream from 1. Crawl down to aven, and then large passage to T-junction. To left is choked, to right is narrow rift becoming too tight, with tube communicating with 1 on left.

AYLEBURN MINE CAVE NGR NY 728498 Grade III
Alt. 330m Length 1.7km Depth 30m
Entered by lead miners in the 18th century; re-discovered 1948, CUCC; extended DCC; 1969/75, MSG; 1975, CDG.

WARNING – Sections of this cave may flood after heavy rain. Loose boulders are a hazard in some parts. Rescue of an injured person through the squeeze would be extremely difficult.

GL. On N bank of Ayle Burn a few metres upstream from Clargill bridge is mine level entered through collapse on N side of quarry track. Level with deep mud for 150m to fork. Right branch ends in collapse after 30m, straight ahead ends after 210m. Above the fork is a 9m rise. Advisable to send best climber in party up first, to belay ladder for the remainder (timbers wedged across passage serve as belay). At top of rise turn left and climb down 4m into natural stream passage.

Upstream Series

Upstream after 15m is 1.5m waterfall. Above fall a route through boulders, and a squeeze, lead into the upstream passage. On right where passage is entered is the 130m long Gutgrinder Inlet, very tight and tortuous initially. Beyond The Contortions, on the left, Coward's Entry is an easy link back to the streamway. Other tight side passages in this area.

Main way is continued easy walking, passing another side passage on right which becomes very tight. Streamway lowers to stooping height, and sandy oxbow on right avoids a long duck. At end of oxbow, stream is rejoined in a low, wide bedding. Flat-out crawl leads to Far Upstream Passage, hands-and-knees crawling in a shallow canal with some formations, eventually ending too low only a few metres from Ayleburn Pot.

Downstream Series

Downstream from point of entry, stream flows into a low passage which sumps, but on left is a 3m climb into a dry by-pass. Where this turns right to re-join stream, straight ahead is entrance to Upper Grotesque Passage, a series of narrow crawls.

Continuing downstream, an opening on the left leads into Lower Grotesque Passage, communicating with Upper Grotesque Passage via a

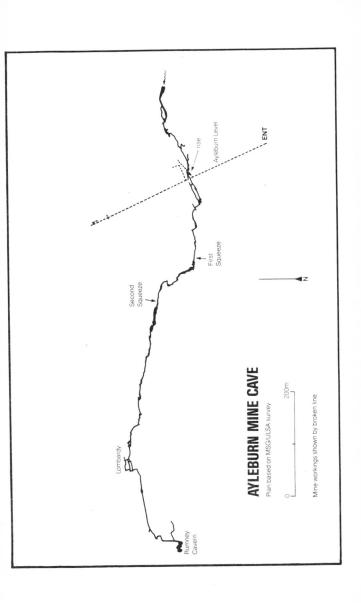

AYLEBURN MINE CAVE

Plan based on MSG/ULSA survey

0   200m

Mine workings shown by broken line

ENT

Ayleburn Level

rise

First Squeeze

Second Squeeze

Lombardy

Rumney Cavern

N

narrow fissure. Following the streamway down, Overhead Crawl is reached (stream flowing in an impassable lower level), and several boulder ruckles, with passage gradually lowering to a crawl. Eventually where stream flows under right wall, in impassable bedding, is route on through dry tube. After small chamber, this tube becomes very tight and low—The Squeeze.

Beyond, the downstream passage continues as hands-and-knees crawling, and down several small cascades, gradually developing into a high rift passage again. On left is High Level Oxbow, and 30m further downstream are three entrances into a series of interconnecting sandy crawls, Lombardy. Streamway lowers to an acute bend, then gains height, passing an inlet on the left, which is a tight crawl, becoming too narrow after 45m. A 1.2m waterfall drops into Rumney Cavern, which is 15m long, and then a short crawl leads to a boulder-choked aven and Sump 1. This sump is 8m long, constricted and should not be free-dived. After 17m of low, muddy canal is Sump 2—low, muddy and over 15m long, leading to Sump 3, not yet dived. Water is presumed to rise at Saffron Well, NGR NY 693515, 2.5km from and 80m lower than the final sump, but impenetrable.

Tackle—9m ladder; 3m belay; 12m lifeline.

AYLEBURN POT   NGR NY 730499   Grade II
Alt. 350m   Length 203m   Depth 12m
Main exploration 1977, Oxford University Caving Club/ULSA.

GL. Old entrance is rift in shakehole above scar, with easy climb down to stream in low bedding. Dry branch on left links to passable downstream crawl; before this gets too low, dry crawl up to left leads into complex of dry passages with some formations, with several holes down into stream in low beddings. One crawl leads to New Entrance 20m up-valley from Ayleburn Cave 2.

BACKSTONE EDGE POT   NGR NY 705361   Grade II
Alt. 685m   Depth 6m
Explored 1978, MSG.

GL. On limestone bench beneath Backstone Edge, in small shakehole N of larger one taking a stream. Open hole in peat to shaft in spiky corroded limestone; squeeze to second drop which is probably too tight.

CLARGILL CAVE   NGR NY 727496   Grade I
Alt. 350m   Length 8m

GL. At foot of prominent small scar across field S of bridge over Ayle Burn. Low crawl to small chamber.

CLARGILLSIDE CAVES   NGR NY 771367   Grade II
Alt. 560m
Explored 1975, MSG.

1. Lower Cave   Length 20m
ScL. Dry Entrance E of where Clargill normally sinks in its bed. A small

stream is met sinking in floor, and upstream an easy crawl leads to second entrance beneath a fence, then further crawl into bedding chamber, ending choked where daylight visible.

2. Upper Cave   **Length 25m**
   ScL. Stream sink 50m SE of 1. Narrow crawl with formations, ending too low.

DOUPS BURN CAVE   NGR NY 728368   Grade II
Alt. 620m   **Length 8m**
Explored 1978, MSG.
   4FL. Small entrance at rising on S of old hush. Crawl into pool chamber.

DRY BURN CAVES   NGR NY 722422   Grade I
Alt 340m   **Length 30m**
   ScL. In long, dry gorge above road. Longest cave is at the above grid reference, on W side of the stream bed, a through trip with three entrances, all easy crawling. At times this may be choked by shingle. Further downstream on the W side of the gorge is an oxbow cave 9m long. Opposite is a small resurgence cave (explored 1985, MSG), a 9m tight wet tube ending too tight.

FORESHIELD BURN CAVES   NGR NY 753473   Grade I
Alt. 400m
Explored 1974, MSG.

1. Length 8m
   GL. Rising at head of eastern gorge where Foreshield Burn divides. Low bedding leads to cross rift and narrow fissure to where daylight can be seen.

2. Length 9m
   GL. Dry cave on W side of northern gorge above where burn divides. Stooping-height passage to collapse where daylight is visible.

HIGH DRYBURN HOLE   NGR NY 724422   Grade II
Alt. 350m   **Length 5m**
Explored 1981, YURT.
   ScL. Entrance in shallow shakehole about 20m from road. Tight slot drops 2m to short section of passage which doubles back and chokes.

HOTTON HOLE   NGR NY 659415   Grade II
[Hunter's Hole]
Alt. 490m   **Length 110m**
Extended 1975, CDG.
   ScL. On Rowgill Burn, where the stream rises at foot of gorge, on N bank. Roomy stream passage with short, choked branches, leading to sump. Low silty sump of 43m with airbell to large chamber; continuing bedding crawl becomes too low. Further up gorge on N bank is 8m long dry cave.

HOWBURN CAVE   NGR NY 710433   Grade II
Alt. 310m   Length 58m
Explored 1980, YURT.

ScL. Through Howburn Farm yard and over boundary wall is rising from culvert. This is start of approximately 30m of crawling through a stone culvert, concrete pipes and oil drums to the cave entrance which is now buried under farm yard extension. A low wet start enlarges into wide bedding plane. At first corner small fissure passage on right with deep water ends in cobble blockage. Upstream continues as crawling to flat out section and collapse and cobble blockage.

Permission – Howburn Farm.

HUDGILL BURN MINE CAVERN   NGR NY 751456
Alt. 410m

GL. Extensive natural cavern found by lead miners; level now badly collapsed at entrance.

INCISOR CAVE   NGR NY 758405   Grade II
At. 400m   Length 27m
Explored 1987, Haymarket Caving Club

ScL. On N bank of Ashgill by path below waterfall. Loose wriggle down under boulders to large chamber; upstream passage ends in tight bedding, with high level above blocked by boulder and side passages choked with mud.

LAMBGREEN POT   NGR NY 712362   Grade II
Alt. 680m   Length 8m   Depth 5m
Explored 1978, MSG.

GL. On E side of Lambgreen Hills is large rocky shakehole near E end of row of shakeholes. Squeeze under slipped block to 2.5m drop constricted by chert ledges.

LITTLE GILL CAVES   Grade I

GL. A group of small caves in Little Gill. Sink may feed Priorsdale Cave.

1. NGR NY 778391   Alt. 545m   Depth 4.5m
Where stream sinks in gully on W side of gill. Climb down boulder slope to small passage on right ending in choke.

2. NGR NY 779391   Alt. 545m   Length 8m   Depth 3m
Explored 1972, MSG.

On E side of gill 3m above stream level, a short distance N of most obvious entrance on that side of stream, which is Little Gill Hole. Narrow crawl to 3m climb down into small chamber, crawl into second small chamber and choke.

3. NGR NY 799391   Alt. 550m   Length 4.5m   Depth 3.4m
Explored 1969, MSG.

On E side of gill a few metres S of Little Gill Hole. Narrow climbable shaft opens into small chamber, where a stream can be heard through an impassable fissure.

4. NGR NY 779391   **Alt. 550m**   **Length 4.5m**
  On E side of gill at head of gorge. Flood sink, drop through boulders into low chamber, outlet choked by collapse.

5. NGR NY 778395   **Alt. 550m**   **Depth 6m**
  In gorge where tributary cuts limestone outcrop. Near head of cascades part of stream sinks in hole on N side of gorge. Easier entrance just upstream leads to climbable descent into rift chamber, where water sinks to reappear at foot of cliff. In cliff on N side of the gorge further downstream is an old resurgence cave, becoming very tight after 3.5m

LITTLE GILL HOLE   NGR NY 779391   Grade II
Alt. 550m   **Length 30m**   **Depth 12m**
Explored DCC.

  GL. Entrance in scar on E side of Little Gill. Climbable descents in rift passage and where rift becomes too tight turn right into second rift chamber. At far end of this is difficult 6m climb on right into passage at roof level, which leads to 6m climbable pitch into third rift chamber and impassably-tight rift.

PRIORSDALE CAVE   NGR NY 778410   Grade III
Alt. 500m   **Length 310m**
Explored DCC; extended 1971, University of Newcastle Caving Club & MSG.

WARNING—This cave contains a tight squeeze through which rescue of an injured person would be impossible. There are also dangerous loose boulders in much of the system.

  GL. On S bank of Ashgill below Priorsdale farmhouse is large rising from cliff and boulder ruckle. Entrance lowers to bedding with crawl up on left into high rift passage, then short crawl and turn left along mined passage into small chamber. Crawl ahead and to right, and after constriction 4.5m from the chamber squeeze up into roof bedding. Tight squeeze through bedding and into small chamber with solid roof. Passage amongst boulders on left here runs almost back to the cliff face at the rising—many loose boulders. Turn right down boulder slope to Stalactite Chamber. At far end of this follow right wall, up slope and into large Tilted Slabs Chamber. At far side of this, hole in floor drops into short passage, then 1.2m drop into large passage in solid rock. To right 15m of large passage to massive boulder ruckle, penetrable for some distance at various levels. To left, passage lowers and upstream passage enters on right. Straight ahead (downstream) water sinks in choked fissures after 12m. Upstream passage is wet crawl for 25m to very tight double bend, then crawl in deepening water for 45m through ducks to final sump.
  May be fed by sinks in Little Gill, 1.6km away and 60m higher, and Sally Grain Cave, 3km away and 70m higher.

RABBITSKULL CAVE   NGR NY 778931   Grade II
Alt. 550m   **Length 20m**
Explored 1969, MSG.

GL. Where Little Gill valley narrows is entrance at foot of scar on E side, behind nettles. Small chamber closes to tight tube, then low crawl to narrow squeeze, and aven on left provides room to turn round, where passage ahead becomes too tight. Dripping water is cutting through the mud floor to reveal a layer of calcited rabbit bones beneath.

SIMSHOLM WELL   NGR NY 672528   Grade I
Alt. 230m   **Length 6m**
Explored 1985, MSG.

GL. Obvious rising. Tubular wet crawl to collapse from surface, with tree roots.

TUTMAN'S HOLE   NGR NY 680460   Grade III
Alt. 355m   **Length 615m**
Explored by lead miners; extended 1969, YURT; 1975, DUSA.

WARNING – Liable to flooding; the ducks readily sump.

ScL. Resurgence from collapsed scar on SE bank of Gilderdale Burn, close to wall. Hole above collapse enters roomy chamber with bouldery passage leading upstream. At sharp right bend into pools is joint on left, giving access to wriggle into East Avens Passage, 45m of varied going to two avens and excessively-tight continuation. Main passage continues walking size through pools to Dry Chamber, beyond which is a steadily-lowering passage through two canals to a third in a wide, low crawl continuing below cross-joints to two low ducks, then long hands-and-knees crawl in canal with fine formations, Venice. Further crawling and ducks lead to Turtle Chamber and then junction. To right ends too tight. To left, upstream bedding crawl eventually ends in impassable bedding only about 50m from sink in bank of Gilderdale Burn. There is a 4.5m deep climbable pot on the other side of the wall to the cave.

WINDY HALL POT   NGR NY 700505   Grade II
Alt. 290m   **Depth 9m**
GL. Small stream sink just E of Ayle-Barhaugh road. Climb down through boulder ruckle to choke; rope useful. Loose boulders.

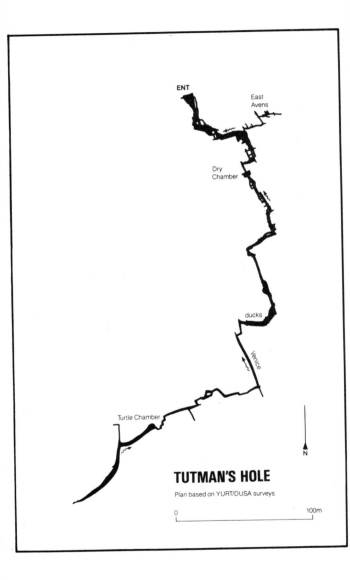

ENT

East
Avens

Dry
Chamber

ducks

Venice

Turtle Chamber

N

TUTMAN'S HOLE

Plan based on YURT/DUSA surveys

0   100m

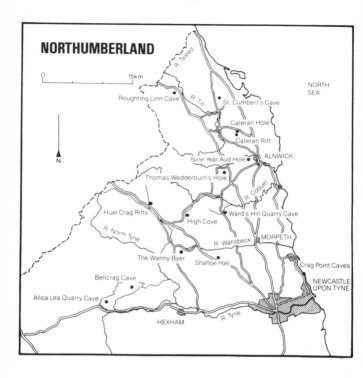

NORTHUMBERLAND

ALLOA LEA QUARRY CAVE NGR NY 684665 Grade I
Alt. 220m   **Length 10m**
Explored 1987, MSG.

5YL. In old quarry above ruined limekiln beside farm road from Walltown to Alloa Lea. Up-dip tube to junction; left is squeeze up into choked tube with daylight visible; right is squeeze to tiny chamber.

BELLCRAG CAVE   NGR NY 772720   Grade I
Alt. 320m   Length 8m

Limestone. Below road on right where stream sinks is narrow passage between peat banks. Roof lowers to blockage of peat and rocks. Formed in thin limestone bed and fills to roof in flood.

CATERAN HOLE   NGR NU 102237   Grade I
Alt. 250m   Length 45m   Depth 6m

Gritstone. On N slope of Cateran Hill; difficult to find! Walk 1.1km S from the North Charlton-Chillingham road at Quarry House. Correct line to walk is such that, when looking back, the tall radio aerial beyond the house appears just inside the edge of the wood beside the farm. Shallow crater with cut steps leading down into easy rift passage; short muddy crawl at end to total choke. Once used as smugglers' hiding place.

CATERAN RIFT   NGR NU 102232   Grade II
Alt. 260m   Length 15m   Depth 5m

Gritstone. In obvious slip trench 120m SW of Cateran Hill cairn. Wriggle down through boulders into chamber with daylight entering.

CRAG POINT CAVES   NGR NZ 343762   Grade I
Alt. Sea level

Sandstone. Three sea caves at Crag Point, between Seaton Sluice and St. Mary's Point, numbered from S.

1. Length 18m
Nearest St. Mary's Point is opening 2.7m wide and 3.5m high, reached by climbing over slippery boulders to cliff face. Tall square-cut passage with rocks on floor ends at blank wall with 2m long undercut at floor level.

2. Length 13m
Near angle in cliff N of 1 is scramble up cobble slope at back of large undercut, to 1.2m square passage ending at step down into slight enlargement, with small stal flow on right wall.

3. Length 34m
Large entrance in outer end of rock buttress immediately N of 2. Climb over rocks in rift passage averaging 3m high and 1.5m wide. Pebble slope rises to within 1m of roof where cave pinches out.

HIGH COVE   NGR NY 953958   Grade I
Alt. 250m   Lengths to 18m   Depths to 6m

Gritstone. Major slip feature on W side of Grasslees Burn; several small rifts and caves.

HUEL CRAG RIFTS   NGR NY 829995   Grade I
Alt. 230m

Gritstone. Slip rift caves in massive slipped block below crag N of Hillock Farm, High Rochester.

1. Length 16m
Entrance at N end of block; easy through trip.

2. Length 28m
Low entrance a few metres E of 1. Roomy passage divides into boulder-choked rifts.

3. Length 30m
Near roofless rift splitting S part of block; several entrances to a little complex of tilted rifts.

NINE YEAR AUD HOLE   NGR NU 156146   Grade I
Alt. 170m   Length 12m

Gritstone. In Hulne Park (pedestrian access only; permit from Estate Office) on N side of Cave Drive on Brizlee Hill. Large entrance guarded by stone friar; scramble through boulders to exit round corner to E.

ROUGHTING LINN CAVE   NGR NT 902368   Grade I
Alt. 90m   Length 12m
Explored 1985, University of Bristol Speleological Society.

Sandstone. Below the track to Roughting Linn, 20m downstream of waterfall on E side of stream just above path. Tube narrowing to squeeze and earth choke.

ST. CUTHBERT'S CAVE   NGR NU 059353   Grade I
Alt. 150m

Sandstone. Follow metalled road to Holburn Grange, then track up to open moor and right to plantation. Half way along foot of wood, path leads up to cave which is an impressive rock shelter 20m wide, 3m high and going back 5m from the cliff face.

SHAFTOE HALL   NGR NZ 055817   Grade I
Alt. 180m   Length 8m

Gritstone. In crag to W of East Shaftoe Hall, directly beneath the prominent Punchbowl Stone. Roomy rock shelter.

THOMAS WEDDERBURN'S HOLE
NGR NU 077100   Grade I
Alt. 185m   Length 10m

Gritstone. Beside footpath in Thrunton Wood, signposted. Slipped mass of rock with a couple of short through caves.

THE WANNY BYER
Alt. 290m

NGR NY 934835
Length 35m

Grade II
Depth 8m

Gritstone. Rift on summit of escarpment towards E end of crag; at W end where rift meets cliff face is a 10m long through trip. Another 30m E a hole under a boulder drops down a tight 5m chimney into a narrow rift ending in boulder blockages.

WARD'S HILL QUARRY CAVE
NGR NU 079965
Alt. 170m   Length 104m

Grade II

Explored 1977, MSG.

GL. On SE side of minor road 5.7km SSE of Rothbury is old quarry. Follow track down into deepest part of quarry and on right, limestone is exposed beneath Whin Sill. Obvious entrance leads into a series of bedding passages and chambers connecting with a second entrance, which may be blocked. Generally low and muddy and the various ends are too low and choked.

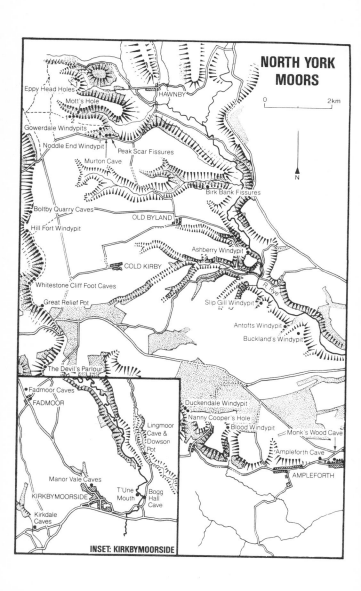

NORTH YORK MOORS

0   2km

N

Eppy Head Holes
Mott's Hole
HAWNBY
Gowerdale Windypits
Noddle End Windypit
Peak Scar Fissures
Murton Cave
Birk Bank Fissures
Boltby Quarry Caves
OLD BYLAND
Hill Fort Windypit
Ashberry Windypit
COLD KIRBY
Whitestone Cliff Foot Caves
R Rye
Great Relief Pot
Slip Gill Windypit
Antofts Windypit
Buckland's Windypit
The Devil's Parlour
Duckendale Windypit
Nanny Cooper's Hole
Blood Windypit
Monk's Wood Cave
Ampleforth Cave
AMPLEFORTH

INSET: KIRKBYMOORSIDE

Fadmoor Caves
FADMOOR
Lingmoor Cave & Dowson Pot
Manor Vale Caves
KIRKBYMOORSIDE
T'Une Mouth
Bogg Hall Cave
Kirkdale Caves

NORTH YORK MOORS

All caves in this area are in Corallian Limestone

AMPLEFORTH CAVE   NGR SE 591789   Grade I
Alt. 150m   **Length 8m**
Explored 1972, ACVSU.

In quarry at left side of road going uphill from Ampleforth-Ampleforth College road. Low entrance at cliff base leads down over large boulder into low cross-passage, which chokes to right and ends similarly to left after 6m.

ANTOFTS WINDYPIT   NGR SE 582829   Grade III
Alt. 150m   **Length 250m**   **Depth 43m**
Explored 1949, BSA; extended 1955, ACVSU.

WARNING – Danger of falling rocks in many places.

A variety of archaeological material was found during the further exploration of this windypit, including a skull dated from 1700-1500BC. Permission to descend the hole is not granted at present.

Entrance surrounded by high wooden fence 20m E of Antofts Farm. Steep mud slope leads to a series of superimposed rift chambers; a ladder is useful but not essential. The lowest chamber intersects the impressive Main Fissure in a roomy chamber from which a traverse in the oblique Branch Fissure can be entered. The Main Fissure continues NW with various climbs up, down and through boulders. An oblique branch on the right after 20m leads to the Crossroads and a tall chamber. The Main Rift ends where it steps to the right into a choked parallel fissure. This section, the deepest point, is both geologically recent (see broken calcite) and disturbingly unstable.

Tackle – 20m ladder; stake and sling belay; 30m lifeline.

ASHBERRY WINDYPIT   NGR SE 570850   Grade II
Alt. 150m   **Length 320m**   **Depth 27m**
WARNING – Loose rock in places.

On Ashberry Hill, just below crest of wooded slope facing Rievaulx Abbey. Follow track branching left from Old Byland to Rievaulx road and about 100m before gate into open field, turn left into wood and search for hole. An intricate and extensive windypit.

1. Entrance is an obvious crater beneath tree. Series of roomy rifts and chambers spiral down to head of 9m pitch into Main Rift. Pitch can be avoided by using Dowson's Route – take first left before head of pitch, and series of small descents and final 4.5m drop, where a handline is useful, provide an easier route into Main Rift. To N is climb up boulder slope, short crawl, and 5.5m climb down into short further section of Main Rift. To S, below foot of climb on Dowson's Route, is smaller passage, a hole in the floor of which is deepest point in the system, ending in choke close to Ammonite Rift in 2.

2. Small entrance 9m S of 1 is 4.5m descent (rope useful) into chamber. To N is very tight rift connecting with 1, to S a low crawl leads into very complex series of chambers and rifts. Route to deepest point found by taking first possible branch on left (not hole in roof), and right at first junction along narrow rift, dropping into a chamber with false floor. Climb down into chamber beneath, then down slope onto rock bridge in Ammonite Rift – this area is very unstable. Climb down 3.6m to floor of rift; to N boulder choke, to S crawl into Lower Windlet Chamber, with narrow rift on left in floor draughting strongly – the Windlet. Various other passages and chambers, too complex to be easily described.

BIRK BANK FISSURES   NGR SE 555868   Grade II
Alt. 185m

Two slip rift caves on S edge of Caydale.

1. Dog Rescue Fissure (Caydale Hole)   Length 27m   Depth 10.5m

Twin entrances at foot of main scar. Climbable descents through rift chambers. Archaeological remains found here in 1952.

2. Shelob's Lair   Length 17m   Depth 3.5m
Explored 1981, MSG.

Opposite Dog Rescue Fissure in the S face of the slipped block of land below the main scar. Narrow rift linking two entrances, with just inside W entrance a sloping side passage ending in a chamber. Arachnophobes will not like it.

BLOOD WINDYPIT   NGR SE 565799   Grade II
Alt. 200m   Length 90m   Depth 16m
Explored 1972, ACVSU.

WARNING – Danger everywhere from loose rocks.

Three entrances on W side of Shallowdale; W entrance among boulders in a hollow 65m NNW of farm at head of valley; 10m E is E entrance, round hole covered with boulders. No. 3 entrance is 9m E again, in side of bank and is tight and unstable. Latter two entrances should be covered securely. A complex and unstable windypit-type cave with many passages lying close to the surface.

From W entrance an 8m climb among boulders (handline advisable) leads to small chamber. To right, short climb and traverse lead via crawl into main passage. Ahead through crawl and up climb is E entrance. To left various ways lead to Main Chamber. From here a squeeze leads to a T-junction. To left and down a letterbox is the bottom fissure, the deepest point. To right a climb leads to 9m high chamber. Various crawls, only partially explored, lead off. Entrance 4 drops into this chamber.

Tackle

Entrance	Ladder	Belay	Lifeline
Main (W)	–	–	15m handline
3	11m	3m	12m

Permission – Farm at head of valley.

BOGG HALL CAVE   NGR SE 709865
[Spring Head]

Alt. 40m   **Length 200m**

Explored 1981, Scunthorpe Caving Club,

Obvious rising on E bank of river Dove. First sump 9m to airbell, second sump 9m to two passages which rejoin. Beyond is duck and The Wedge, complex of small passages reuniting in streamway 3m wide and 1-2m high. After large fallen blocks and oxbow, passage ends in The Font, chamber with underwater pitch explored to 12m depth, continuing down. No accessible cave for non-divers.

BOLTBY QUARRY CAVES   NGR SE 507863   Grade II

Alt. 300m

Three small caves in disused quarry on the edge of the Hambleton escarpment.

1. Length 25m   **Depth 8m**

Obvious tube entrance just above quarry floor. Short crawl to junction with high rift, with boulder chokes at each end.

2. Length 11m

Explored 1975, MSG.

A few metres S of 1. Very tight passage turns left into roomier crawl ending choked. Vocal connection with 1.

3. Length 21m   **Depth 8.5m**

Explored 1975, MSG.

Further N along face, just beyond step in the quarry floor. Squeeze down onto pitch into rift ending in boulder ruckles.

Tackle – 8m ladder; stake and sling belay; 12m lifeline.

BUCKLAND'S WINDYPIT   NGR SE 587828   Grade III
[Buckland's Deer Park Windypit] [Helmsley Windypit]

Alt. 130m   **Length 366m**   **Depth 38m**

WARNING – Danger of falling rocks in many places.

Important archaeological deposits in some passages. Permission to descend is not normally granted. In wire fence in recent conifer plantation a few metres uphill from a new forestry track crossing Far Moor Park is entrance marked by a large fallen tree trunk.

Carefully slide down the N entrance onto a traverse ledge; old iron chain should not be trusted. Climbing down from a boulder bridge gains the floor of the larger S entrance shaft. S from here is a short passage opening onto a pitch into Fissure S. N is a climb down to a junction where a crawl into Fissure S runs back under the entrance area; this has two side rifts, Fissure T on the left and, a little further on, Fissure U on the right. The main rift continues as a steep chute down onto a 5m climb to where Fissure J goes off on the right. Straight ahead is a climb up into the spacious Oxtail Chamber; at the far end Fissure F3 climbs steeply to a boulder ruckle on the left. Fissure F1 (Dead Man's Gulch) drops down a traverse and climbs to the deepest point and Fissure F2, to the right, drops down a 6m pitch but soon gets too tight. Turning sharp right upon entering Oxtail Chamber one enters Fissure F4. An ascending traverse here leads to Hayes Hall and the New Series, a series of very large rifts.

Tackle – 30m lifeline advisable for entrance.

CROPTON CAVE NGR SE 755892 Grade I
Alt. 130m Length 4.5m

Obvious entrance in small scar adjacent to N side of road near top of Cropton Bank. Single small chamber largely occupied by rusting ironmongery.

(For location see Northern England map on front endpaper).

THE DEVIL'S PARLOUR NGR SE 512816 Grade I
Alt. 250m Length 9m

In Roulston Scar, most easily approached from footpath above scar by scrambling down a steep gully just beyond two wooden gateposts on the path; cave is on right at foot of gully. A rift passage becoming too tight.

DOWSON POT NGR SE 710877 Grade I
Alt. 80m Depth 5.5m
Explored 1941.

At top of N end of cliff in which Lingmoor Cave lies. Small entrance below tree, to squeeze and climb down choked shaft.

DUCKENDALE WINDYPIT NGR SE 553805 Grade II
Alt. 230m Length 20m Depth 17m
Explored 1981, MSG.

In dense woodland halfway up steep stepped rock slope on E side of valley. Tight rift drops round corners to blind chamber.

Tackle – 20m ladder; stake and sling belay; 20m lifeline.

EPPY HEAD HOLES NGR SE 520900 Grade I
Alt. 330m

On Eppy Head, S of Arden Hall and directly opposite ruins of cottage just above top of S corner of plantation.

1. Explored 1949, BSA   **Length 6m**   **Depth 4.5m**

Open pot-like rift in shattered rock above point where slope begins to decrease. Walk down and wriggle along obvious rift to drop into small chamber to one side with boulder floor and no way out.

2. Length 6m

Small hole covered by timbers 50m NW of and slightly higher than 1. Drop into fissure which chokes one way and becomes too tight in the other direction.

FADMOOR CAVES   NGR SE 674896   Grade I
Alt. 160m

Obvious entrances in SE corner of disused quarry on E side of road a short distance N of Fadmoor.

1. Length 33m

Bedding entrance; hands-and-knees crawling to crawl over roof fall, with 2m high aven on left. Passage becomes flat crawl and ends too low.

2. Length 14m

Larger entrance higher in quarry wall. Roomy passage to boulder ruckle; further short crawl amidst ruckle to total choke.

3. Length 11m
Explored 1974, MSG.

In N side of quarry. Very constricted tube leads to slightly larger passage, ending too low.

GOWERDALE WINDYPITS   Grade II
Alt. 302m
Explored 1936, YRC.

WARNING – Both holes contain loose boulders, rubbish and dead sheep. Danger of falling objects. Gloves are advisable as a protection against cuts which could become infected.

From bend in road at head of Peak Scar Gill follow track N to emerge in large field. In small fenced enclosure 50m E from the NW wall corner is 2; about 80m SW in the next field W is 1.

1. South Gowerdale Windypit   NGR SE 517889
Length 12m   **Depth 33m**

Hole in middle of level field is usually covered over and has a few stakes around it. Single fissure 0.6m-0.9m wide with numerous wedged boulders against which the ladder rests. About 21m down a landing where dead sheep may have accumulated is followed by steep slope and further pitch with take-off over rubbish and barbed wire. From bottom of ladder a slide down lands on dead sheep resting on boulders. The rift closes at each end.

Tackle – 30m ladder; stake and sling belay; 36m lifeline.

2. NGR SE 518889   **Length 88m**   **Depth 27m**

Overgrown hole within wire fence. Pitch descends onto steep earth and rubbish slope and continues below constriction down one end of pleasant chamber 2.5m wide, 9m long and high with wedged boulder floor. At the far end of chamber, traverse over drop gains fissure passage which rounds a few corners and chokes. A slide to right of ladder enters descending fissure which pinches out while a further pitch near the ladder enters a choked lower rift below the upper level traverse. Pitches laddered as one.

Tackle – 25m ladder; stake and sling belay; 30m lifeline.

GREAT RELIEF POT   NGR SE 511832   Grade I
Alt. 300m   **Length 3.6m**   **Depth 3m**
Explored 1972, ACVSU.

NW of head of Sutton Bank, 400m from road and 10m from path down nature trail. Small, draughty opening to right of path is tight squeeze into small fissure with excessively-narrow cross rifts at each end. There are a number of other small holes in this area.

HILL FORT WINDYPIT   NGR SE 505857   Grade II
Alt. 320m   **Length 15m**   **Depth 11m**
Explored 1968, YURT.

Small hole about 12m below top of Boltby Scar where bank and ditch of hill fort reaches cliff edge. Pitch of 3m into Chamber 1 followed by 4.5m pitch into Chamber 2 with short crawl to N into 2a. From opposite end of 1 is 3m climbable descent into Chamber 3 which is choked with collapse debris, like the other chambers in the pot, which is in shattered rock. Pitches laddered as one.

Tackle – 8m ladder; stake and sling belay; 9m lifeline.

KIRKDALE CAVES   NGR SE 678856   Grade I
Alt. 58m

Entrances in quarry NW of ford across Hodge Beck, about 2.5m from foot of cliff, 2 nearest the road and 1 about 30m further on.

1. Length 175m
An extensive series of interconnecting muddy passages, mostly stooping height, with several 'round trips' possible. The various ways all choke eventually, save for one passage which leads to a sump, dived for 9m to 45m of muddy passage which becomes too tight. Cave fauna are in abundance.

2. Length 8m
Single passage which chokes.

LINGMOOR CAVE   NGR SE 710878   Grade I
Alt. 70m   **Length 9m**
Explored 1942.

Wide, formerly walled, entrance at base of cliff on W side of Hutton Beck, 200m downstream of farm. Crawl along upper bedding plane ends in earth-floored chamber with no way on. Lower crawl can be entered at end and also stops in an earth-floored chamber.

MANOR VALE CAVES NGR SE 694868 Grade I
Alt. 70m

In Manor Vale County Council Yard, Kirkbymoorside.

1. Length 4.5m

Obvious entrance in cliff on W side of valley; roomy passage runs to a choke which may be artificial. A few metres further N is a small cave 2.5m long ending in a blank wall.

2. Length 26m

In cliff face behind main building on E side of yard. Entrance used as a rubbish tip. Crawl down debris slope into roomy passage, lowering to a flat-out crawl to a 2.5m high aven, bedding beyond being choked with calcite and fill.

MONK'S WOOD CAVE NGR SE 597790 Grade II
Alt. 170m **Length 33m**

Explored 1971, ACVSU.

Entrance at foot of a cliff 10m N of ruined wooden hut in Monk's Wood of Ampleforth College. Very low crawl into wide, low passage. Short climb and left turn lead to two chambers. From the second an impassable tube connects with the passage near the entrance.

Permission — Ampleforth College.

MOTTS HOLE NGR SE 518889 Grade II
Alt. 290m **Length 70m** **Depth 21m**

Explored 1962, BPC.

Entrance 50m E of Gowerdale Windypit 2 and 20m N down side of Gowerdale is hole below dead silver birch tree. Take care not to fall down hole, which is well concealed from above. Climb into rift; obvious descending passage to crawl through boulders and further descending fissure, eventually turning right and ending too narrow. In opposite direction from foot of open shaft climb up into narrow passage ending in choke. Hole in floor here leads down chute into a short, choked rift. Rope useful.

MURTON CAVE NGR SE 528883 Grade II
[Peak Scar Fissure B]
Alt. 240m **Length 43m**

High rift entrance in corner of Peak Scar, below Boltby — Hawnby road. Short climb up into entrance fissure, which contains boulder bridges and slopes up and then down to top of 3.5m climb down into lower rift, choked in one direction and too tight in the other. Traversing upwards above boulders near entrance gains short, higher level ending in a blank wall.

NANNY COOPER'S HOLE NGR SE 553804 Grade I
Alt. 230m **Length 6m**

In dense woodland on E side of Duckendale, in cliff face 50m S of Duckendale Windypit. Fissure at right angles to cliff enters small chamber.

NODDLE END WINDYPIT NGR SE 526885 Grade II
[Hawnby Windypit]
Alt. 273m   Length 175m
                                            Depth 29m
WARNING – Danger of falling rocks.

In open field 100m SSW of barn at E extremity of Noddle End, a head of
land to S of Gowerdale running E-W. Entrance is hole 0.6m × 0.3m, easily
missed. Pitch lands on broad ledge in main fissure. To right, traversing over
sheep remains gains a branch fissure on right ascending to within 3m of
surface. Straight on 12m from ladder, rift turns left and can be followed at
several levels, all ending choked; lowest level requires a ladder.

Below ledge level, entrance pitch continues to floor of main rift and
descends to T-junction. To right can be followed to chokes at two levels. To
left tight squeezes open into high rift with flowstone formations. Just before
rift ends a 5m pitch drops to a junction, all routes from which soon pinch
out.

Tackle

Pitch	Ladder	Belay	Lifeline
Entrance	20m	Stake and sling	25m
Others	6m	Bar and sling	10m

PEAK SCAR FISSURES NGR SE 530883 Grade I
Alt. 240m

Two small caves E of Murton Cave, in mass of slipped rock beside path at
Peak Scar.

1. Peak Scar Fissure A Length 9m
Large entrance lowers to crawl which is impassable where daylight is seen.

2. Length 6m
Obvious entrance in mossy gully E of 1. Wriggle down to passage ending
at blank wall in each direction.

SILPHO QUARRY CAVE NGR SE 957917 Grade I
Alt. 170m   Length 6m
Explored 1974, MSG.

In N wall of large disused quarry reached by lane running SW from Silpho
village. Low, muddy passage ending too low.
(For location see Northern England map on front endpaper).

SLIP GILL WINDYPIT NGR SE 575835 Grade III
Alt. 150m   Length 171m
                                            Depth 43m
Extended 1981, MSG.

WARNING – Danger of falling rocks throughout.

Archaeological material has been found here on several occasions.
Permission to descend is not normally granted. Entrance beneath tree a few
metres down slope from a forestry track on the summit convexity of the E
slope of the Slip Gill valley (Snip Gill on O.S. maps).

Broken 23m pitch into Main Rift. To NW rift closes to very tight fissure; to SE climb down and then up to massive choke. Before choke on left is route to New Series, a crawl with two squeezes ending on a boulder bridge in another big rift. Climb down to rift floor; ahead leads to undescended 9m pitch, with two branches on right, the first leading to a 5m climb down to the deepest point.

Tackle — 25m, ladder; stake and sling belay; 30m lifeline.

SUTHERBRUFF RIGG POT   NGR SE 860867   Grade II
Alt. 155m   **Depth 18m**
Explored 1972, BACC.

Entrance in pinewood left of forest road is hole 2m x 0.6m with fence round. Drop of 3.6m to inclined rift 25cm wide which descends steeply to T-junction where passage becomes too narrow to follow but lower (shale) passage might be extended by digging. A very constricted hole.

(For location see Northern England map on front endpaper).

T'UNE MOUTH   NGR SE 707867   Grade I
Alt. 50m   **Length 9m**

In Ravenswyke Park, in cliff on W side of normally dry bed of river Dove, obvious entrance 3.5m above river. Passage lowers to a crawl, becoming too low and choked after a small joint aven.

WHITESTONE CLIFF FOOT CAVES
NGR SE 507835   Grade I
Alt. 280m

A series of interesting little caves at the foot of the impressive Whitestone Cliff, all adjacent to a footpath which winds amongst the slipped blocks at the foot of the cliff.

1. Whitestone Cliff Rift   Length 30m   Depth 8.5m
At extreme N end of cliff foot; obvious entrance in angle in cliff. Descending rift to fork; both routes reunite, and interesting scrambling into small chambers at higher levels in rift.

2. Whitestone Cliff Through Cave   Length 36m   Depth 8.5m
About 80m S of 1 is obvious entrance beneath large boulder just out from the foot of the cliff. Roomy rift passage to turn right to exits amongst boulders.

3. Whitestone Cliff Pot   Length 11m   Depth 12.8m
50m S of main entrance to 2, up steep slope and directly at cliff foot. Scramble down, easier on a rope, to narrow descending rift which chokes.

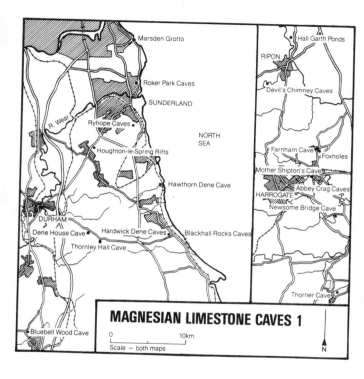

0   10km

Scale – both maps

N

MAGNESIAN LIMESTONE CAVES

COUNTY DURHAM

BLACKHALL ROCKS CAVES   NGR NZ 473389   Grade I
Alt. 3m

Second small headland to S of track descending to beach.

1. Length 38m

Immediately N of headland is obvious circular entrance 4.5m across 4.5m up from base of cliff. Small entrance at beach level directly below leads to chimney up into entrance chamber above. At rear of chamber smaller passage continues for 25m before suddenly ending. Might be partly artificial.

2. Length 140m
Several entrances in headland. Roomy passages and large chamber; some smaller passages about 3m above beach level.

BLUEBELL WOOD CAVE   NGR NZ 266258   Grade II
Alt. 110m   **Length 39m**
Explored 1970, BACC and MSG.

In disused quarry in wood, on E side of road from Newton Aycliffe to Middridge, just before garage and junction, at edge of built-up area of Newton Aycliffe. Small entrance in the E side of the quarry. Squeeze into tight rift passage with small chamber and tight climbs up and down, ending too tight and silted. Quarry has been turned into a small park and cave entrance has been filled with earth.

DENE HOUSE CAVE   NGR NZ 347393   Grade I
Alt. 180m   **Length 12m**
Obvious entrance in small cliff across the valley and visible from Dene House Farm. Roomy passage suddenly shuts down to impassable tubes.

HARDWICK DENE CAVES   NGR NZ 453394   Grade I
Alt. 60m

1. Length 20m
Just upstream of small waterfall on E side of gorge. Large entrance with remains of door, on E bank of stream. Walking-size passage to second entrance in side of gorge a few metres further downstream. May be partly artificial.

2. Length 3.5m
On side of stream about 200m farther downstream. Prominent circular entrance about 6m above stream. Opens into single small chamber.

HAWTHORN DENE CAVE   NGR NZ 441459   Grade I
Alt. 15m   **Length 6m**
On S side of Hawthorn Dene, directly beneath railway viaduct at mouth of dene. Large and obvious entrance to rock shelter, with second smaller entrance to E.

HOUGHTON-LE-SPRING RIFTS
NGR NZ 345505   **Grade III**
Alt. 140m
WARNING—These holes are all in very friable and unsound rock, and are extremely dangerous.
On hilltop to E of cutting through which Durham–Sunderland road

passes, immediately N of Houghton-le-Spring. A series of open rifts and holes running E from the cutting for 800m, all apparently slip features. Some fissures seem to be up to 30m deep but descents of these would be extremely hazardous. Further E is a smaller hole, 9m long and 6m deep, a scramble down a loose slope leading to a small chamber. Halfway down the steep slope between the moor top and Houghton-le-Spring is an impressive open rift formed by slipping, running parallel to the line of the escarpment, easily descended at several points, and up to 15m deep.

MARSDEN GROTTO   NGR NZ 399649   Grade I
Alt. 10m   Length 20m

Restaurant built into enlarged natural cave, first inhabited by Peter Allan in the early 1800s; access by lift from cliff top or by staircase. In the cliffs nearby are several short sea caves, and there are small caves and natural arches in the detached Marsden Rock.

ROKER PARK CAVES   NGR NZ 406593   Grade I
Alt. 10m

Walled and gated entrances on either side of ravine at foot of Roker Park. Follow signs to Doggy Toilet.

1. Spotty's Hole   Length 16m
Two entrances on S of ravine, adjacent to Doggy Toilet. Large phreatic tube; in 1987 contained tableau with polystyrene flowstone blocks, mushrooms, elves and unicorn. Ends in wall; another 20m of passage beyond infilled c.1983 after collapse of footpath above. Spotty was a tramp who used to live in the cave.

2. Length 4m
Entrance on N of ravine; single chamber with cardboard elf. Other entrances, totally walled up, adjacent.

RYHOPE CAVES   NGR NZ 400537   Grade I
Alt. 45m

Entrances were in railway cutting in valley bottom near disused colliery. Cutting has been filled by tipping and caves are now inaccessible.

1. Length 9m
Entrance on right side of cutting, through hole in brick wall (opposite a larger entrance which is bricked up). Roomy, sandy passage closing down to choke.

2. Length 60m
About 55m further E along cutting, on left side. Low entrance into 1.5m high passage descending into chamber 3.5m high, 9m wide and 27m long. On right is small crawl to choke, across chamber to slope up to second entrance, originally large but choked by tipping. Low crawl up debris slope formerly emerged in old quarry.

3. Length 12m
About 18m further E along cutting on left side was entrance formerly blocked by three parallel brick walls, all now pierced. Low passage leads to slope up into choked rift.

THORNLEY HALL CAVE   NGR NZ 362383   Grade I
Alt. 140m   **Length 5m**

Entrance in gully due S of Thornley Hall, overlooking dry valley. Short crawl to choked tube; reputed to be an old escape route from the Hall.

NORTH & WEST YORKSHIRE

ABBEY CRAG CAVES   NGR SE 357557   Grade I
Alt. 45m

Two small caves in Abbey Crag, Knaresborough, E of the house called The Abbey. Both entrances are near the top of an old quarry.

1. Length 5.5m
The W cave is a roomy opening, probably artificially enlarged, and ending at a collapsed bedding.

2. Length 3.5m
The E cave is a fissure which quickly closes in to an impenetrable joint.

DEVIL'S CHIMNEY CAVES   NGR SE 284690   Grade I
Alt. 60m

In Studley Park, SW of Ripon, at base of prominent scar 400m down valley from lake, on right side of river.

1. Length 12m
Right-hand entrance enlarges to easy crawl into chamber 4.5m across, with the apparent way on collapsed.

2. Length 5.5m
Wider entrance in corner of scar becomes too low but can be seen to continue for another 3m at least.

FARNHAM CAVE   NGR SE 353603   Grade III
Alt. 70m   **Length 110m**   **Depth 18m**

Explored 1974, Cave Projects Group.

Entrance is on prime parkland and access permission must be sought in writing from the landowner at least two weeks before an intended visit.

Gated entrance shaft close to prominent water tower on Limekiln Hill. Belay ladder to suspect fence or with long belay to nearest tree. Unstable shaft sidesteps to rift and easy chimneying down to mud floor. Up mud slope to E is chamber with massive blockfall and many small formations ending beyond depression in floor at an unstable boulder choke.

Other way from foot of shaft leads immediately to 2nd pitch, free climbable but tight and awkward; ladder belayed to huge jammed block is recommended. Rift below is up to 2m wide and 9m high, leading over blockfalls and under jammed blocks until floor rises steeply and rift narrows. Where floor drops away, awkward chimneying regains lower level. Back towards entrance is sandy crawl into small boulder chamber and in other direction the passage closes down to a boulder blockage after 8m. Take care to avoid formations, including mud spikes, below 2nd pitch.

Tackle

Pitch	Ladder	Belay	Lifeline
Entrance	4.5m	1.5m	—
2nd	8m	Sling or 6m	12m

Permission—Write to Mr M.J.R. Cowling, Quarry Farm, Farnham, Knaresborough.

FOXHOLES NGR SE 355600 Grade I
Alt. 60m Length 17m

Wide entrance 2.5m high in old quarry 600m SE of Farnham. Entrance enlarged by quarrying leads to slabs on floor and inner chamber with scramble by blocks at far end into fissure 3.5m long which becomes too narrow.

HALL GARTH PONDS NGR SE 318747
Alt. 25m

Collapse in gypsum belt NW of Nunwick, in 1939, formed hole 30m x 20m, full of water which is said by local sub-aqua club to be 7m deep. Rock is apparently exposed under water in the sides, with water flowing out of fissures, and a tree remains rooted in the floor of the hole.

MOTHER SHIPTON'S CAVE NGR SE 347565 Grade I
Alt. 40m Length 8m

On SW side of river Nidd at Knaresborough, near the Dropping Well, a 'petrifying' spring. A single blind chamber about 3.5m high, formed between a bank of tufa and the Magnesian Limestone cliff.

NEWSOME BRIDGE CAVE NGR SE 379515 Grade I
Alt. 33m Length 4.5m

Obvious entrance in quarry beside Spofforth—North Deighton road. Short cave formed at unconformity between Millstone Grit and Magnesian Limestone pinches out into fissure. Probably artificially widened.

THORNER CAVE NGR SE 382413 Grade I
Alt. 84m Length 6m

In W end of small, old quarry S of foot path from Thorner to Wothersome. Wide entrance contracts to crawl ending at shattered rock and earth bank to one side.

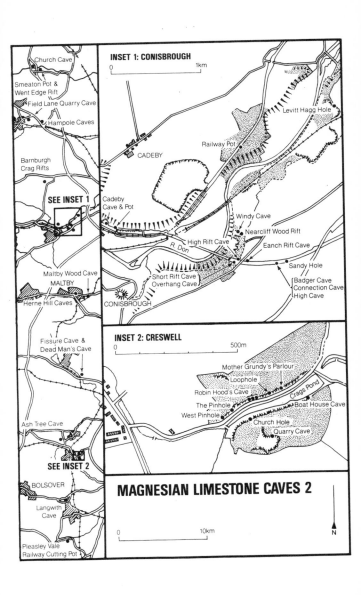

INSET 1: CONISBROUGH

0 ___ 1km

Church Cave

Smeaton Pot &
Went Edge Rift

Field Lane Quarry Cave

Hampole Caves

Barnburgh
Crag Rifts

SEE INSET 1

Cadeby
Cave & Pot

Maltby Wood Cave

MALTBY

Herne Hill Caves

Fissure Cave &
Dead Man's Cave

Ash Tree Cave

SEE INSET 2

BOLSOVER

Langwith
Cave

Pleasley Vale
Railway Cutting Pot

Levitt Hagg Hole

Railway Pot

CADEBY

Windy Cave

Nearcliff Wood Rift

High Rift Cave

Eanch Rift Cave

R. Don

Sandy Hole

Short Rift Cave
Overhang Cave

Badger Cave
Connection Cave
High Cave

CONISBROUGH

INSET 2: CRESWELL

0 ___ 500m

Mother Grundy's Parlour

Loophole

Robin Hood's Cave

Crags Pond

The Pinhole

Boat House Cave

West Pinhole

Church Hole

Quarry Cave

MAGNESIAN LIMESTONE CAVES 2

0 ___ 10km

N

SOUTH YORKSHIRE

BADGER CAVE   NGR SK 532992   Grade I
Alt. 60m   Length 12m

Tight entrance about 14m W of High Cave is 1.2m drop into passage and
low bedding chamber. Higher passage with avens and draughting tubes ends
at a choke. Entrance now covered by tipping.

BARNBURGH CRAG RIFTS   NGR SE 500037   Grade I
Alt. 100m

A group of small caves about 1.5km ENE of Barnburgh, in a small scar W
of the Marr-Mexborough road, on N side of bridle track.

1. Length 10m
Tight rift passage 20m W of road ends at clay choke.

2. Length 13.5m
Entrance 20m W of 1 leads into 3.5m high rift which lowers and becomes
too tight.

3. Length 9m
Further W again is small, very tight hole at base of crag, becoming too
tight.

CADEBY CAVE   NGR SK 515996   Grade I
Alt. 52m   Length 12m

About 800m W of W end of disused viaduct is small quarry on N side of
old railway cutting. In E side of quarry is entrance 3m high and 1.5m wide
leading to chamber. In left wall behind slab is squeeze into low boulder
chamber 6m long. Small rift leading off becomes too tight.

CADEBY POT   NGR SK 516996   Grade II
Alt. 55m   Length 45m   Depth 14m
Explored 1974, YSS.

About 550m W of railway viaduct along disused railway line, and 200m
beyond small footbridge. The pot is three-quarters of the way up the cutting
side and difficult to find.

W entrance needs 9m rope and descends in steps to boulder-floored rift.
To W ascends and ends at earth choke after 8m. To E is passage up to 2m
wide and 6m high, ending at a boulder fall after 20m. Roof passage near fall
can be reached by chimneying and crawls at two levels separated by climbs
end in chokes, while further ascent reaches E entrance.

CHURCH CAVE   NGR SE 490175   Grade I
Alt. 45m   Length 11m

In small scar at rear of Wentbridge church is entrance 2m high by 1m wide,
reached by 5m climb. Passage quickly becomes too tight.

CONNECTION CAVE   NGR SK 532992   Grade I
Alt. 60m   Length 7.5m

Tight entrance 10m E of High Cave leads into chamber with low passage continuing to impassable connection with low bedding plane at end of High Cave. Entrance now covered by tipping.

DEAD MAN'S CAVE   NGR SK 533831   Grade I
Alt. 85m   Length 9m

In Anston Stones, crags E of South Anston and adjacent to Sheffield–Worksop road. Entrance 2.5m wide and 1.5m high. Passage narrows and then opens into long, low chamber. Archaeological remains have been found here and at several rock shelters in the crags; no digging should be done.

EANCH RIFT CAVE   NGR SK 528993   Grade I
Alt. 60m   Length 26m
Explored 1975, 14th Doncaster Scout Troop.

Entrance on N side of disused railway cutting about 25m E of main A630 Doncaster–Sheffield road is best reached from above. Slope down into 6m high rift which closes to a squeeze into a narrow rift, widening and ending at loose boulders.

FIELD LANE QUARRY CAVE   NGR SE 483116   Grade I
Alt. 52m   Length 27m
Extended 1976, YSS.

Entrance in quarry S of road, 1.2km ENE of centre of South Elmsall. Hands-and-knees crawl to timbered dig through choke into passage up to 3.5m high ending at a choke. Quarry now filled in and entrance blocked.

FISSURE CAVE   NGR SK 535830   Grade II
Alt. 80m   Length 10m

In crags called Anston Stones, E of South Anston and adjoining Sheffield–Worksop road. Coffin-shaped depression 2m long and 1m deep is followed by 2m long squeeze into chamber 3m high, 2.5m wide and 8m long with tight passage leading off.

HAMPOLE CAVES   NGR SE 498112   Grade I
Alt. 55m

Two caves on NE side of A638 Wakefield–Doncaster road in old quarry about 1.2km NW of Hampole. Quarry now filled in and entrances blocked.

1. Length 11m
Scramble up rubble to high, inviting entrance. Narrow rift up to 6m high becomes excessively choked although it can be seen to continue.

2. Length 12m
Scramble up loose and shattered rock to entrance 2.5m high and 0.6m wide, which soon opens into spacious chamber terminated by a choke. Second smaller chamber below is reached by grovel in floor.

HERNE HILL CAVES   NGR SK 533922   Grade II
Alt. 105m

1. Explored 1975-78, MSG.   **Length 170m**   **Depth 11m**

Small gated entrance in rock outcrop to rear of supermarket on N side of main street, Maltby. Low descending crawl into First Chamber. Boulder slope spirals down into series of chambers connected by crawls, with several short side passages, some interlinked. Enlarged tube (Chips Squeeze) gains sixth and final chamber.

Permission and key—South Yorkshire County Council Environment Department.

2. Length 64m

Explored 1980, South Yorks, County Archaeology Service.

Entrance in narrow gap between E wall of supermarket and rock face, probably buried by cardboard boxes and rubbish. A series of interconnected small chambers, with some formations. Partly infilled by concrete pumped in to prevent supermarket collapsing.

HIGH CAVE   NGR SK 532992   Grade I
[Conisbrough Cave 2]
Alt. 60m   Length 30m

Entrance high up on S side of old railway cutting 400m E of bridge on A630 Doncaster—Sheffield road. Roomy entrance with large slab leads into chamber with a low, choked chamber off to the right. Ahead is a further chamber with various digs and a small aven and crawl to flowstone choke at its far side. To left is the excessively low bedding plane link to Connection Cave. About 3m E of entrance is an extremely tight entrance to a tortuous passage linking with the first chamber in the main cave. Entrance now covered by tipping.

HIGH RIFT CAVE   NGR SK 528993   Grade I
[Conisbrough Cave 1]
Alt. 60m   Length 27m

On N side of cutting near large viaduct on NW side of A630 road. Entrance just W of road bridge is reached by scramble up cutting side. Just inside is a short climb down to floor of higher fissure with boulder roof. Fissure closes to small chamber and continuing sandy crawl which appears to end at a choke. Tight squeeze to left enters bedding chamber with no way on.

LEVITT HAGG HOLE   NGR SE 538009   Grade I
Alt. 27m   Length 24m

In disused quarry just N of railway line and W of Warmsworth—Sprotborough road. Entrance leads to junction. Right chokes almost immediately, ahead is crawl to series of chambers and chokes and left is rift parallel to cliff and ending at an awkward climb and choke.

MALTBY WOOD CAVE   NGR SK 549917   Grade II
Alt. 70m   **Length 37m**

Explored 1982, MSG.

On N side of railway cutting 30m E of bridge. On left of entrance arch, crawl down into roomy chamber; on right is smaller chamber and dug-out crawl to clay-floored bedding and final collapse chamber.

NEARCLIFF WOOD RIFT   NGR SK 527995   Grade II
Alt. 40m   **Length 88m**   **Depth 12m**

About 400m N of E end of disused railway viaduct in old quarry are two entrances, difficult to locate. Follow track under railway to path slanting up on right over old tips. Follow this path back towards railway, to branch path on left into thick woodland. With luck the entrances will be found nearby, near foot of scarp, lower entrance 10m down the bank from the upper.

Crawl into upper entrance enlarges to 4.5m climbable drop into chamber with three routes leading off. First is high level link into upper entrance passage; second is lower and leads to other entrance; third is lowest, reached by a further 4.5m descent, and ending in choke after link to lower entrance passage.

OVERHANG CAVE   NGR SK 528993   Grade I
Alt. 60m   **Length 8m**

At top of fault above Short Rift Cave, left of overhang at top of slope. Roomy entrance lowers and enters small chamber with two choked passages in right wall.

RAILWAY POT   NGR SE 527005   Grade II
Alt. 45m   **Length 35m**   **Depth 10m**

Explored 1976, YSS; extended 1983, MSG.

In E side of disused railway cutting 1.2km E of Cadeby is rift ending at climbable descent to passage which doubles back under entrance and chokes. On other side of climb is squeeze to descending rift and choke.

SANDY HOLE   NGR SK 533992   Grade I
Alt. 60m   **Length 9m**

On S side of disused railway cutting about 500m E of main road bridge, and E of High Cave. Small tube which became too tight has been covered by tipping.

SHORT RIFT CAVE   NGR SK 528993   Grade I
Alt. 60m   **Length 15m**

On S side of disused railway cutting opposite High Rift Cave is difficult climb up fault. Small entrance near top followed by 2m drop into 2.5m high rift with boulder roof and ending at a choke.

SMEATON POT
NGR SE 499172
Grade III

Alt. 55m
Length 300m
Depth 34m

Explored 1960 and 1979-86, YSS.

Entrance in old quarry, now stockyard, is capped by concrete pipe and locked lid. A major slip-rift system of some antiquity, with excellent formations in parts. Entrance is 19m pitch down calcite flows into tall rift passage. To N is choke, to S second 5m pitch and varied going in rift, with climbs, traverses and one squeeze, reaches T-junction. To right is large rift for 60m to choke. On right before choke is 30m branch with constrictions. To left at T-junction is climb and traverse down into bottom of rift. Tight cross rift on right 8m before end leads into parallel rift passage, closing down at both ends. A constricted climb into the roof leads into large passage with fine flowstone formations, eventually ending in a choke after 120m.

Tackle – 30m ladder; bar and sling belay; 35m lifeline.

Permission to visit this cave must be arranged via A. Speight, 63 High Green Road, Altofts, Normanton, West Yorkshire, WF6 2LG. Send s.a.e. Do not attempt to gain access by contacting the quarry/steel stockyard owners direct, or by unauthorised trips. Any inconvenience or annoyance to the owners will jeopardise the limited access that has been negotiated and will result in the complete destruction and sealing of the entrance.

WENT EDGE RIFT
NGR SE 498171
Grade II

Alt. 55m
Length 29m
Depth 12m

Explored 1973, YSS.

Entrance pitch is narrow fissure opening out into large rift and lies at E end of same quarry as Smeaton Pot. SW from pitch the rift closes in after 9m. To NE a series of squeezes through jammed boulders can be by-passed by traversing above and lead to a deep fissure chamber with choked floor. Short climb up calcited boulders leads to second small chamber with fine stalactites and curtains. Hole in floor leads to lower part of rift and chokes.

Tackle – 11m ladder; bar and sling belay; 15m lifeline.

Permission – All as Smeaton Pot.

WINDY CAVE
NGR SK 527996
Grade I

Alt. 30m
Length 10m

Entrance in same quarry as Nearcliff Wood Rift lies in area of limestone debris under large overhang. Crawl into 2m high rift which lowers to crawl and choke.

DERBYSHIRE/NOTTINGHAMSHIRE

ASH TREE CAVE
NGR SK 515762
Alt. 120m   Length 7m   **Depth 3m**
Excavated 1950-1956.

Obvious entrance in cliff on south side of shallow valley 200m W of road. Slope down into chamber. Continuation is choked by fill although further open passage can be glimpsed beyond.

BOAT HOUSE CAVE
NGR SK 537742   **Grade I**
Alt. 75m   Length 55m

Obvious low arched entrance near E end of crags on S side of gorge. At rear of entrance chamber gently winding 1.2m high passage leads beneath a variety of small avens to a sandy choke. Important archaeological site – do not disturb fill or deposits.
Permission – Derbyshire County Council, Derby.

CHURCH HOLE
NGR SK 534741   **Grade I**
Alt. 75m   Length 75m

Obvious large entrance on S side of gorge; gated, smaller entrance a short distance to W. Entrances unite in a roomy tunnel, gradually lowering, to easy climb up sloping tube to final small chamber and calcited choke. Important archaeological site – do not disturb fill or deposits. Now gated.
Permission – Derbyshire County Council, Derby.

LANGWITH CAVE
NGR SK 518695   **Grade I**
Alt. 90m   Length 30m

Large entrance on N bank of river Poulter a few metres W of a public footpath and almost due N of Upper Langwith church. Entrance drops into roomy chamber from which much fill has been removed by archaeologists. Several sandy crawls lead off; longest is to left, ending in small chamber with tree roots.

LOOPHOLE
NGR SK 535742   **Grade I**
Alt. 75m   Length 15m

Small entrance at cliff foot E of Robin Hood's Cave. Small, spidery cave with upper entrance on ledge. Important archaeological site – do not disturb fill or deposits.
Permission – Derbyshire County Council, Derby.

MOTHER GRUNDY'S PARLOUR
NGR SK 536743   **Grade I**
Alt. 75m   Length 15m

Large and obvious rock shelter near E end of N side of gorge. Small

passage at rear soon ends in a little chamber. Important archaeological site – do not disturb fill or deposits.
Permission – Derbyshire County Council, Derby.

THE PINHOLE   NGR SK 533741   Grade I
Alt. 75m   Length 52m

Obvious large entrance, gated. High but narrow passage opens into lofty chamber with short, low branch to right. Ahead, climb through wedged boulders into narrow passage with stalagmite flows, choking after a squeeze and 2m drop. Important archaeological site – do not disturb fill or deposits.
Permission – Derbyshire County Council, Derby.

PLEASLEY VALE RAILWAY CUTTING POT   Grade III
NGR SK 520649
Alt. 137m   Length 90m   Depth 23m

WARNING – Continuing rock movements mean that visits to the chamber below Rift Chamber Pitch are not recommended.

An unusual slip-rift system. Obvious entrance on S side of disused railway cutting. Drop of 3m into rift. Straight ahead is rift with hole in floor leading back into Main Rift; back under cutting is T-junction with Main Rift. Right is climb down to feet-first squeeze into chamber, with various short rift passages beyond. Left is climb down through boulders onto 4.5m rift chamber pitch; belay to any safe boulder above boulders. Ahead is unsafe high level chamber, rift on left to choked chamber, and scramble up to lip of 6m second pitch into final chamber.

Tackle

Pitch	Ladder	Belay	Lifeline
Entrance	–	–	6m
Rift Chamber	6m	6m	12m
2nd	6m	1.5m and stemple	18m

QUARRY CAVE   NGR SK 535740   Grade I
Alt. 90m   Length 15m

In N wall of large disused quarry 90m S of Creswell Crags. Obvious entrance drops into large passage with much sandy fill, which meets roof after a short distance in each direction.

ROBIN HOOD'S CAVE   NGR SK 534742   Grade I
Alt. 75m   Length 290m

Three obvious entrances, all gated. Series of roomy, dry chambers and galleries, owing much of their size to archaeologists' removal of fill. At end of passage running straight in from E entrance is 6m aven leading only to short, choked passage. Two routes from rear of large chamber just inside central entrance connect in an interesting 'round trip' including an easy

chimney and a squeeze. In floor of large chamber is climbable 3.5m shaft to short, lower passage. More complex low level series is reached via 2.5m shaft at the side of the portal of the W entrance. Important archaeological site – do not disturb fill or deposits.
Permission – Derbyshire County Council, Derby.

WEST PINHOLE   NGR SK 533741   Grade II
Alt. 75m   **Length 60m**

Several entrances near W end of N side of gorge; those to right into semi-daylight chamber, that to left into high rift passage pinching out after 15m. On right of rift passage is a low chamber; on left two routes into a series of low crawls, with squeeze, and small avens.

Between West Pinhole and Pinhole, and again between Pinhole and Robin Hood's Cave, are a few short small caves, up to 9m in length. All the caves are important archaeological sites – do not disturb fill or deposits.
Permission – Derbyshire County Council, Derby.

OTHER CAVES

For location of these caves see Northern England map, on front endpaper.

ALMSCLIFF CRAG CAVE   NGR SE 267490   Grade II
Alt. 180m   **Length 67m**
Extended 1976/77, Royal Park Middle School Caving Club.

Almscliff Grit. Prominent rock tor 1.2km W of North Rigton. Entrance adjoins left end of lower crag just below top of scarp and is partly-walled fissure. Crawl to scramble down into 2m high passage. Left is narrow fissure to low exit NW of main entrance. Ahead beneath poised blocks to T-junction. Right is Cole Passage, tight crawl into wider bedding cave leading to very narrow descending fissure. Left from junction is Thornton Passage, fissure to violent dog leg (more difficult on way out) into chamber with boulder choke at far end. Up to left is narrow fissure rising towards surface but becoming narrow. Ahead over choke is Royal Park, chamber with narrow fissure. Other short caves in main crag.

BUTLER'S FOLLY   NGR SE 079598   Grade I
Alt. 475m   **Length 5.5m**   **Depth 2.5m**
Explored 1977, Royal Park Middle School Caving Club.

Gritstone. At far end of rocks E of track from Valley of Desolation, just short of Simon's Seat. Cave in huge grit boulders facing summit. Drop of 2m then slide forward to chamber going back for 3m on left. Tight exit from chamber blocked with small boulders.

CULVERIN CAVE   NGR SE 205650   Grade I
Alt. 290m   **Length 8m**

Brimham Grit. Entrance 80m W of Brimham House at uphill side of crag to W of Dancing Bear. Tubular crawl at ground level into small chamber choked in both directions.

DRUID'S CAVE   NGR SE 205649   Grade I
Alt. 275m   **Length 20m**

Brimham Grit. Cave entrances are below Lover's Leap, 120m SSW of Brimham House. Main entrance at N end of crag is walking fissure emerging partway up Lover's Leap Chimney and continuing again to lower entrance just beyond cannon tube on right. To left is step up to further exit, with small choked chamber on left, and descent of steps to foot of crag.

FLAMBOROUGH HEAD CAVES

Chalk. A series of sea caves at Flamborough Head. Explore at low tide only, leaving time to return before the tide turns. There are dangerously strong currents in places; be cautious at all times. The caves are at or close to sea level unless stated, and there are other short caves in addition to those listed.

THORNWICK BAYS

1. NGR TA 231725   Length 30m
Roomy fissure passing through Long Ness headland.

2a. East Side Cave   NGR TA 233725   Length 13m
Spacious passage running through buttress behind natural arch.

2b. West Side Cave   NGR TA 233725   Length 9m
Cave ending in small chamber, in cliff beside natural arch.

3. NGR TA 233725   Length 6m
Through arch is cave ending at 4.5m blockfall aven.

4a. Smugglers' Cave   NGR TA 236724   Length 100m
On E side of Thornwick Bay is massive entrance, reached only by boat in calm weather at low tide, because of turbulent sea conditions at entrance. Vast chamber 75m long with rift on E side at back wall. Rift is 23m long, to exit on ledge next to 4b. No landing in cave at high tide.

4b. NGR TA 236724   Length 40m
Large cave entrance; straight passage to dead end contains no dry land.

NORTH LANDING

5. NGR TA 239721   Length 10m
Shattered cave with 4.5m x 4.5m entrance on W side of North Landing is dead end.

6. NGR TA 238722   Length 6m
Beyond deep gully where stream descends on W side of North Landing.

Two entrances, the larger 6m high and 2m wide, into cave with small window out of collapse chamber 2m up in right wall.

7. NGR TA 238722   Length 12m
Entrance beyond 6 is 5m high and 2.7m wide, with poised block above. Floor is flooded at high tide.

8. NGR TA 238724   Length 30m
Short cave through pillar near N end of cliff on W side of North Landing gives access to 55m long collapsed cave forming canyon running back from sea. Spacious cave at S end slopes up to end. On E side 6m before end is 6m high rift aven.

9. NGR TA 238724   Length 13m
Half-way along E side of canyon is 5m high fissure leading to narrow exit and 2.5m drop down slabs onto W side of North Landing.

10. Robin Lyth's Cave   NGR TA 240772   Length 90m
Grid reference is for landward entrance, which is on E side of North Landing, 5m high and 2m wide. Walking for 14m to 1.5m drop into main chamber, 78m long and up to 14m wide and 18m high, with massive exit into the sea. All of the cave is flooded at high tide.

11. NGR TA 240722   Length 17m
About 20m beyond 10 and 7m above low water is 3m square entrance to straight passage.

12. NGR TA 240722   Length 25m
Canyon in cliff on E side of North Landing is 50m long to hading cave entrance 9m high and 2m wide.

12a. NGR TA 240722   Length 20m
At seaward end of canyon is through cave with large rock-pool.

STOTTLE BANK NOOK
13. NGR TA 255713   Length 37m
Fissure cave just N of Stottle Bank Nook. Entrance 3m above shore is 7m crawl to 1.5m drop onto boulders in Main Cave, blocked by boulders at seaward end. Beyond boulders in landward direction is 1.5m deep water in passage 3m-6m wide, ending in narrow fissure. Flooded at high tide.

14. Scout Hole   NGR TA 254714   Length 22m
Around corner to NW of Stottle Bank Nook is cave with two entrances into chamber 16m x 22m and 8m high. Flooded at high tide.

15. NGR TA 254714   Length 54m
At base of steep cliffs just beyond 14. Straight cave 2m high and 3m wide, flooded at high tide, ends narrow and choked.

SELWICKS BAY
16. Blow Hole Cave   NGR TA 255708
On S side of Selwicks Bay. Blow Hole can be descended to enter passage which opens out at foot of cliffs. Descent needs tackle and better approach is from the sea.

The cliffs between 12 and 13 are known to contain at least two caves, Petrel Hole and Fall Hole, but this section is inaccessible except by a longer and more difficult boat journey. No details are known at present.

FYLFOT FISSURE
NGR SE 094470
Grade I
Alt. 295m　　　　　Length 9m

Addingham Edge Grit. About 20m W of Swastika Stone at Ilkley, in face of scar. Small stream sinks at top of scar in impenetrable hole and runs through narrow rift cave to flow out of fissure entrance on corner of crag.

PAN HOLES
NGR SE 084392
Grade II
Alt. 240m　　　　　Length 200m
Depth 26m
Extended 1964, ULSA.

Rough Rock. On highest part of St. Ives Estate at Harden above Bingley, 140m W of Ferrand Memorial in third depression. Small cave entrance to little chamber and bedding plane ending in 8m deep pit, which is climbable direct or via a traverse. NE Passage is scramble down into two high rifts with chockstones and a square, muddy crawl to a chamber with a manhole in the floor. Manhole is an awkward chute into another high rift and shale crawl to a choke of glutinous mud.

SW Passage is entered by crawl under blocks to climbs up and down until a twisting fissure leads to tight chimney. Below the chimney a low bedding plane breaks out into a chamber back under the false floor above, but forward is a further drop down a very tight L-shaped crack to a low level passage. Crawl over blocks leads back towards entrance and a wide passage ahead ends in a boulder choke.

RIPON STATION HOLE
NGR SE 318726
Alt. 35m
Depth 11m
Explored 1987, MSG.

Sherwood Sandstone. Collapse in gypsum belt, in field E of N end of site of Ripon Station, occurred in 1834. Pothole about 14m wide with vertical sides of loose sandstone. Floor of boulders and rubbish sloping down to E, where water ponds in shallow undercuts.

Tackle – 15m ladder; long belay; 30m lifeline.

TOM BELL'S CAVE
NGR SD 978291
Grade II
Alt. 220m　　　　　Length 43m

Grit. Follow path down beside Slack Post Office to top of crag and then go round W of crag to entrance below cliff, in boulders. Passage leads to pitch and then through chambers to choke.

Tackle – 8m ladder; bar and sling belay; 9m lifeline.

INDEX

The Legend Grows

SPECIALISTS

SETTLE WATERSPORTS

OUTDOOR CENTRE & CAVING SHOP

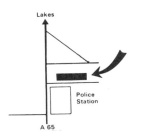

2 CHAPEL STREET,
SETTLE, N. YORKS
TEL: 07292 2760

Sat	8	————	6
Sun	8	12.30	
Mon	9	————	6
Tues	9	————	6
Wed		CLOSED	
Thurs	9	————	6
Fri	9	————	7.30

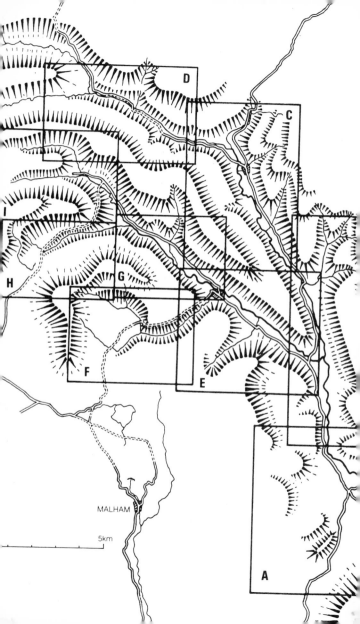

D

C

I

H

G

F

E

A

MALHAM

5km